D0984489

BEFORE WATERGATE:
PROBLEMS OF CORRUPTION
IN AMERICAN SOCIETY

EDITED BY

ABRAHAM S. EISENSTADT, ARI HOOGENBOOM
and HANS L. TREFOUSSE

BROOKLYN COLLEGE PRESS, BROOKLYN, N.Y.

Distributed by Columbia University Press
New York

1978

Fened. 17,50/ 15,75/ 9/30/81

Library of Congress Catalog Card Number 77-90630
ISBN 0-930888-01-4

Printed in USA

BROOKLYN COLLEGE

OF

THE CITY UNIVERSITY OF NEW YORK

SCHOOL OF SOCIAL SCIENCE

DEPARTMENT OF HISTORY

STUDIES ON SOCIETY IN CHANGE, No. 4.

BROOKLYN COLLEGE STUDIES ON
SOCIETY IN CHANGE
—Editor in Chief Béla K. Király—

For Oscar Handlin
Distinguished Alumnus

PREFACE

The "Third Annual Brooklyn College Conference on Society in Change" was held at the College in May 1977. The proceedings, presented in this book, represent an already established tradition for these conferences and the publications that have flowed from them: they are investigations of major issues in modern society; the research, presentations and conclusions relate to the life of our nation, our generation and our community; the studies, taken together, constitute an interdisciplinary approach; and they concern our actual educational processes.

It is also characteristic of these conferences that the scholarship presented at them is the product of the talents and expertise of our own colleagues at Brooklyn College, those of our sister colleges in CUNY, and those of other distinguished colleges and universities. This volume includes papers by Arnold Heidenheimer (Washington University), Morton Keller (Brandeis University), Mary-Jo Kline (New-York Historical Society) and Linda Levy Peck (Purdue University). From CUNY institutions there are papers by Edward Pessen (Distinguished Professor, Baruch College) and Arthur Schlesinger, Jr. (Albert Schweitzer Professor of the Humanities, The Graduate School and University Center). From our faculty at Brooklyn College there are papers by Edwin G. Burrows, Abraham S. Eisenstadt, Ari Hoogenboom, James P. Johnson, Robert H. Muccigrosso, James L. Sternstein, Hans L. Trefousse and Melvin Williams. Among these contributors, as is the tradition in these books, are leading scholars in the fields represented as well as scholars at the beginning of their academic careers.

The subject of the conference that produced these papers must be among the least well understood aspects of American history and political culture. The studies, taken together, cannot claim comprehensiveness—that was not their goal—but their contribution to our understanding can be regarded, I believe, as an incisive one.

With the publication of this volume, Number 4, the series on "Society in Change" is becoming a fixture in the academic

life of Brooklyn College and well beyond it. We look ahead now
to the annual conference and its scholarly product.

Brooklyn College
October 23, 1977

Donald R. Reich
Professor of Political Science
Vice President and Provost

EDITORS' FOREWORD

The Watergate affair, more than any other single series of events in recent decades, dramatized the fact of corruption in American politics. On the eve of our bicentennial celebration, it posed for our attention, perhaps more pointedly than it otherwise would have, a number of urgent questions: What have been the principal modes, patterns and events of the history of American corruption? How far does corruption inhere in the democratic process—in the institutions, that is, of a liberal democratic polity such as ours? To what extent have our principal political leaders been men of virtue or of vice? What, indeed, do we mean by the concepts of probity and corruption? Looking at the problem from a comparative perspective, to what extent is corruption a basic feature of every polity? And if it is, how have the modes and sources of corruption in our society been similar to and different from those of other polities?

To attempt an answer to these questions, at least in some measure, we held a conference on the theme of "Before Watergate: Problems of Corruption in American Society." The conference met at Brooklyn College on May 2 and 3, 1977. The essays that follow are revised versions of the papers that were read at several sessions. We invited scholars to participate in our discussions on the basis of their interest and expertise in the questions we were considering. Our panelists were given the widest latitude in defining and addressing their particular subject. Inevitably, because of the embracing theme of the conference, they were primarily concerned with exploring the nature and incidence of American political corruption. But, as several of them have said, corruption is far from being a uniquely American phenomenon or, indeed, more characteristic of the American polity than of other political systems. The participants in our conference were, for the larger part, professional historians. We regret that, owing to stringent cost limitations, we have not been able to include the remarks of our commentators, some of whom were members of other disciplines. Because our subject is historical, the order in which the essays are being presented in this volume is a simple chronological one.

The subjects our contributors address may be classified under several major rubrics. Professors Schlesinger, Heidenheimer, Keller and Eisenstadt offer general considerations about political corruption in American history. Professors Peck and Burrows suggest the relevance of European ideas and developments to understanding corruption in our own society. Professors Klein, Williams and Johnson deal with problems of corruption during critical periods of our past. Professors Pessen and Hoogenboom venture revisionist suggestions about the nature of political morality during periods—the Jacksonian and the Gilded Age—traditionally regarded as corrupt. Dr. Kline and Professors Trefousse and Sternstein probe the theme of corruption by analyzing the roles of three prominent political figures: Aaron Burr, Carl Schurz and Nelson Aldrich. And Professor Muccigrosso considers the impact of corruption on some groups of American intellectuals during the late nineteenth century.

We are grateful to all the individuals who helped make the conference possible. These include our colleagues at Brooklyn College: President John W. Kneller, Provost Donald Reich, Associate Provost Marilyn Gittell, and Dean Nathan Schmukler; Profesor Béla K. Király, the editor in chief of the "Studies on Society in Change" series in which this book belongs; Mr. Theodore M. Lauer; Professor Jerome L. Sternstein, who suggested the theme and many of the specific papers of the conference; and Mr. Peter J. Beales, who edited the essays in this volume as he has the previous books in this series. Our greatest thanks go to the scholars whose contributions this volume contains.

This collection represents a concerted effort by specialists in American history to study the theme of political corruption in our past. It has been, to the best of our knowledge, the only such effort in recent years. We do not pretend to have canvassed all, or even most, of the problems which the theme presents. Our answers to the questions before us are, we are keenly aware, tentative and incomplete. Indeed, we would not wish to claim more than to have laid the subject before our colleagues and the public. The essays that follow are offered, then, not as the conclusion of an inquiry but rather as its beginning. It will satisfy

the goal of our own venture if it stimulates others into this
challenging domain.

A. S. Eisenstadt
Ari Hoogenboom
Hans L. Trefousse

TABLE OF CONTENTS

Arthur M. Schlesinger, Jr.

INTRODUCTION

And God looked upon the earth, and, behold, it was corrupt;
for all flesh had corrupted his way upon the earth.

Genesis 6:12

Historians are bound to approach the problem of corruption
with a double vision. On the one hand, they must as citizens
deplore so serious a subversion of individual integrity and social
trust. On the other, they must as students of society see in
corruption, its rhythms and permutations, clues to some deeper
social mystery. Of course, corruption arises in the first instance
from human freedom and frailty. Even in the blameless Garden
of Eden the serpent was able, without undue difficulty, to corrupt Eve. But variations in the nature and quantity of corruption
illuminate broader problems and tendencies. For a historical
epoch, as Lord Acton contended, reveals itself above all in its
crimes—and in the particular temptations and pressures that
corrupt particular men in particular situations.

Never was the astute Edward Gibbon more wrong than when
he pronounced corruption "the most infallible symptom of constitutional liberty." We know now that corruption is most intense
of all in authoritarian regimes where ambitions and rivalries
find no acceptable outlet and where there are no institutional
checks on men in power. Still one imagines what Gibbon had
in mind before he succumbed to epigram. The very looseness
of a liberal polity offers unusual scope for fallen human nature—
and corruption is inevitably evidence of the failure or ineffec-
tuality of authority. Beyond such spacious reflections, however,
the task of the historian is to relate corruption to specific social

environments. The operative question is: what function, beside the exercise of greed, does corruption serve at one or another time?

There is an abundance of theories to explain criminality and corruption. Marx, for example, offered an economic interpretation, finding a role for crime in the maintenance of capitalism. "The criminal," he wrote, following (and citing) Mandeville, "breaks the monotony and everyday security of bourgeois life. In this way he keeps it from stagnation, and gives rise to that uneasy tension and agility without which even the spur of competition would get blunted. Thus he gives a stimulus to productive forces. While crime takes a part of the superfluous population off the labor market and thus reduces competition among the laborers— up to a certain point preventing wages from falling below the minimum—the struggle against crime absorbs another part of this population. Thus the criminal comes in as one of those natural 'counterweights' which bring about a correct balance and open up a whole perspective of 'useful' occupations."

Walter Lippmann saw crime as a growth industry providing services that people desire but are debarred by moral tradition from acknowledging and legalizing. He distinguished the old-fashioned *laissez-faire* crook, American individualism turned sour, from the systematic corruptions of a corporate society. The first, he observed, is merely predatory. But organized crime "offers something in return to the respectable members of society." This is why

voters in our large cities have as yet shown no disposition to get thoroughly rid of the politicans who submit to, profit by, and fumble with the activities of the underworld. . . . We are all so much addicted to lawbreaking that the existence of a great underworld which lives on lawbreaking is not wholly alien and antagonistic to the working assumptions of our lives.

Corruption is a way of performing "services for which there is some kind of public demand."

Robert K. Merton traced criminality and corruption to the differential opportunities in a society that places the highest premium on success but denies part of the population a chance at this supreme goal except through illegal short cuts. "Social structures," he wrote, "exert a definite pressure upon certain

persons in society to engage in nonconforming rather than con-
forming conduct." Daniel Bell, ruminating on "crime as an
American way of life," saw the criminal career as one of our
"queer ladders of social mobility," used particularly by ethnic
minorities shedding traditional restraints in avid pursuit of the
American dream. Noting how Irish, Jews, Italians, blacks had
succeeded each other in the parade of crime and the passage
to respectability, he concluded, "Any group on the way up finds
old ties loosened, and some of its members turn to crime."

The contemporary experience of modernization in the Third
World suggested another perspective. Rapid change, as Samuel
Huntington has noted, disrupts ancestral folkways and values.
Dislocation leads to demoralization and deviance. Corruption
becomes a means of social accommodation for aggressive and
previously excluded economic groups exploiting new sources of
wealth. By giving concrete benefits to otherwise restless people,
corruption may "be functional to the maintenance of a political
system in the same way that reform is. Corruption itself may
be a substitute for reform and both corruption and reform may
be substitutes for revolution." Emerging as an ailment of the
transition process, corruption thereafter finds new lodgement
as a means of coping with the crowded, mass, anonymous, in-
human world of the twentieth century city.

This is only a sampling of theories as to the diversity of
social functions that corruption might serve—a factor in economic
equilibrium, a response to consumer demand, a disapproved
path toward an approved goal, an escalator for minorities, a
facilitator of economic growth, a response to frustrations due
to growth. Doubtless it performed all these functions, except
probably the first, at one time or another in the United States.
At the same time, corruption, however functional it might in
some sense be, rested uneasily on the American conscience. For
few nations had been more saturated in the idea of life as
perpetual warfare between corruption and virtue.

Calvinism, by instilling in the American psyche an abiding
conviction of man's propensity to wickedness, had created an
enormous sensitivity to symptoms of human depravity. The
seventeenth century colonists were dedicated to the dream of a
pure and regenerative commonwealth, a redeemer nation. The
dread of corruption received a powerful secular infusion in the

eighteenth century when Americans set out to establish an independent republic. Steeped in the history of antiquity, they saw corruption not only as individual but as public evil—as the ineluctable fate of all previous republics. This dread was reinforced by a flood of political tracts from British oppositionists portraying the progress of corruption in the motherland. The Founding Fathers viewed corruption not as a superficial malady, easily curable by laws and constables, but as a wasting disease fatal to the state. "Commerce, luxury and avarice have destroyed every republican government," said John Adams. "We mortals cannot work miracles; we struggle in vain against the . . . course of nature."

This apocalyptic theory of corruption had its sustenance in the accompanying sense of the instability and perishability of republics. As the United States began to feel secure and self-doubt gave way to complacency, corruption no longer seemed the organic threat perceived by the Founding Fathers. By mid-century it had become a conspicuous feature of the American scene. As the novelist George Lippard put it,

Could Washington and his hero-band, could the immortal throng of Signers, once more assemble, . . . what would be their emotions, as they gazed upon the fruits, which the republican tree has borne? We left you pure, they would say, we left you happy, and now we find Bribery on the Bench of Justice, the Knife and the Torch in place of Law, a people beggared by dishonest Banks, and a city disgraced by Riot, by Robbery, by Murder! Are these the fruits for which we fought and bled? Was it for this we dared the rebel's gibbet, the traitor's doom?

Still a moral concern lingered. "There is no country in the world," observed Colonel Sellers in *The Gilded Age,* "that pursues corruption as inveterately as we do." The result was the contradiction that provoked Baron Jacobi's famous outburst in Henry Adams's *Democracy*:

You Americans believe yourselves to be exempted from the operation of general laws. . . . I have lived seventy-five years, and all that time in the midst of corruption. I am corrupt myself, only I do have the courage to proclaim it, and you others have it not. Rome, Paris, Vienna, Petersburg, London, all are corrupt; only Washington is pure. Well, I declare to you that in all my experience I have found no society which has had elements of corruption like the United States. The children in the street are corrupt, and know how to cheat me. The cities are all corrupt, and also the towns and the counties and the States' legislatures and the judges. Everywhere men betray trusts both public and private, steal money, run away with public funds. . . . And you gentlemen in the Senate very well declare that your great United States, which is the head of the civilized world, can never learn anything from the example of corrupt Europe. You are right—quite right! The great United States needs not an example. I do much regret that I have not yet one hundred years to live. If I could then come back . . . the United States will then be more corrupt than Rome under Caligula; more corrupt than the Church under Leo X; more corrupt than France under the Regent!

A hundred years from the publication of *Democracy* will find the United States in 1980. If Adams had let Jacobi settle for ninety-two years, the prediction would have been on target.

Corruption in American society represents one more of several notable struggles between the theory and practice of American life. The essays in this volume offer a valuable account of the vicissitudes of this schism in the national soul.

Morton Keller

CORRUPTION IN AMERICA:
CONTINUITY AND CHANGE

The word "corruption" itself, as the numerous definitions attached to it in the *Oxford English Dictionary* attest, is an elusive and ambiguous one. For some it is a strongly normative concept, describing an illegal or immoral transgression of prevailing mores for the benefit of oneself or one's group. In this sense the presence of corruption usually is as much dependent upon the stance of the observer as it is on the act of the transgressor: I am reality-oriented; you are self-interested; he is corrupt. Often the corrupt do not regard themselves as such; and rightly so, by their own frame of values. Often enough (as in tyrannies) the most corrupt act is to accord with law and custom; to violate or subvert authority may well be the higher morality. Nor is corruption, even when accepted as such, necessarily harmful. No less than reform, as Samuel Huntington observed, it "may . . . be functional to the maintenance of a political system."[1]

Corruption has been understood in yet another sense: as something natural, organic, an ineluctable part of the business of living. The trouble with the house of politics, Mr. Dooley observed, "is that it is occupied by human bein's. If 'twas a vacant house it cud aisily be kept clean."[2] Lord Acton's more elegant aphorism about power and corruption conveys the same meaning, but it does so in the darker, more pessimistic sense of the inevitable decay and degeneration of institutions—a process that has been commented upon by political philosophers since Plato.

These semantic and philosophical problems, and indeed the

larger question of the functional or dysfunctional character of corruption, can be left to those better suited to deal with them. The intention here is to offer instead a historian's-eye view of the place that corruption in the popular sense of the word—the misuse of power for personal gain—has had in the history of American public life.

Historians appear to have an unconquerable affinity for triads. They speak of ancient, medieval, and modern history; or, in the more parochial American case, of the colonial period, the nineteenth century and modern America. The following remarks, too, will focus on these three stages of the American past.

✿   ✿   ✿

Along with their Bibles, their charters and their desires for freedom and fortune, the early English settlers in America brought with them a distinctive set of attitudes toward government. In light of what was to follow, their outlook was a strikingly traditional one, steeped in the social assumptions of late medieval and early modern Europe. Huntington has observed that in many respects early American government was a Tudor polity. As such it inherited principles of deference, of hierarchy—and of public office being one's property rather than a public trust— which were characteristic of English and other early modern European governments.[3]

John Winthrop may have had religious attitudes that upset his Church of England contemporaries, but there was nothing avant-garde about his view of power and authority. For all his Puritan sense of early seventeenth century England as a corrupt society (he was convinced that he lived in "evil and declining times"), his belief in hierarchy and good order would have gladdened the heart of Marsilius of Padua. "God Almighty," he wrote on his way to the New World, "in His most holy and wise providence has so disposed of the condition of mankind, as in all times, so some must be rich, some poor, some high and eminent in power and dignity; others mean and in subjection."[4]

The closed, aristocratic system of politics in eighteenth century England, like that of seventeenth century France, fostered a rich system of corruption. Crown offices, parliamentary votes and the franchise of the sparse electorate were openly and expensively for sale. What Bernard Bailyn has called a "private, informal constitution" of patronage and influence prevailed in that hermetic public life.[5]

The upper levels of colonial American government closely paralleled eighteenth century England in developing an elaborate system of nepotism, sale of offices and kept supporters in the legislature. What has been called the anglicization of American society, that is, the self-conscious aping of the mores and institutions of the mother country, was well advanced by the mid eighteenth century. It is revealing that the same political vocabulary—faction, clique, junto—flourished on both sides of the Atlantic. Great New York families like the Delanceys and the Livingstons, Crown and assembly (or "country") parties in the colonies everywhere, jousted for place and perquisites as did Whig and Tory magnates in Sir Lewis Namier's England. As late as 1811, the Virginia planter John Campbell wrote to his son David in terms that would have been quite familiar to an English squire sitting for a rotten borough: "I have heard with much pain that you have not recovered your health yet. Would a session in the legislature be of benefit to you?"[6]

Those opposing the Crown in eighteenth century England often focused their attention on political corruption. John Trenchard and Thomas Gordon, who wrote the influential "Cato Letters" of the 1720s, declaimed: "Public corruptions and abuses have grown upon us; fees in most, if not in all, offices are immensely increased; places and employments, which ought not to be sold at all, are sold for treble values." This was an attack not only on the abuse of aristocratic politics but on aristocratic politics itself. As such it struck a responsive note with those who were creating the American Revolution, and the "Cato Letters" became a rhetorical model for the growing colonial assault on the imperial system.[7]

In fact the American colonies were remote and different enough from the motherland to be spared the full impact of this politics of aristocracy and monarchy. The special qualities of American life—the availability of land, the shortage of labor, the lack of a past—already were stripping that system of much of its force. Refractory colonial legislatures steadily chipped away at the patronage powers of the royal governors; the electoral system by the mid eighteenth century was far broader and more representative than its English counterpart.

Given the changing character of American public life and
the nature of eighteenth century English government, it is
understandable that the American revolutionaries teamed corruption with tyranny as the major themes in their assault on
the colonial system. They found particularly congenial a view
of themselves as incorruptible advocates of republicanism, in
the imagined mold of the ancient Roman Republic. The great
popular hero of the early United States was not Benjamin
Franklin, that lovable man of humble origins and ready adapter
to the corrupt ways of eighteenth century politics and court
life. Rather it was the austere, incorruptible, classically republican George Washington who was first in the hearts of his
countrymen.

Of course the American revolutionaries were doing more than
recreating republican Rome. The emerging model of American
government, where power and legitimacy were held, as it were,
on loan from their ultimate repository—the people, was in fact
a dramatic inversion of the hierarchical, deferential theory that
underlay the politics of the rest of the eighteenth century
western world.

Yet this turned out to be a mixed legacy. Republicanism,
liberty, sovereignty stemming from the people remained important underlying principles of American public life. The accompanying model of austere public incorruptibility met a far
less happy fate. None of the Founders (except perhaps Alexander
Hamilton) would have thought of doing what President Kwame
Nkrumah of Ghana did: have inscribed on the base of his statue
in front of the Law Courts in Accra the inscription "Seek ye
first the Kingdom of Politics and all else shall be added unto
you." But in the democratic politics of nineteenth century America this would not have been inappropriate at all.[8]

*   *   *

The corruption that so thoroughly permeated American politics
and government in the nineteenth century had certain things
in common with the misdoings of the eighteenth century public
order. It reflected and enhanced the constant inflow of new
men and new interests into public life and it served as a means
of perpetuating established interests. But there the resemblance
ends. Nineteenth century American corruption in fact was part

of a very different political system, far more democratic and far more deeply worked into the life of the society than any that preceded it.

Massive, popular political parties and an elaborate system of local, state and national officeholding, related to the needs of the party system rather than to the needs of government, rose through the nineteenth century. It was estimated in the 1870s that one in twelve heads of households in New York City had a public position. The lawyer David Dudley Field, an opponent of efforts to prohibit civil servants from participating in politics, pointed out in 1877 that there were more than 140,000 federal, state and local officeholders in New York—one in eight voters. "The exclusion of public servants from political action," he concluded, "would disfranchise a great body of our fellow-citizens."[9]

The vocabulary of nineteenth century American politics is that of a vigorous, active institution, filled with words drawn from the home, the farm, the factory. By the 1820s American candidates were running for office; in England they still stood. Politicians did more than run: they dodged, bolted, backed and filled, bluffed. There were planks, platforms, favorite sons, party wheelhorses and lots of buncombe—soon to be shortened to bunk. And very soon there were gerrymanders, bosses, machines, lobbyists, repeaters, floaters, graft, boodle, loot and rakeoffs.

This democratization of politics—and of corruption—served purposes beyond the timeless one of enriching the participants. Widespread payoffs lessened the need for prior wealth as a condition of entry into politics or government. And the monetary lures of a public career may have kept the level of nineteenth century American politics and government from being worse than it was—or, occasionally, made it as good as it was.

Nineteenth century American political corruption was closely linked as well to the sustenance of increasingly large and costly political parties, which for all their faults did provide broader representation of a diverse (if white and male) electorate than any previous system. As political machines became more and more highly organized, so too was the collection of the funds that sustained them. The machines and their bosses became what James Russell Lowell called "majority manufacturers" and like their counterparts in industry they needed growing amounts of capital to pay for an ever larger and more complex system of production. As Tammany boss William Tweed observed: "The money . . . was distributed around in every way, to everybody, and paid for everything, and was scattered throughout the community." Officeholder kickbacks and political workers on the public payroll—in the customhouses, post offices and the like— were the primary sources of party support during the mid-century decades. In 1878 the secretary of the Republican Congressional Campaign Committee asked all federal officeholders making $1,000 a year or more to contribute at least 1% of their salaries. Twelve separate dunning letters went from the New York Republican Committee to federal employees in 1880. Payments for congressional, judicial and other party nominations were more and more systematic, with fixed schedules.[10]

Massive contractor kickbacks for public works and payments to avoid the growing licensing and regulatory apparatus of late nineteenth century America were increasingly important sources of funds. And by the turn of the century large-scale corporate contributions had become a major source of money for state and national elections.[11]

Gilded Age corruption in government, as in politics, is a familiar theme. The dreary litany of wrongdoing includes the Crédit Mobilier affair, in which a number of prominent men (including Vice President Schuyler Colfax and Congressmen James G. Blaine and James A. Garfield) accepted stock in the Union Pacific's construction company; the Belknap scandal, in which the secretary of war took bribes from an Indian post trader; the Whiskey Ring, an elaborate system of collusion between internal-revenue agents and whiskey distillers designed to avoid the federal excise tax on alcohol; and the Star Route scandals, where lucrative western mail delivery franchises were given to favored contractors.

This surge of scandal usually is linked to the slackened morality of post-Civil-War American life and to a burgeoning capitalism that contaminated the political system. But it had another dimension as well. It involved activities that were part of the post-Civil-War expansion of the national government: the Pacific Railroad, Indian policy, excise taxes, the postal services. The late nineteenth century American polity had neither the ideological nor the organizational means to deal with this growth. Elitist manipulation and control belonged to the rejected aristocratic governmental model of the past; the bureaucratic, administrative state lay in the future. Bribery and kickbacks were a form of accommodation, a way of getting things done—much as the raw bribery required of and provided by multinational corporations today is an apparent necessity in the anarchic world of international dealings.[12]

The American polity by the late eighteenth century was unique in the western world in its commitment to republican rule, popular sovereignty and civic rectitude. By the same token its yeasty mix of administrative weakness and large-scale corruption seemed to set the United States apart by the end of the nineteenth century. In nineteenth century America the springs of government were weakened, in Moisei Ostrogorski's phrase. Government in nineteenth century England underwent a dramatically different evolution: from its eighteenth century state—what Edmund Burke called a "loaded compost heap of corrupt influence"—to a model of probity and efficiency, one fit to rule an empire. Elsewhere in Europe too (in Prussia, Austria, France) the professional civil servant and the bureaucratic world in which he moved became the governmental norm. European government went more or less directly from the nepotism and purchased offices of the seventeenth and eighteenth centuries to the routinized, professional bureaucracy of modern times.[13]

This is not to say that the civil-service concept failed to take root in nineteenth century America as well. Civil-service reform in the United States was close in time and spirit to its British counterpart. Rule by an educated social elite, the ideals of government economy and efficiency, a new attitude toward morality in government derived from the religious and social values of middle-class Victorian culture—these were the stock in trade of American civil-service reformers no less than of their opposite numbers in England.

But there was a revealing difference in the English and American civil-service-reform movements. The object of the British assault was the old system of aristocratic nepotism and sale of office. The target of the American movement was democracy— or at least its excesses. Insofar as civil-service reform and a professional bureaucracy succeeded in England, they coincided with the values, interests and growing political power of that country's middle class. The American equivalent was far less successful because it went against the grain of increasingly powerful mass party machines and a deep popular distrust of government divorced from politics. England's aristocratic past made possible the triumph of efficient, honest bourgeois government; America's democratic polity assured its failure. American critics of civil-service reform could argue persuasively that competitive written examinations would be "practically limiting entry to the graduates of colleges" and thus narrow, not broaden, access to government. Indiana Senator Oliver P. Morton condemned the "restlessness and the spirit of change" of elite reformers in comparison with the broad, middle-class "balance wheel in our political machine."[14]

*   *   *

The classic nineteenth century modes of American political and economic corruption—graft, bribery, kickbacks and the like—continue to lead a hearty life in American society, but other modes of corruption have become conspicuous in the twentieth century world. They are the concomitants of the rise of large bureaucratic institutions in both the public and the private sectors and of the spread of political ideology as a primary form of self-definition.

The corruption that characterizes bureaucracies consists of intricate webs of nepotism, subtle forms of favoritism and preferment, fierce jockeying for place and status, and an assumption on the part of the participants that they are entitled as of right to tenure in office and a certain level of income, status and perquisites. In this sense the twentieth century world of public and private bureaucracy is reminiscent of nothing so much as the early modern state.

But there is something new that is peculiarly the province of our own time, and that is the presence as well of strong ideological commitments—sometimes in conjunction with bureaucracy, sometimes against it—that generate their own forms of malfeasance.

The corruption attendant upon bureaucracy and ideology has gone furthest in the twentieth century totalitarian states: Fascist Italy and Spain, Nazi Germany, the Marxian Socialist states of

Eastern Europe. *The New Class* by Milovan Djilas is perhaps the best formulation of the prevailing style of governance and its characteristic corruption in those societies.

But the "new class" may be found in the more open societies of the West as well: in government, business corporations, foundations, universities. The behavior of those who staff these institutions is for the most part muted and benign, but they are still susceptible to the temptations that beset any member of a. large, impersonal, amorphous bureaucracy. Consider, for example, the activities and life style of the Ford Foundation: the expensive lunches and expansive expense accounts; the not unostentatious headquarters on Forty-Second Street in New York City, complete with the world's largest greenhouse—according to Martin Mayer, the most stunning piece of architectural symbolism in the twentieth century.[15]

And then there are the government bureaucracies of the West: vast grey units where nothing is very dishonest but which are highly susceptible to the occasional buccaneer like the "educational entrepreneur" that Congresswoman Edith Green described several years ago in *The Public Interest*. This academic grantsman sliced through the soft bureaucracy of the Office of Education like a knife through butter. Congreswoman Green's account of heavy funding and sparse results recalls George Washington Plunkitt's classic description of the big city as a spoilsman's Garden of Eden:

It's an orchard full of beautiful apple trees. One of them has got a big sign on it, marked: "Penal Code Tree—Poison." The other trees have lots of apples on them for all. Yet, the fools go to the Penal Code Tree. Why? For the reason, I guess, that a cranky child refuses to eat good food and chews up a box of matches with relish. I never had any temptation to touch the Penal Code Tree. The other apples are good enough for me, and O Lord! how many of them there are in a big city![16]

Another and more sinister form of modern corruption has been very evident in recent years. Revelations about the Central Intelligence Agency fall into this category, as does that collection of attitudes and actions with the generic name of Watergate. It is instructive to compare this latter episode with its major counterparts of the past: the scandals of the Ulysses S. Grant administration or Teapot Dome. During the Grant years two things were being greased: the workings of government and the pockets of the participants. Much the same can be said of Teapot Dome: corrupt politicians and oilmen worked their way through problems posed by the conservationist movement of the early twentieth century and the growing role of the national defense establishment.[17] But Watergate¹ was different. The principals took the law into their hands not because they saw a quick buck to be made or because they felt a need to circumvent administrative obstacles but because they were driven by a vision of what was right and true.

The Watergate conspirators were odious and maladroit and the scale of what they did rightly outraged public opinion. But purloining documents and betraying a public trust to serve one's own higher goals hardly began in 1972. During the 1950s an incredulous Senator John McClellan taxed Senator Joseph McCarthy for calling on government employees to turn over to him confidential documents that in their view revealed subversion in high places: "You are advocating government by individual conscience as against government by law." McCarthy's response was: "The issue is whether the people are entitled to the facts."[18]

This view and its implementation by such as the State Department's Otto Otepka earned the censure of the right-thinking in the 1950s. Its implementation by others for other reasons in the 1960s and early 1970s often earned a different judgment. But the point is not the morality or immorality of these acts. Rather, it is that they are threads in a pattern of behavior that can be seen as a characteristic and perhaps at times quite functional part of a polity in which bureaucracy and ideology play commanding roles.

❖ ❖ ❖

In one sense the character of public corruption has changed enormously over two centuries of American life. It has moved from the patronage and nepotism of the essentially aristocratic polities of early modern times, through but not out of the full-throated graft and bribery of a democratic politics and a burgeoning market economy, into the more subtle and complex deviations of an age of bureaucracy and ideology.

These changes have occurred, however, in a social system

whose character and values have shown great tenacity over centuries of enormous socioeconomic change. The distinctive characteristics of American life—its persistent individualist ethos, the distrust of centralized, indeed, of any, authority, capitalist materialism, democratic political theory, a plenitude of contesting groups—have tended to constrain the baleful impact both of pre-1776 aristocratic government and post-1900 bureaucracy and ideology, even while they fed the modes of corruption that flourished in the nineteenth century. As William Allen White once observed, with some sadness but more relief, the United States "is a country where you can buy men only with money."[19]

This does not dictate complacent acceptance of those forms of corruption that are as American as apple pie or that, because everything can be understood, it can be forgiven. The tendency of people and their institutions to fix things to suit themselves, whether that self-suiting be status, or wealth or power, must always be resisted, even if it will always be present. "Continuity with the past," said Oliver Wendell Holmes, "is only a necessity and not a duty."[20] It may well be a necessity that such things exist, but it is no less a necessity—and more, a duty—to try to counter them. The point is not that corruption then will cease to exist but rather that without that endless counterthrust it will be far worse than it is.

One final word. Disorder, dishonesty and the like are not necessarily proof that now, finally, the American sky is falling in and the American way of life is past redemption. The cause for concern but not despair was eloquently put a century ago— also a time of corruption in high places and a widespread sense that the system had failed—by the Russian novelist Ivan Turgenev:

In my opinion, he who is weary of democracy because it creates disorder, is very much in the state of one who is about to commit suicide. He is tired of the variety of life and longs for the monotony of death. For as long as we are created individuals, and not uniform repetitions of one and the same type, life will be motley, varied, and even disorderly. And in this infinite collision of interests and ideas lies our chief promise of progress. To me the great charm of American institutions has always been in the fact that they offer the widest scope for individual development, the very thing which despotism does not and cannot do.[21]

18 BEFORE WATERGATE

NOTES

1. Huntington quoted in Arnold J. Heidenheimer, ed., *Political Corruption: Readings in Comparative Analysis* (New York, 1970), p. 3.

2. Dooley quoted in Carl J. Friedrich, *The Pathology of Politics* (New York, 1972), p. 171.

3. Samuel Huntington, "Political Modernization: America vs. Europe," *Political Order in Changing Societies* (New Haven, 1968), pp. 93–139.

4. Winthrop, "A Modell of Christian Charity," *Winthrop Papers*, II (Boston, 1931), 282.

5. Ronald Wraith and Edgar Simpkins, *Corruption in Developing Countries* (London, 1963); Bernard Bailyn, "The Origins of American Politics," *Perspectives in American History*, I (1967), 26.

6. Campbell quoted in Anthony F. Upton, "The Road to Power in Virginia in the Early Nineteenth Century," *Virginia Magazine of History and Biography*, LXII (1954), 275.

7. Bailyn, *op. cit.*, 36–37.

8. Wraith and Simpkins, *op. cit.*, 14.

9. David D. Field, "Corruption in Politics," *International Review*, IV (1877), 85.

10. Lowell quoted in George F. Howe, *Chester A. Arthur* (New York, 1934), p. 204; Tweed quoted in Alexander B. Callow, Jr., *The Tweed Ring* (New York, 1966), p. 196; Thomas C. Reeves, "Chester A. Arthur and Campaign Assessments in the Election of 1880," *Historian*, XXXI (1969), 573–582. See also Morton Keller, *Affairs of State: Public Life in Late Nineteenth Century America* (Cambridge, 1977), pp. 238–258, 522–544.

11. Morton Keller, *The Life Insurance Enterprise, 1885–1910* (Cambridge, 1964), pp. 227–230.

12. Keller, *Affairs of State*, p. 245.

13. Burke quoted in Heidenheimer, *op. cit.*, p. 17. On Europe, *ibid.*, pp. 90 ff.

14. Keller, *Affairs of State*, pp. 272–275, 313–314; William M. Dickson, "The New Political Machine," *North American Review*, CXXXIV (1882), 42–43; Oliver P. Morton, "The American Constitution," *ibid.*, CLVI (1887), 343–345. See also Ari Hoogenboom, *Outlawing the Spoils* (Urbana, 1961).

15. Mayer, "What to Do about Television," *Commentary*, No. 53 (May 1972), p. 69.

16. Green, "The Educational Entrepreneur," *The Public Interest*, No. 28 (Summer 1972), pp. 12–25; William L. Riordon, *Plunkett of Tammany Hall* (New York, 1948), p. 41.

17. J. Leonard Bates, *The Origins of Teapot Dome* (Urbana, Ill., 1963).

18. Michael P. Rogin, *The Intellectuals and McCarthy* (Cambridge, 1967), p. 230.

19. White, "The Old Order Changeth," *American Magazine*, LXVII (1909), 218.

20. Holmes, *Collected Legal Papers* (New York, 1920), p. 211.

21. Hjalmar H. Borgeson, "A Visit to Tourguénoff," *Galaxy*, XVII (1874), 459–460.

Arnold J. Heidenheimer

POLITICAL CORRUPTION IN AMERICA:
IS IT COMPARABLE?

Any discussion of political corruption is by nature deeply
grounded in values and much of the problem of potential
analysts has consisted of disentangling the value systems manifested and expounded by the actors, intermediaries, monitors
and observers of the actions deemed corrupt. As soon as transactions are labeled corrupt, they engender rhetorical and ideological descriptors that tend to remain only loosely linked to
the actors accused of the questionable relationships. Analysis
of the monitors' claims to moral superiority or the prosecutors'
partisan motivations may elicit greater interest than the nature
and value of the material advantages that were illicitly traded.
Since many of these components seem so tied to culture and
situation, some may seriously question whether evidence of
corruption can be effectively gathered and analyzed over time
and compared across political cultures.

These obstacles are not insurmountable, however, and analysis of the incidence of various kinds of corrupt transactions *can*
be pursued both through varying historical periods and potentially also across national and even broader cultural boundaries.
At least for the modern period, since the duties and obligations
of public office have become legally and otherwise institution-
alized in Western countries, it is possible to attempt an objective
definition of political corruption that can be applied transnationally and, properly adjusted, also through time. Such a
definition might state:

Corruption is behavior which deviates from the formal duties of a public
role because of private-regarding (family, close family, private clique)
pecuniary or status gains; or violates rules against the exercise of certain

types of private-regarding influence. This includes such behavior as bribery (use of a reward to pervert the judgment of a person in a position of trust); nepotism (bestowal of patronage by reason of ascriptive relationship rather than merit); and misappropriation (illegal appropriation of public resources for private-regarding uses).[1]

Historians and social scientists who choose to utilize such a definition have for some time had the opportunity to compare the occurrence of corruption in American settings with its incidence elsewhere, particularly western Europe. However, an extensive examination of the literature has indicated that very few writers have succeeded in realizing that potential. European scholars have often looked in vain to their American colleagues for good descriptive studies they could build on. Thus Jacob van Klaveren complained that it was "a well-known fact among those studying American history" that "corruption is systematically practiced even today . . . yet it is difficult to obtain more specific explanations and information from American scholars." Elsewhere Colin Leys characterized most writing on American corruption as being "inquisitional" in nature, in contrast to the more solid historical studies of the eclipse of corrupt practices in Britain.[2]

A contemporary frame of reference will be used here to examine some of the reasons that have impeded the comparative analysis of American corruption.

✦   ✦   ✦

Students of political corruption need to be intensely concerned about the problem of comparing different phenomena, say bribery and inefficiency, if for no other reason than that they are included by some under an overarching label of corruption. Careful lexicographers, such as those who edit the *Oxford English Dictionary*, identify a dozen or more definitions of corruption in past and present usage.[3] In America the range of practices to which the term is applied by publicists and even scholars has tended to vary more with cycles of public equanimity and arousal than in Europe. In periods of more intense and widespread concern with the morality and legitimacy of government, the variety of practices labeled corrupt tends to multiply. Thus Robert Brooks noted for the Progressive period that scholars, journalists and reformers displayed little discrimination in using the term to stigmatize "transactions and conditions of very different kinds."[4] He warned that the constant repetition of unclearly applied concepts tended to blur the popular conception of corruption. In the post-Watergate period the number of meanings which writers encompass under the corruption label seems to have expanded again. Typical of the broadened concept urged by some is one that calls for "the need to widen the conceptual approach to the study of corruption" by including a wide variety of actions and relationships that in one way or another "comprise a threat to the constitutional order and to the values of the democratic society."[5]

Even if researchers could agree on transnationally applicable definitions of political corruption, they still face problems of applying them to varying political jurisdictions. American national political institutions differ from European ones. To think of the powers of U.S. congressional committees or the discretionary power of U.S. regulatory agencies is to suggest contextual differences crucial to corruptibility that find only limited counterparts in European capitals. From many perspectives, as well as the simple matter of scale, American state systems might most fruitfully be compared with European national and regional governments. It can be appreciated how greatly the incidence of corruption at the state and local level varies between and within regions. It would therefore matter a great deal whether a researcher undertook a comparison of Belgian corruption with corruption in Louisiana or Oregon. Students of the mores of state legislatures can distinguish fairly evident gradations in the incidence of corruption: in the Midwest, for example, most would expect corruption to increase as they moved from Madison, Wisconsin, to Jefferson City, Missouri, to Springfield, Illinois. These variations in the tolerance of corruption at the subnational level are surely much greater than within the larger European countries, both the centralized ones like Britain and the federal ones like West Germany. In fact it is quite possible that an American state like Minnesota might be distinguished from other U.S. states by virtue of the low incidence of corruption almost as much as a European nation like Sweden might be distinguished from the nations and regions of western and southern Europe as a whole.

Another impediment to measuring corruption comparatively

may be attributed to the greater visibility of much American corruption, especially at the local level. In America it is highly likely that information about corrupt arrangements will sooner or later come out not just in corridor gossip but also in public print and possibly in subsequent investigation. There are many interrelated reasons for this. In Europe bureaucracies are more tightly knit and insulated, and much medium-level official malfeasance may be discovered and punished without the general public ever becoming aware of it. The exposure of inefficiencies and corruption constitutes a vital theme of American local newspapers, more so than in Europe with the greater predominance of national media there. American journalists were more enterprising in this respect than their European equivalents even before the New Journalism turned them into superferrets. Typically they have inside information sources, such as the challengers who want to upset incumbents in primary elections, or the candidates for elected district attorneys and judges, for which there are few equivalents in Europe. The appointed jobholder in many American local and state governments, more used as he is to frequent job changes, is also probably more willing to divulge incriminating information than a European equivalent loath to endanger a lifelong career in his civil service. Once aspersions and accusations are public, there are in America half a million individually elected local and state politicians, who can hope to enhance both their personal reputations and the public interest by calling for or expanding investigations. An American writer claimed in 1910 that the combating of more political corruption in the democratic, decentralized American setting implied the existence of greater political virtue than it did in Prussia of that day, where "the local government of the country is kept closely in the leading strings of the state."[6] Some of that difference has remained.

*   *   *

Toward the end of the period of "normalcy" that preceded Vietnam and Watergate, some observers believed that, when all the factors making for escalation of talk of corruption had been discounted, the United States was actually going through "a period of unexampled honesty in public administration."

These were the words of a dean of the Stanford Law School, who was particularly concerned lest tightened conflict-of-interest statutes were keeping able corporate executives and lawyers from accepting government positions. The prototypical political outs, he held, had continued to blow up isolated instances of impropriety so that they appeared to illustrate massive, pervasive political corruption, causing "yesterday's peccadillo to become today's enormity." Conflict of interest had for him become "a modern political obsession" because of the American proclivity toward "morality escalation." In an era of unparalleled honesty he saw Americans indulging in the luxury of worrying about harms that were only potential.[7]

Bayless Manning's concern for the restraints on the mobility of American political elites might well be different after the experiences of the Lyndon Johnson and particularly the Richard Nixon administrations. The numerous and disastrous instances of malfeasance, misfeasance and abuse of power, particularly by officials in the White House, the intelligence agencies and the military complex, have certainly destroyed many illusions about the functioning of institutional controls. But neither the cause of social science nor of reform is well served by including all these offenses indiscriminately under an expanded umbrella definition of political corruption. On the contrary, the enormity of some of these abuses can too easily be lost from view if they are labeled as only one variety of a large family of corruption techniques. Corruption charges should continue to be restricted to those who have abused their offices of public trust for the purposes of direct or indirect material enrichment. Fresh analyses of the systemic implications of the revelations of the past decade would be instructive but those who undertake them should distinguish the incidence of the standard forms of corrupt practice from other abuses of public office.

Comparative research or, in the absence of good data, comparatively oriented thinking or even speculation can be helpful in this respect. For instance, suppose a really probing European-American study of the incidence of corruption had been sponsored by a foundation in, say, the late 1950s, a period of relative normality and fairly stabilized concepts among both elites and masses. What such a survey would have shown would have depended very much on how questions were asked and responses translated. It would have been fairest then as now to include all of the present European Economic Community together with Scandinavia and other reasonably competitive political systems such as those of Austria and Switzerland. In other words, a Europe extending from Narvik to Syracuse would have been matched against a United States extending from Bangor and Key West to San Diego and Tacoma.

Making some educated guesses what such a survey would have revealed would constitute a sporting proposition, since the Jersey Cities and St. Pauls of America would be matched with the Gothenburgs and Palermos of Europe. Especially since no one will soon develop the technology needed to prove them, the findings of such a survey can be revealed on the basis of intuition. They might well show:

• Press mentions of the incidence of political corruption would be several score times more frequent in the United States than in Europe.

• Knowledge that there was "considerable or extensive" corruption in American state and local, and European national and local, government would vary widely in both settings: it would be more sharply polarized on a north-south dimension in Europe than in the United States.

• The identification of petty corruption would take different forms, such as traffic-ticket fixing in the United States and petty administrative bribery in Europe, but would be more uniformly reported from around the United States than in Europe, where it would rarely have been reported from northern urban areas.

• The pervasiveness of more serious forms of police corruption, as indicated for such cities as New York and Chicago, would not be widely ascertainable in Europe.

• Vote-buying and other forms of electoral corruption would be more widely reported in interviews with older Americans, while their European equivalents would more frequently report memories of other forms of electoral intimidation.

• Where financial contributions by business were believed to have swayed policies corruptly, American reports would usually mention individual firms while European ones would mention more industry and business associations.

The canons of scholarship do not presently punish aggravated historical fabrication much more severely than simple one-shot cases of supposition, so historians could also hypothesize about how the incidence of corruption has developed over time on both sides of the Atlantic. Suppose a data repository containing roughly comparable surveys since the late nineteenth century had been found. The shape of the curves of corruption incidence in Europe and America as they developed in the last three generations can be imagined.

What would these curves look like? Would they be similar, for instance, to the curves of car ownership, with the American incidence ratios higher at the start but with the Europeans gaining to narrow the difference over time? Or would they be more similar to the curves reflecting rates of infant mortality, with both American and European rates declining over time, but with the European rate declining more rapidly, so that almost all West European countries now have lower infant mortality rates than does the United States? Or maybe they would be cyclical in shape, somewhat akin to unemployment rates, with a tendency toward lower levels and lesser oscillation in the more recent periods. A set of curves closer to the infant mortality model seems most likely.

＊　　＊　　＊

While the honest historian will reject the above extrapolations, the behavioral social scientist may claim that they unfairly malign Americans. The higher American rates of incidence of corruption, they may say, can still mean that a larger proportion of Americans than Europeans have over time virtuously forgone corruption opportunities. They will be thinking of the countless petty and large-scale bribers and favor-exchangers among businessmen, home owners, taxpayers and middlemen, department chairmen and other components of the large unwashed masses of corrupters. Corruption, they will say, can meaningfully be measured only as a proportion of opportunities to corrupt that were taken advantage of.

They have an arguable point. More Americans have probably had more opportunities to corrupt officials than have Europeans. In Germany civil servants traditionally displayed such disdain for the favors of other classes that in one German scholar's words, businessmen "did not even dare to offer any favors."[8] In the Netherlands the citizens' opportunity to bribe the police is limited by the pervasive way in which policemen live up to the legal provisions that forbid them to accept even cigarettes as gifts.[9] The American citizen's more direct involvement in administration gives him more opportunities for evading or breaking the rules. Thus the "tax morality" of most individual American taxpayers has to be evaluated differently, for our system of having the income-tax-payer figure out his own assessment is different from the practice followed in Europe, where the assessments are made by tax officials on the basis of documents submitted by the taxpayer. Faced by a more disciplined and professionalized bureaucracy and fewer opportunities to interpret rules for themselves, most Europeans may indeed face fewer opportunities to engage in corruption.

Are there, for instance, any European countries or regional jurisdictions where the knowledgeable businessman faces as few impediments to bribery to achieve his ends as in Chicago and Illinois, to take a state toward the top of the corruption scale? There the citizens found in the course of a recent six-year period that there was scarcely a single state or city elective official where the incumbent was not on the take. The governor took $300,000 from the racetrack interests. The secretary of state took from so many donors that his apartment overflowed with payoff envelopes. The Cook County clerk was convicted of receiving kickbacks from voting-machine manufacturers and numerous Chicago aldermen were convicted of extortion, embezzlement and conventional bribe-taking in zoning cases. State legislators, metropolitan district commissioners and appointed officials were shown to have formed numerous syndicates to take and distribute bribes. Thus in one five-year period alone several hundred public officials were convicted in more than 100 individual cases.

If a determined opposition party had won control of the Italian justice ministry, would it have racked up so vast a record even in Sicily? Possibly, though it is doubtful whether even there it would have been as sweeping. Elsewhere in central and northern Europe there has been no approximation to the incidence of corruption on this scale. There are, of course, regions there where the get-rich-quick opportunities of a commercial metropolis occasion successful attempts at corruption. Perhaps the state of Hesse with the metropolis of Frankfurt is a close approximation to Illinois in this respect. There, too, insiders greased the way for favorable action on contract bids for city and airport-building construction and concessions. But the scale of influence-buying did not touch all levels of the political and administrative hierarchies as it demonstrably did in Illinois. The scale of corruption payments in some notorious British cases would have aroused interest with difficulty in even the cleaner American states. Thus the main culprit in the Lynskey Tribunal case in the 1940s was shown to have been influenced by gifts of several dozen bottles of wine, a suit of clothes, a gold cigarette case and a week's hotel hospitality. To one American it "seems surprising that so much excitement was aroused in England about so little."[10]

The decline of Tammany in New York apparently reduced certain techniques of favor-buying in New York City politics but it evidently did not diminish the proclivity to bribe-taking of large sections of the New York police, as subsequently documented by the Knapp commission. The vast publicity given to its revelations produced a public scandal of the type that has forced reluctant administrators in many cities to shake up their departments to reduce corruption. The cyclical nature of attempts to reduce administrative corruption seems to be pronounced in American cities, even those lacking dominant party machines. The pattern seems to work as follows. Prior to the scandal corruption may reach pretty far up the police ladder, with assistant chiefs and inspectors joining captains and sergeants in taking corrupt payments. The reform administration then uses various devices, including dismissals from the force and incentive pay increases, to try to eliminate corruption at least at the higher and middle levels. During such phases promotion can be won by reporting bribe offers to superiors. But once the cleanup wave ebbs, there is a tendency to return to the pre-reform pattern of behavior, and the readiness to accept bribes or to sell protection once again rises up the command level within the police force.

*   *   *

What are the major reasons why attempts to compare the scale and nature of American corruption must remain so predominantly based on guesswork and piecework? The paucity of good-quality anaylses of corruption cannot be explained entirely by the lack of encouragement from governmental and private research organizations. Rather it seems as though political phenomena that have embraced corruption have been largely ignored as research topics by recent generations of social scientists and historians. Relevant contributions from historians seem to have seldom surmounted the limited frameworks provided by focusing on particular organizations, bosses and eras. The contributions from legal scholars have been limited to the point of nonexistence. A perusal of work in political science, sociology and economics shows that at least some scholars have realized that there were big and important questions to be explored from both empirical and theoretical perspectives. In these disciplines corruption has never been anything like a mainstream research favorite, but at least there have in each decade been several people who tried to mount reasonably ambitious individual research projects.

These initiatives have stimulated rivulets of academic interest, but perhaps in no area less than that of American politics above the level of the ethnic ghetto or the city ward. In the 1930s V. O. Key devoted his Ph.D. dissertation to an interesting attempt to develop an analysis of corruption in America.[11] It largely sank from public view and he treated the subject only peripherally in his subsequent career as one of the most widely recognized scholars of American parties and elections.

In the 1940s and 1950s sociologists like Robert K. Merton and Daniel Bell opened new perspectives which remolded academic views by purporting to demonstrate the positive functions of corruption and patronage from the standpoint of social integration. In the 1960s there was a relative profusion of studies, many of them more comparative and incorporating much new material derived from the study of politics in developing non-Western countries. Many of these studies applied theoretical constructs, derived from the study of machines and patronage, with more insight and in more convincing ways than similar work being done on earlier or contemporary American politics. But very few scholars made any reasonably ambitious or comprehensive attempts to treat the nature and scope of American corruption comparatively. The very few article-length efforts at comparative treatment in historical contexts were written by European and not by American scholars.[12]

A striking characteristic of most of the writing on American corruption by both historians and political scientists of the past several decades is how predominantly it has been linked in particular to the rise and fall of urban party machines. The development and employment of this machine paradigm has no doubt been fruitful, serving as a vehicle for linking the concepts of several disciplines and schools, but it has also inhibited the progress of research in a number of ways.

First, it has served to perpetuate a synecdochic research focus, in which the part looms bigger than the whole. Even as their middle-class inhabitants were fleeing to the suburbs, city machines were being subjected to much more searching and interesting analyses than were the politics at the state capitol or the shifting coalitions of national party coalitions. Historians argued over whether New Deal welfare programs helped or hurt the city machines. The ward was infinitely more closely scrutinized than the corporate board room; the boodle traditions of Philadelphia and San Francisco became much better known than the practices of the steel and construction industries.

Secondly, concentration on the machine paradigm perpetuated a kind of technological lag among social scientists. While they argued over how much of the exactions of party organizations constituted "dirty" or "clean" graft, or induced inefficiency rather than corruption, they were failing to keep abreast with newer, more subtle, indirect forms of favor-exchanging. These techniques typically involved the exchange of highly technical information at the interface of public and private economic spheres. Such newer forms of favor-trading operated much more characteristically between company officials and bureaucrats outside the relatively stagnant cities. If social scientists were as surprised as Republicans that a nice suburban politician like Spiro T. Agnew had to resign to avoid impeachment, it was partly because so much of their attention was focused on whether Mike Royko would ever be able to incriminate Mayor Richard Daley.

Finally, concentration on the machine model has focused attention one-sidedly on how manpower based on patronage

and support-chaneling has imposed coordinated policies within
a given political market across only one particular set of juris-
dictional boundaries. It was long thought that the interests that
procured acquiescence among some scores of governmental
boards in a single American metropolitan area faced unique
challenges. Revelations about supranational corporations have
demonstrated that companies like Lockheed have been treating
national governments around the world much as a turn-of-the-
century traction magnate treated local governments. But what
differences are there behind these similarities? It used to be
held that lack of data prevented an assessment of the global
behavior of international companies, when they were challenged
by critics like Gunnar Myrdal.[13] Now, rather suddenly, there
are plenty of data. But, partly because our "machine" tools do
not seem applicable, the conceptual apparatus to process them
is generally lacking.

*　　*　　*

The increments in objective perspective that can be gained
by relativizing cultural biases through cross-cultural examination
are especially important to a value-laden research topic like
corruption. That is why students of American corruption are
well advised to become knowledgeable about the definitions
and incidence of political corruption in other places and other
times. If such analyses are pursued, invaluable insights will
also be gained into the costs of corrupt practices relative to
other social goods and evils. Thus the arguments that in certain
situations the toleration of corruption by the few can in the
long term lead to economic benefits for the many is certainly
worth considering.

More than seventy years ago Henry Jones Ford derided Lincoln
Steffens by claiming that future cultural archeologists might
praise America for its willingness to accept corruption. "Most
assuredly," he wrote, they would "rejoice" that "men of affairs
in our time corrupted government in securing opportunities of
enterprise," because "slackness and decay are more dangerous
to a nation than corruption."[14] Today many are more likely to
agree with Max Weber that America has flourished economically
not because, but in spite of, its toleration of lax political and
administrative morality. "A corruption and wastefulness second

to none could be tolerated by a country with as yet unlimited economic opportunities."[15] As the limits earlier visible in Europe have become more evident also in this country, the drain of corruption becomes more critical.

Part of the wisdom the student of corruption needs to develop will also relate to considering how corruption as a social evil relates to other social evils. Is it occasionally preferable as a lesser evil to the more widespread incidence of societal violence? Scholars like Huntington and Friedrich argue that the two phenomena may indeed be mutually substitutable. The conservative may be willing to tolerate patterns of police corruption as an alternative to attempts to storm and seize police stations. Even the tender-hearted liberal might accept the bribing of concentration-camp guards if it might lessen the death or mutilization toll of the political or ethnic deviants who may constitute the bulk of camp inmates.

Fortunately such trade-offs need not be given prime consideration in an essay comparing corrupt patterns in the post-industrial societies of Europe and North America. But if one attempts to answer the larger question of "what difference" the supposed higher levels of United States corruption make in terms of the dominant goals of these political systems, he should attempt to perceive how the widespread toleration of corruption affects the manner in which governments are able to approach their larger social goals as implemented in their social welfare programs.

Even the New Deal might not have been able to break through the resistance to social legislation, had it not included the big city machines within its coalition. These machines in turn would not have delivered crucial congressional votes if the do-gooders had not been tolerant of a certain level of corruption at local and state levels. Advocates of the welfare state in northern Europe did not have to make such accommodations to expand their programs. Rather they have always emphasized tough standards of administrative probity. Although the Nazis attacked the Social Democratic welfare bureaucracies as self-serving instruments in the 1930s, such grounds for attacking the expansion of the welfare state have not been successful in recent decades. Scarcely any European politicians have won elections on the basis of attacks on welfare "chiselers." Those concerned with how voter backlash and other reactions have set political limits on the development of social reform legislation in the 1960s might reconsider the priority given to the problem of corruption.

NOTES

1. This definition is employed by Joseph S. Nye in "Corruption and Political Development: A Cost Benefit Analysis," *American Political Science Review*, LXI, No. 2 (June 1967), 419, and is cited in Arnold J. Heidenheimer, ed., *Political Corruption: Readings in Comparative Analysis* (New York, 1970), pp. 566–567.

2. Jacob van Klaveren, "Corruption: The Special Case of the United States" in Heidenheimer, *op. cit.*, p. 269; Colin Leys, "What Is the Problem about Corruption?" *Journal of Modern African Studies*, III (1965), No. 2, 215–224.

3. Heidenheimer, "Definitions, Concepts and Criteria," in Heidenheimer, *op. cit.*, pp. 3–9.

4. Robert C. Brooks, "The Nature of Political Corruption," in *ibid.*, p. 56.

5. Larry L. Berg *et. al.*, *Corruption in the American Political System* (Morristown, N.J., 1977), pp. 7, 80.

6. Henry Jones Ford, "Municipal Corruption: A Comment on Lincoln Steffens," *Political Science Quarterly*, XIX (1904), 673–686.

7. Bayless Manning, "The Purity Potlatch: Conflict of Interests and Moral Escalation," *Federal Bar Journal*, XXIV, No. 3 (Summer 1954), 243–249.

8. Theodore Eschenburg, "The Decline of the Bureaucratic Ethos in the Federal Republic" in Heidenheimer, *op. cit.*, p. 259.

9. H. H. Brasz, "Administrative Corruption in Theory and Dutch Practice" in *ibid.*, p. 247.

10. Madeline R. Robinton, "The British Method of Dealing with Political Corruption" in *ibid.*, p. 254.

11. V. O. Key, Jr., *The Techniques of Political Graft in the United States* (Chicago, 1936).

12. Cf. Samuel E. Finer, "Patronage and the Public Service: Jeffersonian Bureaucracy and the British Tradition" in *ibid.*, pp. 106–127; Van Klaveren, *op. cit.*

13. Gunnar Myrdal, "Corruption: Its Causes and Effects," in *Asian Drama: An Enquiry into the Poverty of Nations* (New York, 1968), II, 937–951.

14. Ford, *op. cit.*

15. Max Weber, *Politics as a Vocation* (Philadelphia, 1965), p. 108.

Linda Levy Peck

THE BRITISH CASE:
CORRUPTION AND POLITICAL DEVELOPMENT
IN THE EARLY MODERN STATE*

If corruption has been the most powerful issue within American politics in recent years, it was even more explosive on the
eve of the American Revolution. The most frequent political
charge pressed against the British by the colonists was that of
moral and political corruption. In 1775, Benjamin Franklin
wrote from England:

When I consider the extreme corruption prevalent among all orders of
men in this old rotten state, and the glorious public virtue so predominant
in our rising country, I cannot but apprehend more mischief than benefit
from a closer union. Here numberless and needless places, enormous
salaries, pensions, prerequisites, bribes ... devour all revenue and produce continual necessity in the midst of natural plenty. I apprehend,
therefore, that to unite us intimately will only be to corrupt and poison
us also.[1]

After close examination of the extensive elaboration of such
charges in colonial newspapers and pamphlets, Bernard Bailyn
concluded that to most informed colonists "by 1774, the final
crisis of the constitution, brought on by political and social
corruption, had been reached."[2]

Yet it is important to note that the practices cited with
outrage by the colonists were normal political practice in early

---

* Thanks are due to Lester Cohen, Darlene Hine, Charles Ingrao,
Philip VanderMeer and Carl Zangerl for their helpful comments on an
earlier draft of this essay.

modern England, a very part, as Patrick Henry suggested pejora-
tively, of its system of government.[3] Why was this the case?
One answer has been suggested by analysts of corruption in
developing nations. Social scientists following the influential
writings of Samuel Huntington have created a new orthodoxy in
the last ten years, equating corruption with the process of
modernization.[4] Modernization, the argument goes, is characterized by the development of new forms of wealth that are not
encompassed by the traditional norms of society. Corrupt practices provide access and control over resources for groups that
have hitherto been excluded from power. Huntington himself
suggests: "Political life in seventeenth-century Britain and in
late nineteenth-century Britain was, it would appear, less corrupt
than it was in eighteenth-century Britain. Is it merely coincidence
that the high point of corruption in English and American public
life coincided with the impact of the industrial revolution, the
development of new sources of wealth and power, and the
appearance of new classes making new demands of government?"[5] Drawing on Huntington's approach, James C. Scott in
his examination of corruption in early Stuart England, em-
phasizes the role of what he calls wealth elites (by which he
seems to mean well-to-do merchants), themselves outside the
political system, who used corrupt means to gain access to
economic privileges and to influence the enforcement of government regulations.[6] The Huntington-Scott view seems to be yet
another invocation of the rise of the bourgeoisie, in this instance
to explain the flourishing of corrupt practices in a period of
political and economic change. This essay will examine corrupt
practices in England from the sixteenth to the eighteenth centuries, tracing the fundamental shift from court-centered to
parliamentary corruption. The aim is to relate corruption to
English political development and to suggest another hypothesis
of who benefited from corrupt practices and why. The definition
of corruption adopted is "behavior which deviates from the
formal duties of a public role because of private-regarding . . . ,
pecuniary or status gains; or violates rules against the exercise
of certain types of private-regarding behavior."[7] Although many
practices later labeled corrupt were standard practice in the
early modern period and might better be labeled proto-
corruption,[8] this use of the contemporary Western definition,

which includes bribery, nepotism and peculation, does allow comparative analysis with societies in other times and places.

What did early modern English government look like? From the 1530s to the end of the seventeenth century, corrupt practices were centered in the sizable administration of Tudor and Stuart England. In the sixteenth century, beginning with the Henrician revolution, the English state took over the functions previously exercised by church and guild, and the period was marked not only by the expansion of offices but also by an increase in laws regulating all aspects of social and economic life. Such an increase in the regulatory side of the state's activities institutionally allowed for an increase in corrupt activities.[9] But it is crucial to note that the notion of a bureaucracy of civil servants serving the public interest did not exist in the period. Public and private interest were hopelessly mixed in what Max Weber described as the early modern patrimonial bureaucratic state.[10] What did this mean in specific terms? The staffing of the bureaucracy proceeded not by merit but by a patronage process in which kinship and client ties were usually more important than ability to perform the job. Since salaries for administrators were pegged either at centuries-old levels or were nonexistent, officials were paid by those who needed to use their services. In the period of price inflation that marked the sixteenth century, money above and beyond traditional fees was exacted. By the 1640s these informal takings amounted to 40% of the government's yearly revenue.[11] In addition, positions on the middle and lower levels of administration carried with them not tenure during good behavior but life tenure, and appointment was often in the hands of middle-level officials. For instance, because England never abolished offices, by the sixteenth century three different royal seals were required for any legal document. The clerkships within these seals' offices were sinecures that offered good pay, little work and the possibility of hiring a deputy. Offices were briskly bought and sold and it was not uncommon to find five or more reversions of interest attached to any one office, sometimes in the names of infants. Royal officials used government property as if it were their own. Thus the two top naval officials used a ship that supposedly accompanied the Lord High Admiral on an embassy to Spain for a private merchant voyage at the king's expense.[12]

This was not, however, unusual. After all, Elizabeth's navy had been made up in part of privateering ships in whose ventures the queen participated when England was not at war. It was cheaper than footing the bill for the navy entirely by herself and in addition "deniability," which is thought of as a contemporary phenomenon, was so much easier for Elizabeth when public and private interest merged. In short, bribery, graft and nepotism were characteristic of early modern bureaucracy in England and elsewhere.

These patterns of administrative corruption parallel those in contemporary developing nations and it is important to cite the positive functions that many social scientists provocatively argue that corruption performs, for similar benefits ensued in early modern England, specifically, increased governmental capacity and national integration.[13] Thus the increased scope of government activity permitted the government to increase its rewards in the form of offices, fees and privileges. The distribution of these spoils served to centralize power, to make the court the center of reward and to integrate those who on the local level were politically important. This was a signal achievement after the disintegrative period of the fifteenth century, the Wars of the Roses and the bane of what contemporaries called "the overmighty subject." The expansion of patronage helped to provide the king with an administrative staff in a period when the monarchy was without the resources to pay its servants. Groups outside the political elite, such as the merchant community, did gain access to power and resources by paying bribes to government officials. Their loyalty was thus assured and, more importantly, their economic resources were made available to the Crown. Given the fact that England lacked a standing army as well as paid local administrators, the allocation of reward was the means by which local elites could be amalgamated to the Crown. In analyzing corruption in Tudor England there can be little doubt that those who benefited from corrupt practices were primarily members of the landed interest and the court itself. Corrupt practices were the cement welding together the Crown and the political elite: the aristocracy, composed of the nobility and gentry.

But in the decades of the seventeenth century before the Puritan revolution, in addition to the administrative corruption endemic to the early modern state, there was a sharp change in corrupt practices, an increase in their extent and variety and the outcry against them. Most important, there was a shift to "market corruption" which tended to generalize the distribution of privileges by putting them within the grasp of those who could pay.[14] Did this mean that corruption now centered on the activities of the merchant community? It did seem as if everything were for sale at the court of James I. Public functions such as taxation and law enforcement were granted to private persons in exchange for cash. Access to economic privileges was granted for money. The customs duties were farmed out and the customs farmers, London merchants, soon became the main source of royal loans. Economic privileges belonging to the Crown, such as patents of monopoly on the manufacture or importation of goods, were granted to favorites and officials who subcontracted them to merchants.

Social privileges too were granted in exchange for cash. In the Jacobean period, knighthoods were sold and later, titles: for £10,000 one could purchase a peerage and have the privilege of sitting in the House of Lords by becoming a baron. Or if that was too expensive, for quite a lot less, £1,095, one could become a baronet. James Scott in his book, *Comparative Corruption*, pinpoints the importance of the rise of an affluent commercial elite that desired influence, protection and status. He suggests that there was a trend under the early Stuarts from decentralized nonmarket corruption to centralized market corruption, "reflecting the growing alliance between the Crown and commercial interests and worked to the disadvantage of the independent aristocratic cliques that had previously controlled much of patronage and spoils."[15] Such a statement seems to be substantially incorrect. It cannot be denied that leading merchants did pay bribes to gain access to monopolies and customs farms, particularly in the Jacobean era. In fact the London financial community became a pillar on which the early Stuart monarchy rested. But it is most important to note that Scott's dichotomy between aristocratic networks and court-merchant relations is not accurate. Most merchants who dealt with the Crown did so through the intercession of those very aristocrats whom Scott is intent on phasing out. In 1604, for instance, in the competition for the letting of the Great Customs,

Lords Dorset, Salisbury and Northampton each had his own merchant clients who competed for the farm.[16] Lionel Cranfield, a successful merchant of the period, was brought into government and later became Lord High Treasurer through the intercession of an aristocrat of the Howard family, and continued his career as the client of the Duke of Buckingham. While there was an outcry against the sale of honors, criticism focused not on the sale itself but on who got what. And at the beginning in 1611, baronetcies were sold only to the leading gentlemen in each county. In fact, sales were considered reasonable so long as the price was kept *up*! Those who were most eager to buy were not wealthy merchants but the landed gentry. Indeed gentry, not members of the merchant community, were the principal buyers of government offices.[17]

Historians have the nasty habit of wanting to look at specifics. The court was not without its reformers.[18] In 1608 court officials seeking to rationalize Jacobean administration established a royal commission to investigate corruption in the navy.[19] These were its findings. At the lowest levels of the navy, supplies such as timber, cordage, tar, pitch were diverted into private hands; good wood was used to build private homes and bad wood substituted for the king's ships. At the middle levels, ship's officers, captain, pursers and victualers, would take on supplies for 100 men when there were only 70 and sell the excess. At the top levels, naval officials placed their own liveried followers in office; took kickbacks from all those who provided supplies to the navy, or were themselves the purveyors and passed the cost on to the king; supplied their own ships for merchant voyages at royal expense; and, in appointments, placed "most for Mony, fewe for Meritte, whereby your Navie is made, as your best Ministers depose, a Ragged Regiment of Tapsters, Coblers and Rogues."[20] This is certainly market corruption, but who were the corrupt? The officials were of impeccably gentle credentials; those who were forced to kick back were small businessmen.

What about the towns, home of the newly well-to-do merchants? Corrupt practices flourished on the local level during the period in the form of loans from town corporation funds, use of public power for personal financial advantage and simple peculation. In large part this was due to the multiplication of

offices required for the administration of the Tudor and Stuart
regulations of the economy and society, in particular the poor
law. Newly wealthy men certainly dominated the government of
many English towns in the period, often because they could
afford the expenses associated with town office. But it is important to note that the sixteenth century also witnessed an
increasing interference by the Crown and local gentry in town
affairs. Borough seats in Parliament were monopolized by gentlemen who often also took over the position of town clerk, "lynch-
pin of civic administration." And the Crown's agents were mostly
county gentlemen or county lawyers. The result was the rein-
forcement of oligarchical power, but shared between the gentry
and the well-to-do merchants of the town.[21]

Again, in the most notorious corruption case of the reign,
the trial of the Earl of Suffolk, son of the Duke of Norfolk (in
short, not a new man), the charges against him included ex-
torting kickbacks of 10% to 20% from those owed money by
the Exchequer and using government funds as if they were
his own private bank account. Even other departments within
the administration were forced to kick back to him in order
to secure their budgetary allotments and even then did not
necessarily receive their money. Having borrowed £10,000 from
the customs farmers, Suffolk arranged for a kickback of £1,500
a year to be applied to his debt.[22] The purpose of the bribe,
however, was not to enable those outside political power to
circumvent enforcement of irksome regulations, as Scott's argument suggests, but rather to reinforce their status as insiders,
as clients of the Lord High Treasurer. Because Scott construes
corruption as influence exercised at the enforcement stage, he
overlooks those practices. But if not simply the result of wealthy
merchants seeking to influence policy, what political function,
then, did "market corruption" fulfill in early Stuart England?

To begin with, it provided needed revenue for the king faced
by a Parliament loath to pass what were, after all, inadequate
subsidies. The Crown could do better by selling titles and
privileges, could reward its favorites more through licensing,
than by granting concessions or giving up such practices to a
tightfisted Parliament.[23] Market corruption also served as a
mechanism of allocation in a situation where the increase in
the political elite made it impossible to distribute reward as

broadly as in the past.[24] If the social structure of Tudor and Stuart England is examined, what is most significant for the question of corruption is the large increase in the size of the gentry and nobility, owing not to the rise of the bourgeoisie (or wealth elite) but to the increasing prosperity of yeomen. Where in 1433 there were 48 gentle families in Shropshire, in 1623 there were 470.[25] In keeping with this, increasing numbers of gentry flocked to the university in the second half of the sixteenth century but there were not sufficient positions in church or state for them. This growth in the political elite had crucial consequences. On the one hand, it meant a greater strain on the Crown's ability to reward and to maintain the Elizabethan balance of patronage. On the other, it meant the need for allocating devices as the scramble for reward intensified under the early Stuarts. In short, market corruption, characteristic of the Stuart period, served to raise revenue for the Crown and its favorites and to allocate rewards in a system in which demand greatly exceeded supply. But while market corruption may have served certain functions, the monopolization of favor by the Duke of Buckingham's faction exacerbated the inadequacy of court rewards to gain the support of all segments of the political elite. In addition, the type of corrupt practices prevalent at the Jacobean court provoked a strong outcry from an important section of the gentry because it affected their vital interests. The indiscriminate sale of honors affected the social structure and threatened the status of the politically preeminent. Bribery formed part of the fiscal grievances of the gentry. The payment of pensions by the Spanish to the most influential courtiers affronted vigilant Protestants. As a result, the court and the king himself were labeled corrupt. In the decades before the English Civil War, as the political elite polarized into factions of Court and Country with differing views on politics and religion, the issue of corruption undermined the legitimacy of the monarchy itself.[26]

What changes did the Commonwealth and Protectorate bring? G. E. Aylmer in the second of his important studies of seventeenth century administration pointed out that there was a massive change in personnel.[27] Where before the Civil War the nobility and gentry had been the principal holders of office, the government of the republic was strikingly less upper-class. There was a considerable change, too, in administrative practices. Salaries were increased, fee-taking was curtailed and offices were not sold on a significant level during the period. The result was a noticeable drop in administrative corruption, but the new elite created by the revolution was unable to entrench itself. With the Restoration, along with Charles II came the restoration of the old elite and the "old administrative system." Aylmer observed that its tenacious continuation into the nineteenth century was due to the victories of oligarchy and constitutionalism in 1660, 1688–89 and 1714, and the later reaction against the French Revolution.[28]

In the period from the Restoration to the American Revolution England experienced great economic growth and a large expansion in government offices which caused changed patterns of corruption too. The "commercial revolution" with increased trade to America, the West Indies and the East, and the development and growth of the home market created new wealth, with the result that the newly well-to-do took power in almost all English towns great and small. Significantly, this economic growth benefited the landed interest too, offering the gentry a variety of new opportunities for money-making as well as increased reward for agricultural products. Furthermore, the landed were becoming more stable as a group and even more entrenched in the countryside, as evidenced by the increasing size of landholdings and the shrinkage of the land market throughout most of the eighteenth century.[29] Where early Stuart England and the Civil War had seen a polarization of the politically important, the political elite of eighteenth century England, much more broadly based, its focus of attention less on the court and more on Parliament, was characterized by remarkable stability, one important factor of which was a "sense of common identity in those who wielded economic, social and political power."[30] What did this mean for corrupt practices? Certainly corruption played an important role in eighteenth century politics. Yet the cause lay not in wealthy merchants *outside* the political system making new demands for political power. Rather it lay in the alliance of the important landed and mercantile interests in a highly stable oligarchy. In combination with the Crown, this oligarchy ruled England well into the nineteenth century. As J. H. Plumb suggested of the period after 1689, "what the revolution did was to confirm the authority of certain men of property, particularly those of high social standing, either aristocrats or linked with the aristocracy, whose tap root was in land but whose side-roots reached out to commerce, industry and finance. . . . Their authority was established . . . because they settled like a cloud of locusts on the royal household and all the institutions of executive government."[31]

With the Glorious Revolution, parliamentary sovereignty was finally established, but there existed neither a constitutional mechanism by which the executive related to the legislature nor a means to finance increasingly expensive political campaigns. As a result, the royal ministers devised the informal but very effective means of using governmental patronage to reward the Crown's supporters in Parliament with offices and contracts. The monopolization of political control by the Whigs from 1720 to 1760 meant that division on issues receded and politics revolved around personality. The "influence of the Crown" was thereby augmented and the division of spoils became the lifeblood of the British system.[32]

The patronage at the disposal of the Hanoverians would have been the envy of James I. Late seventeenth and eighteenth century English government underwent a massive expansion, in conjunction with commercial growth, particularly in the offices of the Treasury which included the customs and excise subdepartments. New taxes brought not only increased revenues but also increased sinecures. In 1718, for instance, there were 1,561 customs officers working in the Port of London alone.[33] And the expansion of the number of officials was as much for political reasons as administrative: the increase in governmental patronage increased the number of those who profited from government employment and those who benefited were drawn from the politically active. As Sir Lewis Namier emphasized, the idea that the politically active part of the nation had a claim to maintenance on the state was generally acepted, tantamount to an eighteenth century version of outdoor relief.[34]

The warfare that characterized the century inflated the size of the War Office, and the army and navy. The result was not only a large increase in government positions but an expansion of government contracts to provision the armed forces. The political importance of these contracts as political favors can be calculated from the fact that 37 of the 50 merchants who sat in the Parliament of 1761 were government contractors.[35] Government office, government contracts and the nepotism, peculation and malfeasance that came in their wake were used by the Crown's ministers to ensure the loyalty of a majority of the Members of Parliament and to pay for the cost of their electioneering. These were the indirect means. In addition, the government maintained a secret fund taken from the Treasury for bribes, pensions and payments for electioneering to its friends in Parliament and out. In five years, £291,000 was paid out of the Treasury for this purpose.[36] In some sense it might be said the parliamentary gentry of the eighteenth century sold their political gains from the revolutions of the seventeenth century for a mess of patronage.

To the extent that the Crown's sharing of the spoils among a wide range of recipients widened participation in the regime, maintained the support of the politically important and increased the ability of the executive to shape policy, it contributed to the political stability of the period. After a century of instability and revolution, this may be deemed political development if considered in terms of the system's needs as opposed to the needs of the populace.[37] The entrenchment of this elite, however, nearly provoked further revolution in the 1830s, as it resisted every movement toward change until unwillingly and under the threat of violence it agreed to share some of its power with other groups. Even the extension of the suffrage, however, did not end the dominance of the landed interest, which continued into the middle of the nineteenth century and later.

To sum up, corruption in England in the sixteenth and early seventeenth centuries tended to be of a nature endemic to a patrimonial bureaucracy. The shift to market corruption under the early Stuarts was due to changes in social structure: the growth if not the rise of the gentry, the shaky finances of the Crown which could more easily be shored up through the sale of titles, patents and licenses, and the tendency of officeholders to maximize short-term gains because of a breakdown in supervision and the monopolization of patronage by one faction. With the development of parliamentary supremacy after the revolution of 1688, corrupt practices were instrumental in maintaining coalitions of interest between royal ministers and the House of Commons, and welded together the aristocracy and major financiers into a single oligarchy. In short, corrupt practices in early modern England served to reinforce the status quo, primarily the interests of the landed aristocracy. Wealthy merchants played their role to be sure, but only in association with the court and later parliamentary aristocracy. They were neither the major initiators of corrupt practices nor the major beneficiaries. Huntington, Scott and other social scientists, bemused by the rise of the bourgeoisie, have not sufficiently taken into account the ability of the English aristocracy to adapt to changing economic and social conditions.

Finally, the role of corruption should be considered in bringing about political change. It has been argued elsewhere that it is the linking of corruption to other vital issues that gives it the power to undermine the legitimacy of a regime. In the decades before the English Civil War, as the nobility and gentry polarized into factions of Court and Country with differing views on religion and politics, the monarchy itself came to be labeled corrupt. The Country opposition thought of themselves as "persons of public spirit, unmoved by private interest, untainted by court influence and corruption—representatives, in short, of the highest good of their local communities and the nation in whose interest they, and they only, acted."[38] With the Restoration such polarization ended and in 1688 there was no such split within the political elite. Although James II was removed from the throne, corruption played little role in the rhetoric of the revolution. While the Country ideology continued to exist in England in the eighteenth century, it found its real home in the colonies. In the years leading up to 1776, a good part of the colonists' rhetoric reflected that of the Puritan revolution. Influenced by the circulation of the works of the eighteenth century Commonwealth men, whose ideas reflected those of the Country opposition, Americans came to look at the English Parliament with the same eyes as the Puritan country gentry had when they looked at James I and Charles I. In Benjamin Franklin's words can be heard the Court/Country polarization across a gap of 125 years and 3,000 miles, in what J. G. A. Pocock has labeled the "revolution against parliament."[39] Tough-minded social scientists sometimes like to think of corruption as the oil that greases the wheels of the political machine. But emphasis on governmental capacity and stability to the exclusion of popular participation may not provide the best definition of political development. It is important to remember that, while corrupt practices may have reinforced the status quo in early modern England and fostered stability, corruption as a political issue was a dissolvent in the 1640s and in 1776 of the political ties that bind.

NOTES

1. Bernard Bailyn, *The Ideological Origins of the American Revolution* (Cambridge, Mass., 1967), pp. 36, 48–49, 130–139.

2. *Ibid.*, p. 132.

3. *Ibid.*, pp. 136–7.

4. Cf. Samuel P. Huntington, *Political Order in Changing Societies* (New Haven, 1968); Nathaniel H. Leff, "Economic Development through Bueaucratic Corruption," José V. Abeuva, "The Contribution of Nepotism, Spoils, and Graft to Political Development," and other selections in Arnold Heidenheimer, ed., *Political Corruption* (New York, 1970), pp. 479–578.

5. Huntington, "Modernization and Corruption," in Heidenheimer, *op. cit.*, p. 492.

6. James C. Scott, "Proto-Corruption in Early Stuart England," *Comparative Political Corruption* (Englewood Cliffs, N. J., 1972), pp. 37–55. Scott uses "wealth elites," "commercial and financial interests" and "bourgeoisie" interchangeably.

7. J. S. Nye, "Corruption and Political Development: A Cost-Benefit Analysis," in Heidenheimer, *op. cit.*, pp. 566–567.

8. Scott, *op. cit.*, p. 4. Scott who accepts Nye's definition suggests the use of "proto-corruption" to describe practices of the pre-nineteenth century period which were only labeled corrupt in the nineteenth century.

9. Cf. Joel Hurstfield, "Political Corruption in Modern England: The Historian's Problem" *History*, LII, No. 174 (February 1967), pp. 16–34. Huntington, *op. cit.*, p. 494.

10. Heidenheimer, *op. cit.*, pp. 10–11.

11. G. E. Aylmer, *The King's Servants* (New York, 1961), p. 248.

12. British Museum, Cotton MSS, Julius F III, fol. 15, 26. Julius F III contains the testimony given before the 1608 naval commission.

13. Cf. Huntington, "Modernization and Corruption," pp. 492–500; David H. Bayley, "The Effects of Corruption in a Developing Nation" in Heidenheimer, *op. cit.*, pp. 521–533; J. S. Nye, *op. cit.*, pp. 564–578.

14. Scott, *op. cit.*, pp. 12, 54.

15. *Ibid.*, p. 54. Lawrence Stone, *The Crisis of the Aristocracy* (Oxford, 1965).

16. A. P. Newton, "The Establishment of the Great Farm of the English Customs," *Transactions of the Royal Historical Society,* 4th series, I (1918), p. 150.

17. Scott is incorrect in his statement, "The sale of office provided an important avenue of social mobility for the growing bourgeoisie. . . . As elsewhere the sale of office led to a tacit alliance between the Crown and a portion of the national bourgeoisie," *op. cit.,* pp. 46–47. Cf, Aylmer, *op. cit.,* pp. 263–265, who stresses the upper-class background of most officials: "It can only be maintained that Tudor bureaucracy was staffed by men of predominantly middle-class origin if the gentry are classified with 'the middle classes'." This classification is not accepted by English historians. Cf. J. H. Hexter, "The Myth of the Middle Class in Tudor England," *Reappraisals in History* (New York, 1961), pp. 71–116.

18. Cf. Linda Levy Peck, "Problems in Jacobean Administration: Was Henry Howard, Earl of Northampton, A Reformer?" *The Historical Journal,* 19 Dec. 1976, 831–858; Menna Prestwich, *Cranfield: Politics and Profits under the Early Stuarts* (Oxford, 1966).

19. British Museum, Cotton MS, Julius C III. The commission's report is Public Record Office, S. P. 14, LXI, 1.

20. Trinity College, Cambridge, MS, R. 5. 1.

21. Peter Clark and Paul Slack, *English Towns in Transition, 1500–1700* (London, 1976), pp. 128–134.

22. A. P. P. Keep, "Star Chamber Proceedings against the Earl of Suffolk and Others," *English Historical Review,* XIII (1898), 716–729.

23. Cf. Conrad Russell, "Parliamentary History in Perspective, 1604–1629," *History,* LXI (February 1976), 1–27.

24. For a discussion of this aspect of corruption, cf. Heidenheimer, *op. cit.,* p. 5.

25. Stone, *op. cit.,* p. 67.

26. Cf. Linda Levy Peck, "Corruption at the Court of James I: The Undermining of Legitimacy," forthcoming in *Festschrift* in honor of J. H. Hexter.

27. Aylmer, *The State's Servants: The Civil Service of the English Republic, 1649–1660* (London, 1973) pp. 324, 328, 373.

28. Aylmer, *The King's Servants,* p. 438. Aylmer makes the following points: "The vested interests of the predominantly gentry and lawyer-staffed administration were perhaps equally at variance with the needs and aspirations of 'Thorough' and of a bourgeois-democratic republic," p. 436; "The Restoration is to be seen above all as an oligarchic victory over any incipient trends either towards 'enlightened absolutism' or towards middle-class democracy." p. 438.

29. J. H. Plumb, *The Origins of Political Stability, England, 1675–1725* (Boston, 1967), pp. 3–10.

30. *Ibid.,* pp. xviii, 18–19.

31. *Ibid.,* p. 69.

32. Cf. Archibald S. Foord, *His Majesty's Opposition, 1714–1830* (Ox-

ford, 1964), pp. 16–19; Sir Lewis Namier, *The Structure of Politics at the Accession of George III* (London, 1963), pp. 16–18.

33. Plumb, *op. cit.*, pp. 116–118.

34. Namier, *op. cit.*, p. 16.

35. *Ibid.*, pp. 45–49.

36. *Ibid.*, p. 234.

37. Cf. Nye, *op. cit.*, p. 566, who defines political development as "growth in the capacity of a society's governmental structures and processes to maintain their legitimacy over time."

38. Pérez Zagorín, *The Court and the Country: The Beginning of the English Revolution* (New York, 1970), p. 37.

39. J. G. A. Pocock, '1776: The Revolution against Parliament," paper delivered at Folger Shakespeare Library conference, "Three British Revolutions," May, 1976. Cf. Caroline Robbins, *The Eighteenth Century Commonwealthman* (Cambridge, Mass., 1959).

Edwin G. Burrows

ALBERT GALLATIN AND THE PROBLEM
OF CORRUPTION IN THE FEDERALIST ERA

In the summer of 1809, with eight years as Secretary of the
Treasury behind him and the prospect of another difficult four
to come, Albert Gallatin confided to former President Thomas
Jefferson, lately retired to Monticello, that he, Gallatin, could
no longer stomach the intrigues and injuries of public life and
wished to resign. Jefferson's reply was swift: your resignation
now, he told Gallatin, would be "a great public calamity," for
it would mean abandoning all hope of extinguishing the
public debt:

[I]f the debt should once more be swelled to a formidable size, its entire
discharge will be despaired of, and we shall be committed to the English
career of debt, corruption, and rottenness, closing with revolution. The
discharge of the debt, therefore, is vital to the destinies of our government, and it hangs on Mr. Madison and yourself alone. We will never
again see another President and Secretary of the Treasury making all other
objects subordinate to this.

Gallatin, in reply, agreed that his immediate departure from
office would be premature and promised to stay on so long as
the other members of James Madison's administration and its
supporters in Congress cooperated in keeping down expenditures. But without such cooperation, he declared to Jefferson,
he would have to quit, since the alternative was to aid and abet
the spread of an evil he too had always fought against:

I cannot, my dear sir, consent to act the part of a mere financier, to
become a contriver of taxes, a dealer of loans, a seeker of resources for
the purpose of supporting useless baubles, of increasing the number of

idle and dissipated members of the community, and of introducing in all its ramifications that system of patronage, corruption, and rottenness which you so justly execrate.[1]

The notable thing about this exchange, apart from Gallatin's effortless appropriation of Jefferson's phraseology, is that Gallatin is not remembered for having taken any special interest at all in the problem of corruption during his long career, much less for crusading against it. His brilliant and relentless attacks on Federal financial policy, his canny leadership of the Republican forces in Congress, his efficient management of the treasury under both Jefferson and Madison, then a memorable decade in diplomacy—this is the familiar substance of his public life and his biographers have always presented it as the product of, among other influences, Rousseauist radicalism, Physiocracy, Protestant frugality, agrarian romanticism, romantic agrarianism, and, inevitably, frontier democracy. Nowhere is there to be found a Gallatin even remotely concerned about corruption. Indeed no one seems ever to have looked twice at Gallatin's professed belief in the existence of an entire "system of patronage, corruption and rottenness" or at the suggestion that its destruction was one of the primary objects of his political career.[2]

The purpose of this essay is to suggest that something very important has been missed, not only about Gallatin himself but also about the nature of post-Revolutionary politics generally. For all the evidence indicates that Gallatin was in fact deeply troubled by the threat and reality of corruption throughout his career, particularly during the unruly 1790s when he was spearheading the resistance to Hamiltonian finance. Indeed, the closer one examines Gallatin's concern with corruption, the more its conquest and elimination appear to lie at the heart of his differences with Hamilton. And although it may push the argument too far, some attention to the origin of Gallatin's interest in the problem of corruption may yield some valuable insights into the social basis of Jeffersonian Republicanism and its relationship to other radical movements in the western world at the end of the eighteenth century.

❖   ❖   ❖

It should first be noted that Gallatin used the word corruption in at least three ways during the controversies of the 1790s.

At times he meant by it a lamentable decline, among the people as a whole, of old-fashioned republican simplicity and selflessness—chiefly, in his mind, as a consequence of the rampant speculation unleashed by Alexander Hamilton's funding and assumption schemes. Running in and out of this first meaning, and closely related to it, was a second: that out of the unseemly scramble for quick riches set in motion by Hamilton there had emerged a class of public creditors whose sudden wealth, essentially fraudulent in nature, made them at once the corrupt dependents of power and yet able as well to influence power illicitly for their own narrow advantage. Indeed, Gallatin would eventually conclude, Hamilton and his followers were deliberately fostering corruption of both kinds in order to destroy the moral and social foundations of republicanism.

Thus, in the early 1790s, Gallatin often harangued the Pennsylvania legislature about "shameful and corrupt speculations" in government paper, about "the spirit of speculation now too prevalent" and about the growing power of "mere speculators."[3] Soon he was toying with the idea of fleeing before he, too, had become corrupted:

The American seaports [he warned a friend] exhibit now such a scene of speculation and excessive fortunes, acquired not by the most deserving members of the community, as must make any person who has yet some principles left, and is not altogether corrupted or dazzled by the prospect, desirous of withdrawing himself from these parts.[4]

Public creditors, he declared a few years later in his famous *Sketch of the Finances of the United States* (1796), constitute a dangerous "artificial interest" that "may at some future period lend its assistance to bad measures and to a bad administration. So far as that interest is artificial, so far as it is distinct from the general interest, it may perhaps act against that general interest."[5] The evil was apparently spreading more rapidly than he had expected, for in 1797 he was moved to "lament the corruption which has already enervated the minds of men" and bitterly abused both Hamilton—"so unprincipled and profligate a creole"—and George Washington—guilty "of the grossest ignorance or the basest treachery"—for programs that had rewarded venality and prostrated virtue:

The spirit which animated our country to resist British tyranny and to declare independence is, alas, paralyzed by systems, artfully contrived to render the mind pliant to the views of an insidious and ambitious administration. Funding and bank systems, with the speculations which have grown out of them, have substituted an avarice of wealth, for the glory and love of country. Had America in the year 1775 been what she is now, a nation governed by stock jobbers, stock holders, bank directors, and brokers, we should have hugged the fetters which Great Britain had then forged for us.[6]

But the corruption that distressed Gallatin most acutely during the 1790s was of a third and different sort, clearer in origin and function and susceptible perhaps of surer correction. This was the process of influence, pressure and subornation by which the executive branch subdued and managed the legislative branch. Though by no means unconnected with purely private depravity or with the venal power of special interests, it was a special species of corruption that jeopardized the equilibrium of the Constitution by destroying the independence of the people's representatives, turning them into the creatures of faction and the accomplices of ministerial ambition. To Gallatin's way of thinking, it too, like the other forms of corruption that troubled him, originated in a diabolical Federalist plot against republicanism. Yet of them all it ranked first in seriousness, for in his mind an uncorrupted legislature could survive the occasional corruption of its constituents, while the reverse was not true and was sure to culminate sooner or later in tyranny.

Gallatin's anxieties over congressional independence had been aroused as early as 1788, when he warned his fellow Antifederalists at the Harrisburg Convention against the "corruption & abuses" that would inevitably emanate from the executive branch under the proposed federal constitution.[7] Not long afterward he was telling the Pennsylvania legislature that as a result of Hamilton's financial program congressional independence had already been seriously undermined: "The power of the executive," he observed, "by the number of offices in its gift, both judiciary, but chiefly belonging to the revenue, [has] enabled it to offer considerable bribes by promise of favors to members of the legislature, so as to gain, if not a majority, at least a considerable number to favor its views."[8] Congress, he repeated even more bluntly some years later, was fast becoming a mere "committee of ways and means—a parliament, somewhat after the ancient regime of France, to register edicts."[9]

What always gave these apprehensions a special accent of immediacy and reality for Gallatin was his conviction that the erosion of congressional independence exactly paralleled the process by which British ministries had recently subjugated Parliament. Remember, he warned the Pennsylvania legislature, "Though the Parliament of Great Britain . . . consists of 500, for want of proper checks, bribery & corruption were there the mainspring—were reduced to a perfect system" that left the representatives of the people no more than tools of administration.[10] He did not actually believe things had yet gone so far in the United States, he assured the House of Representatives in 1798 with unusual restraint. "Upon the whole, our Government was in a great degree pure," he said. "Patronage was not very extensive, nor had it any material effect upon the Legislature, or any other part of the Government." The point was rather to maintain a vigilant guard against the growth of corruption, since what had happened in Britain could also happen in America. To be sure, "the object of a constitution was to secure a proper distribution of power among the different branches of government" and Americans thus enjoyed "a security never possessed by any country" before, but the fate of Parliament should always be a warning against an overconfident reliance on mere forms. Corruption, Gallatin insisted, was no less a danger on this side of the Atlantic:

Look at all Governments where this power [of giving offices] was placed in the Executive, and see if the greatest evil of the Government was not the excessive influence of that department. Did not this corruption exist in the Government which was constituted most similarly to ours, to such a degree as to have become a part of the system itself, and without which, it is said, the Government could not go on?[11]

Indeed, the more he thought about it, the more it seemed that the Federalists were deliberately attempting to reenact the British experience in America, tunneling under the foundations of congressional independence in order to bring down free government. Their entire program, he wrote solemnly, was simply "to assimilate our government to a monarchy. Every measure seems to squint towards this darling object, and hence irredeemable debts, excise systems, national banks, loans, federal cities, reports for raising a revenue by an officer unknown to the Constitution, and dependent upon the Executive"—and more.[12] If ever the Federalists had their way, he declared on another occasion, Congress would be stripped of its power and "our Constitution would become a mere blank; it would be to transform our Government into a Monarchy, or, if gentlemen like the expression better, into a despotic government."[13]

Plainly enough, as Gallatin saw it, everything therefore depended upon detecting and defeating every attempt by the administration or its minions to diminish legislative independence. Nothing mattered more, he told the Pennsylvania House, than that "the guardians of the people's rights . . . put as many obstacles in the way of corruption as possible."[14] The "friends to the independence of the House," he later said in Congress, ought to reject "the doctrine of passive obedience and non-resistance" to the administration favored by the Federalists and refuse to be "deprived of their discretion, of the freedom of their will."[15] "I was opposed to any usurpation of powers by the General Government," he recalled late in life. "But I was specially jealous of executive encroachments; and to keep that branch within the strict limits of Constitution and law, allowing no more discretion than what appeared strictly necessary, was my constant effort."[16] In many cases this meant little beyond refusing to be cowed by administration demands for money to build more frigates, pay more troops, hire more functionaries and the like. It meant insisting on the principle of specific appropriations, so that executive officers would not have loose sums available for mischief, and checking up carefully and regularly to see that public monies were being spent on the objects for which they had been appropriated. And always it meant reducing the national debt so as to dry up the main source of corrupt ministerial influence over Congress as well as the chief corrosive of republican virtue among the people. So thoroughly did these tasks dominate Gallatin's public life in the 1790s that it is no exaggeration to describe the containment and elimination of corruption as his overriding purpose.[17]

Perhaps the closest Gallatin ever came to a comprehensive formulation of his views on corruption was a long and pene-

trating address he made to Congress in March 1798 on a proposed foreign intercourse bill. The immediate issue, as he
pointed out, was merely whether Congress should reduce appropriations for the diplomatic establishment, but looming
behind it was the larger issue of improper executive influence:
did Congress have a right to reject administration requests for
money to do things the Constitution empowered administration
to do and did not excessive expenditures on this and other
matters invite a dangerous corruption? To both questions Gallatin's answer was yes. The Constitution nowhere gives the
executive a right to command money from the legislature, he
insisted, and to believe otherwise is simply to discard the principle of a balanced government. The legislature's ability to
withstand executive pressure on this matter, furthermore, has
already been gravely endangered by a growing patronage. According to his calculations, Gallatin told Congress, the executive
already controls some $2,000,000 a year in salaries and contracts,
"a sum by no means despicable, when compared with our
population and wealth."[18]

What is so ominous about this figure, Gallatin went on, can
be read throughout human history. It is the old story of how
"money accumulated in the hands of a single man, or of a few,
may be applied with success to the destruction of any Government." "The foreign gold of Philip gave the last blow to the
expiring liberty of Athens," for example. "And the same engine
in the hands of the citizens of Rome was not attended with
less fatal consequences." More recently, too, the power of money
had overwhelmed late medieval representative institutions in
Europe and promoted the growth there of absolute monarchies:

What has become of the Cortes of Spain? Of the States General of France?
Of the Diets of Denmark? Everywhere we find the Executive in possession
of Legislative, of absolute powers. The glimmerings of liberty, which for
a moment shone in Europe, were owing to the decay of the feudal system.
When the princes were deprived of the personal services of their vassals,
and of the revenues derived from their ancient domains; when industry
and commerce rendered money the principal engine of power, those
popular assemblies which had the till then 'unimportant right of raising
taxes and granting supplies, arose at once into consequence. And as the
Executive, either by force, or by fraud, or by the folly of the people themselves, succeeded in wresting that power from them, they fell again into
misuse or insignificance.

Far and away the most useful illustration of this tragic process
for Americans, of course, was England in the period since the
Glorious Revolution:

It is during that period that a progressive patronage, and a systematic,
corrupting influence have sunk Parliament to a nominal representation,
a mere machine, the convenience used by Government for the purpose of
raising up supplies; the medium through which the Executive reaches
with ease the purse of the people. And now, when the farce of obtaining
even the nominal consent of Parliament is sufficiently understood, the
Ministry dispense with the ceremony, and have carried so far their contempt for that body, that the sum spent during the last year, without
the consent, exceeds the amount spent with the consent of Parliament.
The Executive there have acquired the unlimited and uncontrolled power of
raising and expending money, and the House of Commons is under a
moral obligation of making the necessary appropriations.

All that he and his friends wanted, Gallatin declared, was
to prevent this dismal fate from overtaking and ruining representative government in America, and what that basically meant
was nothing more complicated than preserving "the equilibrium
intended by the Constitution." "The chief object of our Constitution has been to divide and distribute the powers between
the several branches of Government. With that distribution,
and with the share allotted to us [i.e., Congress], we are fully
satisfied." But, he went on, the Federalists evidently had different
ideas in mind. Through the use of corruption, it seemed, they
were trying to subvert proper constitutional relationships between
the branches of government and to emasculate the Congress:

[Theirs] is the system which seeks for support in the influence of patronage, by increasing the number of offices, and avowing a determination to
distribute them exclusively as rewards, amongst men of a certain description. It is the system which entangles us in new political connexions,
raises standing armies, builds navies, squanders the public money,
swells the public debt, and multiplies the burdens of the people.

Was it so astonishing, therefore, that many persons, observing
the opposition to frugality among the administration's supporters
and their unremitting pressure to break down the constitutional
prerogatives of Congress, should think "there exists in America
a Monarchic, Aristocratic Faction, who would wish to impose
upon us the substance of the British Government?"

The Federalists, Gallatin continued, also stigmatized their enemies as disorganizers, revolutionaries, Jacobins. But the real ground upon which the Republican opposition stood—and here he revealed more clearly than anywhere else his sense of the role he had elected to play in the 1790s—was that occupied by John Hampden, Algernon Sydney and those other immortal adversaries of Stuart tyranny a century earlier. Hampden, in the famous ship-money case, had bravely denied the claim of Charles I to be the sole judge of the need for appropriations, a claim precisely paralleled by the "modern doctrine" of the Federalists and one giving rise to precisely the same dispute: "It is still the power of raising and applying money claimed by, or for, the Executive," Gallatin asserted, "with the only difference that Charles the First exercised it by levying a tax without the consent of Parliament, and that here it is to be carried into effect by depriving the Legislature of the right of withholding their consent" through improper influence. And Sydney, for his part, had subsequently gone to the block for warning his countrymen that, as Gallatin then proceeded to read from the *Discourses Concerning Government* (1698):

Men are naturally propense to corruption, and if he whose will and interest it is to corrupt them be furnished with the means, he will never fail to do it. Power, honor, riches, and the pleasures that attend them, are the baits by which men are drawn to prefer a personal interest before the public good; and the number of those who covet them is so great, that he who abounds in them will be able to gain so many to his service as shall be able to subdue the rest. 'Tis hard to find a tyranny in the world that has not been introduced this way.

The more things change, in short, the more they stay the same: no less in republican America than in monarchical England, corruption remained the greatest threat to liberty, and those who opposed it could never relax their vigilance.

*   *   *

It does Gallatin no disservice to observe that his obvious preoccupation with the problem of corruption was utterly conventional and derivative. It was of course widely shared among his contemporaries in the Republican party, many of whom, like Jefferson, claimed to have first-hand knowledge of corrupt practices in and out of Congress. More to the point—and this could not have been fully grasped until recent years—it belonged squarely in a long tradition of concern for the preservation of political liberty and social stability that originated with classical republican theories of mixed constitutions, acquired new vitality in the turbulent environment of Niccolò Machiavelli's Florence, gave shape and substance to "opposition" or "country party" politics of early eighteenth century England, and scored one of its greatest triumphs in the American Revolution. In this context, "corruption," though it summoned up many of the same scenes of private depravity and political malfeasance that it does today, possessed the additional, more technical meaning of the method by which one element of a balanced government, usually the one exercising executive power, tried to overawe the others and seize complete sovereignty for itself. It thus came to apply not merely to such evils as bribery, graft, pluralism and the selling of offices, but also to things not now considered evil, among them standing armies, national debts and patronage. And its consequences therefore reached far beyond routine issues of law and propriety: they seemed to strike at the very foundations of free government itself, luring men and women away from the self-restraint and independence upon which their liberty rested, destroying the autonomy of their elected representatives, transforming their legislatures into mere machines of extortion and oppression.[19]

But Gallatin's very lack of originality in this regard—his 1798 speech on the foreign intercourse bill may be taken as a model example of "opposition" thinking in America—requires some explaining in its own right. How did it happen that the scion of one of Geneva's most powerful and privileged families could wind up in the United States House of Representatives, admonishing the members to be more careful of corruption by reading, in a thick French accent, excerpts from the work of an executed seventeenth century British pamphleteer? Although this is assuredly not the place for a detailed answer to that question, a few abbreviated remarks on the matter may help to convey its extent and ramifications. They concern what might be called the internationalization of opposition ideology and they make it necessary to reflect upon the social context in which opposition ideas flourished.

It should be remembered as a point of departure that, at the time of Gallatin's birth in 1761, his native Geneva had already maintained for some two centuries the virtually unique reputation of being both Protestant and republican. Both qualities guaranteed it a prominence in European affairs generally out of all proportion to its size and they laid the basis for a rich tradition of cultural affinity and exchange with England in particular that would have major political consequences for both countries. Back in the days of the Marian exiles, England's persecuted reformers had found inspiration and refuge in John Calvin's Protestant Rome and throughout the rest of the sixteenth and seventeenth centuries Genevans followed the progress of English Protestantism with intense interest. Even in the eighteenth century, when religion ceased to be a matter of the gravest concern and commercial expansion began to breed a new cosmopolitanism in both countries, the sense of a special relationship between the two remained: Geneva's rising bankers and merchant manufacturers found English attitudes and institutions the most congenial of any under the *ancien régime,* while well-bred Englishmen on the Grand Tour flocked in to reconnoiter Geneva's sophisticated salons, worldly clergy and urbane patricians. Geneva's "good society," Voltaire proclaimed, "is equal to that of Paris," and his own twenty-year residence in the immediate neighborhood, punctuated with fashionable dinners and amateur theatricals, only enhanced the city's attractiveness to English and other seekers after cultivation and entertainment. It comes as no surprise, then, to learn that the young Gallatin, whose many prominent relations moved easily in the company of *philosophes* and foreign notables, should have received considerable instruction in the English language and English history as well as acquiring a good working knowledge of contemporary English affairs. His later attentiveness to the history of Parliament after the Glorious Revolution was perfectly in keeping with this heavily anglicized upbringing.[20]

Here the story becomes more complex, for not all Genevans read English history in quite the same way. To the aristocracy, with which the Gallatins had always been closely identified, all the peculiar achievements of the English since the Glorious Revolution—a secure Protestant succession, political stability, liberty, prosperity—seemed to flow from their constitution, dividing sovereignty equally among king, lords and commons in a supreme Parliament. Applied to the Genevan political situation, as it was by Jean-Jacques Burlamaqui and other patrician ideologists, the same principle would justify the patrician-dominated ruling councils in refusing encroachments by the General Council of all citizens and thereby preserve political and social equilibrium in the republic.[21]

Other Genevans saw things differently. For the sober and industrious shopkeepers, lawyers, craftsmen and the like, all property-owners who possessed citizenship without the special privileges of the aristocracy, the republic had fallen on hard times. Civic government was no longer, it seemed, a responsibility of those who enjoyed sufficient material independence to govern themselves. It had instead become a mere instrument of a few toplofty families, who preserved their power from one day to the next with a systematic corruption that was ravaging old-fashioned piety and civic virtue even as it undermined ancient constitutional liberties. Over and over again these *représentants,* as they called themselves—the name derived from their insistence on the right to petition for redress of grievances—drew attention to a similar process of decay and degeneration in England and proposed what can only be described as a "country party" program of reform for Geneva: the elimination of official corruption and the restoration of historic constitutional relationships between the General Council and the councils of administration, the reestablishment of such basic rights as those of free speech and taxation by consent, and the revitalization of republican virtue among all citizens. After 1782, when their movement was brutally crushed by the patricians, many *représentant* leaders fled abroad, spreading "opposition" ideas as they went. Étienne Clavière, Jacques-Antoine de Roveray and several others linked up with Jacques-Pierre Brissot de Warville and the Marquis de Mirabeau on a variety of projects, eventually supplying the latter in particular with the research that helped him become the dominant personality in the National Assembly from 1789 to 1791. Clavière went on to become finance minister for the Girondist regime. Still others, such as François d'Ivernois, David Chauvet and Étienne Dumont, found their way to England, where they became closely associated with prominent reformers and coffee-house radicals, among them Richard Price,

Joseph Priestley, Sir Samuel Romilly, Lords Stanhope and Shelburne, their old compatriot Jean-Louis DeLolme and assorted Americans, most notably Benjamin Franklin, John Jay and John Adams.

As for Albert Gallatin, he had known a number of young men of *représentant* views while a student at the Genevan Academy, but though his family accounted themselves enlightened, they had not raised him to think ill of the existing order of things. When he left Geneva in 1780, just past his nineteenth birthday, he had nothing more in mind than taking advantage of the wide-open possibilities of America to make himself rich: in no way was he dissatisfied with the patrician domination of Geneva or partial to the cause of the American Revolution.[22] Only after several years in America did he undergo a sudden and dramatic political conversion, confessing that his views of the Genevan situation had been wrong, that the *représentants* had been right all along about the defects of the Genevan system and that he now intended to stay in America, where correct constitutional principles were more widely understood. Soon he had thrown in with the radical Pennsylvania constitutionalists, then with the Antifederalists and finally with the Jeffersonian Republicans—always keenly aware, perhaps more so than any of his American contemporaries, that he had enlisted in a movement of international scope and membership.[23] Not until this larger context has been fully reconstructed is it really possible to begin to appreciate the urgency, the depth of conviction and the historical sophistication with which Gallatin attacked corruption in the United States.

This is not to suggest that everyone who might be considered part of this "opposition" movement, Gallatin included, necessarily held identical opinions on all subjects. The Genevan *représentants*, for example, were at first deeply suspicious of American resistance to parliamentary supremacy and there were almost endless bitter disagreements on such issues as whether France should have a bicameral or unicameral constitution, whether Gallatin and his American colleagues were too partial to French republicanism under the Convention and Directory, and so on. The point is rather that a preoccupation with the corruption of traditional constitutional relationships was by no means a uniquely American phenomenon at the end of the eighteenth century, that the fate of the English Parliament was a widely recognized case study in the process and consequences of corruption and that English "opposition" ideas supplied much of the conceptual ammunition for resistance to such corruption, however altered to suit local circumstances and usages. The more is learned about this intricate interplay of both principles and personnel, the easier it is to evaluate properly the role that opposition to corruption played in American political development.

The very extent of anticorruption movements should also force reexamination of the conventional wisdom that they were "democratic" in orientation and "agrarian" in origin—the latter assumption figuring very prominently in American historical writing. Their immediate political objective was always the maintenance of time-honored constitutional balances, not the expansion of popular participation in government: not only did "democracy" as such connote the very kind of imbalance they feared but also among, say, the Genevan *représentants*, whose demands for a General Council with vastly enlarged powers appeared to raise the specter of democratic rule, it was repeatedly and violently denounced.[24]

The less a purely American frame of reference is used, moreover, the less adequate it seems to describe this ubiquitous preoccupation with corruption as simply an expression of rural or agrarian disaffection. In America, to be sure, its roots were deepest in the countryside. In Geneva, on the other hand, the fear of corruption ran strongest among the urban bourgeoisie, while rural *sujets*, as they were called, played no role in the political life of the republic. What this suggests is that the familiar distinction between "agricultural" and "commercial" classes is less useful here than one more sharply attuned to underlying similarities in modes of production. Thus American Jeffersonians and Genevan *représentants*—and probably other adherents of "opposition" thought elsewhere—all may well have belonged to the same class of small, independent, property-owning producers. The commodities they sent to market from their shops and farms or the services they provided from their offices and stores clearly varied according to circumstances, but how they lived, the material and human relations with which they forged their survival, appear to have been strikingly similar.

If this is indeed so, then their common resentment against the degradation of ancient constitutional relationships might best be read as one dimension of a still broader opposition to the emergence of capitalist society and capitalist values—to the reorganization of production, to the emergence of new classes and new class relations, to the rise of a money economy and the acceleration of capital accumulation. It is worth recalling, in this context, that Gallatin and other critics of corruption always linked it closely to the growth of the power of money since the end of the Middle Ages and understood it to be part of a larger process of social transformation.[25]

These conjectures and speculations may be far from Gallatin and his attacks on corruption in the Federalist era, yet they suggest finally that he and his colleagues lost the fight in virtually every respect. The rise of cabinet government and political parties, the advent of democracy, and ultimately the triumph of capitalism itself—all of these were signal defeats for the opposition tradition and the world from which it sprang. Perhaps that is why it is so difficult to remember just who they were and exactly what they stood for.

NOTES

1. Henry Adams, *The Life of Albert Gallatin* (1879), pp. 407–10.

2. The only full-length biography of Gallatin since the Adams study is Raymond Walters, Jr., *Albert Gallatin: Jeffersonian Financier and Diplomat* (1957). John Austin Stevens, *Albert Gallatin*, 2nd ed. (1884) is more or less a condensed version of the Adams biography. For more selective studies of Gallatin's career, as well as specific comments on its ideological sources, consult Edwin G. Burrows, "Albert Gallatin and the Political Economy of Republicanism, 1761–1800," unpublished Columbia University thesis, 1974; Henry Cabot Lodge, "Albert Gallatin," *Studies in American History*, 1884, p. 268; Russell J. Ferguson, "Albert Gallatin: Western Pennsylvania Politician," *Western Pennsylvania Historical Magazine*, XVI (1933), 184–85; Henry M. Dater, "Albert Gallatin: Land Speculator," *Mississippi Valley Historical Review*, XXVI (1939–40), 23; Raymond Walters, Jr., "Spokesman of Frontier Democracy: Albert Gallatin in the Pennsylvania Assembly," *Pennsylvania History*, XIII (1946), 4; Walters, "The Making of a Financier: Albert Gallatin in the Pennsylvania Assembly," *Pennsylvania Magazine of History and Biography*, LXX (1946), 260; E. James Ferguson, ed., *Selected Writings of Albert Gallatin* (1967), p. xix.

3. *American Daily Advertiser*, September 3, 5, December 19, 1791; January 7, 15, 1792; Burrows, *op. cit.*, 423–31.

4. Gallatin to Jean Badollet, February 22, 1792, in Gallatin Papers, New-York Historical Society, Box 3 [henceforth cited as GP].

5. Albert Gallatin, *A Sketch of the Finances of the United States* (Philadelphia, 1796), p. 149; cf. also pp. 131, 143–48.

6. [Albert Gallatin], *An Examination of the Conduct of the Executive of the United States towards the French Republic; Likewise An Analysis of the Explanatory Articles of the British Treaty— in a series of Letters* (Philadelphia, 1797), p. 68. The title page bears the inscription: "There's something rotten in the State of Denmark." It should be noted, however, that Gallatin's authorship of this important pamphlet, though widely accepted, is open to serious question, and I intend to comment in more detail on the matter elsewhere.

7. Albert Gallatin, Notes for a Speech to the Harrisburg Convention: GP, Box 2; Burrows, *op. cit.*, pp. 241–44, 509.

8. *American Daily Advertiser,* September 3, 5, 1791.

9. [Gallatin], *Examination of the Conduct . . . ,* p. 40.

10. *American Daily Advertiser,* September 3, 5, 1791.

11. Joseph Gales and W. W. Seaton, eds., *The Debates and Proceedings in the Congress of the United States, 1789–1824,* 42 vols. (Washington, 1834–1856), 5th Cong., 2nd sess., 855–59, 1655 [henceforth cited as *Annals of Congress*].

12. [Gallatin]. *Examination of the Conduct . . . ,* p. 41.

13. *Annals of Congress,* 5th Cong., 2nd sess, 1539.

14. *American Daily Advertiser,* September 3, 5, 1791.

15. *Annals of Congress,* 4th Cong., 1st sess., 464–74; 726–46; 5th Cong., 2nd sess., 1655, 2109–11; 5th Cong., 3rd sess., 2707–08.

16. Gallatin, "Autobiography" quoted in Burrows, *op. cit.*, pp. 467–68.

17. This is the principal argument of *ibid.*, 376–502.

18. For the entire speech, see *Annals of Congress,* 5th Cong., 2nd sess., 1118–1143.

19. The most convenient introduction to the growing literature on this subject is Robert E. Shalhope, "Toward a Republican Synthesis: The Emergence of an Understanding of Republicanism in American Historiography," *William and Mary Quarterly,* 3rd ser., No. 29 (January 1972), pp. 49–80. The most thorough discussion is Lance Gilbert Banning, "The Quarrel With Federalism: A Study in the Origins and Character of Republican Thought," unpublished Washington University thesis, 1971. Also important are Banning's "Republican Ideology and the Triumph of the Constitution, 1789–1793," *William and Mary Quarterly,* 3rd ser., No. 31 (April 1974), pp 167–88; Joyce Appleby, "The New Republican Synthesis and the Changing Political Ideas of John Adams," *American Quarterly,* No. 25 (December 1973), pp. 578–95; Richard L. Bushman, "Corruption and Power in Provincial America," in Library of Congress, *The Development of a Revolutionary Mentality* (Washington, 1972), pp. 63–91.

20. For a more complete discussion of these points, see Burrows, *op. cit.*, pp. 1–11 and passim.

21. This and the following paragraph are based upon *ibid.*, pp. 22–75.

22. See *ibid.*, pp. 11–21, 75–113, 114–22 and passim. The conventional interpretation, for which Henry Adams was chiefly responsible, holds that Gallatin left Geneva out of dissatisfaction with its political circumstances and a desire to examine Revolutionary America firsthand. Consult the various sources in n. 2 above.

23. *Ibid.*, esp. pp. 105–113, 147–81.

24. The notion that the *représentants* and their associates around Europe were engaged in a "democratic" movement is perhaps most thoroughly developed in R. R. Palmer, *The Age of the Democratic Revolution: The Challenge* (1959). It seems evident that the rediscovery of mixed constitutional thinking and its scope will make Palmer's interpretation less and less tenable.

25. Gallatin's views are all the more interesting because he was so conspicuously involved himself in various small business schemes while remaining hostile to the "moneyed men" who traded in government paper, bank stock and the like. See Burrows, *op. cit.*, pp. 114–85. For some especially cogent thinking about modes of production in the American case, see Michael Merrill, "Cash Is Good To Eat: Self-Sufficiency and Exchange in the Rural Economy of the United States," *Radical History Review*, Winter 1977, pp. 42–71. I have also greatly benefited from Robert E. Mutch's unpublished manuscript on "Society and Economy in mid-18th century Massachusetts."

Mary-Jo Kline

AARON BURR AS A SYMBOL OF CORRUPTION IN THE NEW REPUBLIC

The publication of the correspondence and the papers of Aaron Burr, in which I have been engaged for the past two years, may be less important for what it tells about Aaron Burr than for what it reveals about his critics and enemies, men who held higher offices, exerted more power and emerged from political life with less tarnished reputations. This was underlined by a Jefferson scholar's reaction that he hoped that "Burr's papers will explain just why Jefferson distrusted Burr so *thoroughly.*"

Although the remark was made in jest, it has always seemed particularly apt. For what Burr did in his eighty years of life may have had less effect on American history than what other, more influential men did in reaction to Burr and their attitudes toward Burr tell much about their vision of the new nation and the pitfalls of democracy.

To anyone unfamiliar with the details of Thomas Jefferson's relationship with Burr, questions concerning the reasons for the president's "thorough" distrust of his vice-president might seem rhetorical. Did Jefferson not hear rumors that Burr had plotted to insure a tie between them in the Electoral College? Was he not aware of Burr's alliance with Federalists in New York State in 1804? Did he not know of Burr's notorious duel with Hamilton? Did he not see Burr indicted for conspiracy to commit treason?

The answer to each question is, of course, yes. But Jefferson came to distrust Burr long before· he was given any of these "good" reasons and it is the thorough and pervasive quality of his distrust that is remarkable—not merely the fact that such distrust existed.

An explanation of Jefferson's attitude is part of a hypothesis about Burr's spectacular ability to inspire suspicion—even fear —among the more conventional Founding Fathers. The reason for this must be sought in the record left by Burr, not in the writings of his critics, for the suspicion that Burr evoked was peculiarly difficult for his critics to define. This terrible suspicion may not have arisen from anything Burr's contemporaries *knew* that he had done—or even feared that he might do. Rather, this pervasive and thorough mistrust was inspired by the terrible prophecy that Burr embodied.

Jefferson himself seems to have been hard put to analyze his feelings toward Burr. Not until January 1804 did the president confide to his "Anas" any statement about his attitude toward his vice-president and the motives he gave were weak and unconvincing. "I had never seen Colo. Burr until he came as member of the Senate," Jefferson wrote. "His conduct very soon inspired me with distrust. I habitually cautioned Mr. Madison against trusting him too much. I saw afterwards . . . whenever a great military appointment or a diplomatic one was to be made, he came post to Philadelphia to shew himself and in fact that he was always at market, if they had wanted him. . . . With these impressions of Colo. Burr there never had been an intimacy between us, and but little association."[1]

In this account, Jefferson conveniently forgot that the man who had "soon inspired" him "with distrust" was the same one to whom he had appealed for assistance when his friend Dr. James Currie required a legal adviser in New York State.[2] And there is no evidence to support Jefferson's claim that he had "habitually cautioned" James Madison against Burr, although such cautions could have been given verbally.

Indeed it seems unlikely that Jefferson's suspicions concerning Burr could have been roused as early as he claimed—1791 or 1792—without being recorded in some letter or memorandum in the decade that followed. Rather it seems that in 1804 Jefferson indulged in wishful thinking—the wish that he had been wise enough to mistrust Burr at first sight, that he had "cautioned" Madison and others against relying on Burr's support before the New Yorker became an integral part of the Virginia Republican alliance.

Instead Jefferson did not learn to "mistrust" Col. Burr until

1801. It is generally recognized that Jefferson began to withdraw from Burr in the autumn of that year.[3] The materials collected in the Burr Papers give no reason to challenge that point, but they may require a modification of the reasons given for Jefferson's action. The accepted explanation is that Jefferson's patience had been exhausted by Burr's continued demands for offices under the new administration for his political cronies from New York.[4] But by September 1801, when Burr lost his crucial bid to win a naval post for his trusted lieutenant, Matthew Davis, he had already given Jefferson broader and more significant reasons for suspicion.

Burr's correspondence shows that he was not merely a conduit for requests for office for a few dozen old and trusted Jeffersonians from New York. Such demands would have irritated Jefferson. But despite his efforts to remain "above" politics, Jefferson was not naïve; he was familiar enough with New York partisanship to have expected something of the sort from the "deserving" in Burr's home state. What must have genuinely surprised—and shocked—Jefferson was Burr's repeated requests for consideration of the claims of the "faithful" from other states and territories.

The process began in March 1801 when Charles Pinckney, the architect of Republican victory in South Carolina, came to Burr with his list of "some Changes which he wished to take place in certain offices in S.C."[5] Burr handed this list to Jefferson. In the months to come, Burr acted on behalf of Republican politicians and their followers from Massachusetts, Delaware, New Jersey, Kentucky, Connecticut, Rhode Island and from the Northwest Territory.[6]

It has been suggested that Jefferson distrusted Burr because he believed his running mate had not acted forcefully enough to insure Jefferson's choice by the House in 1801. After reviewing the list of the "faithful" for whom Burr acted as spokesman, Jefferson may have felt that the New Yorker had instead worked *too* energetically for a Republican victory—or at least, that his methods left much to be desired.

In weighing Jefferson's reaction to Burr's methods, one must remember what constituted "corrupt" political behavior to men of Jefferson's background. The "corruption" of the English constitution, with a strong emphasis on the evils of "placemen," had

been a rallying point for the theorists of the Revolution. Perhaps
no one expressed their fears better than John Adams in "Novanglus." He compared English political corruption to "a cancer"
which "eats faster and faster every hour." "The revenue creates
pensioners," he wrote, "and the pensioners urge for more revenue.
The people grow less steady, spirited, and virtuous. The seekers
more numerous and corrupt, and every day increases the circles
of their dependents and expectants, until virtue, integrity, public spirit, simplicity, and frugality, become the objects of ridicule and scorn, and vanity, foppery, selfishness, meanness, and
downright venality swallowing up the whole society."[7]

And this view of corruption as a process which could poison
and corrupt an entire society colored such statesmen's views of
political parties as well. Nearly forty years after the publication
of "Novanglus," Adams would define corruption as "a sacrifice of
every national Interest and honour, to private and party objects."[8] Neither Adams nor Jefferson was sanguine enough to
expect that "private" interest could be extinguished in the new
republic. But if parties could be discouraged, then that second
—and possibly greater—temptation to misuse public power could
be eliminated. And so, in devising a plan for America's government, the Founding Fathers adopted what Richard Hofstadter
termed a "Constitution against Parties."[9]

Burr's view of "party," not merely his rather casual acceptance
of the role of patronage in the political process, may have
inspired Jefferson's mistrust. To test this hypothesis, consider
the variety of reasons given for hostility and suspicion by another
of Burr's enemies, Alexander Hamilton. The identification of
good reasons why such bitter political antagonists as Jefferson
and Hamilton came to mistrust Burr may allow some valid
generalizations concerning Burr's remarkable reputation as a
"corrupt" force in the new republic.

Hamilton, of course, practically made a career of being Burr's
political enemy. Still, for many years Hamilton's charges against
his foe were maddeningly vague. Not until the New York guber-
natorial race of 1804 did Hamilton begin to unearth concrete
acts of "corruption" to support the campaign he had waged
against Burr for a dozen years.

Again and again one feels that Hamilton mistrusted Burr by
instinct; he could not articulate his reasons because he may not

have fully understood them himself. In his first known attacks upon Burr, Hamilton could do little better than recite set pieces of Whig and Federalist rhetoric. As a member of the Revolutionary generation, Hamilton believed that a corrupt man *must* be one in need of money, one who was required to provide for improvident and clamorous "connections." And so he charged Burr in 1792 with being "embarrassed . . . with an extravagant family." And as one of the authors of "Publius," Hamilton believed that an evil and corrupt man was one who must have been guilty of the worst heresy known to Federalism—opposition to the Constitution. Even so, the best that Hamilton could muster on this point was: "When the constitution was in deliberation, his conduct was equivocal; but its enemies, who I believe best understood him considered him as with them."[10]

The lameness of his charges seems to have been evident to Hamilton. In a letter of October 1792, he wrote apologetically of his castigations against Burr: "Imputations not favourable to his integrity as a man rest upon him; but I do not vouch for their authenticity."[11]

In the years that followed, Hamilton refined his case against Burr. By 1801 the catalog of sins was firmly established. There were embellishments concerning Burr's private life, of course, including the rather remarkable charge that Burr was "selfish to a degree which excludes all social affections." (Considering Burr's passionate devotion to his family and loyalty to his friends, one wonders whether Hamilton expected any credence for this remark.) And recalling Hamilton's experience with the "Reynolds pamphlet" in 1797, it was rather ill considered of him to accuse Burr of being "decidedly profligate" in 1801.[12]

Beyond these pejorative decorations, one finds a consistent core of accusations centering on Burr's "extreme and irregular ambitions." Hamilton did not fault Burr merely for being ambitious, but more for being ambitious in the wrong way. Burr was willing to use popular support as a "ladder" to power.[13] His ambition was coupled to "no fixed theory."[14] And perhaps most illuminating of all, Hamilton wrote: "Let it be remembered that Mr. Burr has never appeared solicitous for fame, and that great ambition, unchecked by principle or the love of glory, is an unruly tyrant."[15]

Hamilton's perception of Burr was remarkably accurate. Burr

did not see anything wrong in seeking direct popular support
for his views and his candidates. His theories were not so
"fixed" that he was unwilling to compromise demands and
to ally with former opponents. And, as his editors can testify to
their sorrow, Burr was remarkably "unsolicitous for fame." Almost alone among the men who held high office in the early
decades of this nation, Burr left behind no lengthy recrimina-
tions against his enemies (with the exception of one marvelous
letter to his son-in-law about James Monroe's complete lack
of qualifications for any post[16])—no explanations and justifica-
tions for his actions. One cannot imagine Burr engaging in any
correspondence like that between Jefferson and Adams in their
last years when they "explained" themselves to each other.[17]

Burr seems hardly to have cared for the opinions of his contemporaries, much less for posthumous "fame." This was not
arrogance, but the symptom of something much worse from
Hamilton's and Jefferson's point of view.

Since Burr viewed the political process as a means of acquiring
power but not necessarily recognition, he could stand aside while
other men won office as the result of his labors. But he could
also sustain his spirits—and his followers—in time of defeat because he possessed one trait absent from Jefferson's and Hamilton's personalities. Aaron Burr thoroughly enjoyed the game of
politics.

In the last years of his life, Burr wrote to one of the few young
politicians still willing to be known as his friends and closed by
wishing him "a great deal of fun and honor & profit during the
campaign." [18] While Hamilton and Jefferson and men of their
kind would agree that politics could and should bring "honor"
to office seekers, while they would probably admit that victory
could bring "profit," it is inconceivable that either of them
could view politics as simple "fun." But Burr held that view
and seems to have done so without shame or apology.

Burr, then, saw nothing wrong in making promises to secure
political cooperation nor in keeping those promises. His first
political loyalty was to the party in which he had enlisted. He
was willing to forgo "fame" if it would serve the interests of
his party or his friends. He was content to win power through
and for others and to exercise his influence quietly. And he
certainly found "a great deal of fun" in politics—one hopes he

found enough to compensate for the almost total absence of "honor & profit" on his political balance sheet.

To twentieth century readers, this catalog of sins may seem unremarkable. Indeed, it might even be argued that men of Burr's breed were a prerequisite for American political development. Men like him would make it possible for America to pay the "price of Union" described by Herbert Agar a quarter century ago—the creation of nationwide, popularly based political parties.[19] The creation of that system demanded men who were willing to forgo "fame" for their parties, men willing to bargain regional alliances, men able to climb the ladder of popular support and to convey their own enjoyment of the "fun" of politics so that the governmental process might become a spectator sport that would engage the interest and commitment of voters at large.

But if the picture seems innocent enough to us, our acceptance of that image only bears out Hamilton's and Jefferson's worst fears. They recognized Burr as a "corrupt" man in their own terms. More significantly, they must have recognized him as a prototype, not as an isolated sport in political genetics. If America could produce a politician like Burr in the first decade of existence under the Constitution, if these "corrupt" and "corrupting" traits could emerge in a gentleman, the grandson of Jonathan Edwards, a Princeton graduate, an officer in the Revolution, a successful member of the bar—then Hamilton and Jefferson would have had to be blind to ignore the possibility, indeed, the certainty, that Burr was only the first of many such politicians. Burr embodied every trait that could in their terms "corrupt" the political system they had nurtured.

If Hamilton and Jefferson perceived Burr as clearly as it appears, their "thorough distrust" was understandable. And so too was their inability to articulate their feelings, for they responded to the "Ghost of Politics Yet to Come."

The very theme of this volume may prove them right. "Corruption" is discussed here calmly, as a fact of our nation's history. Readers will find tales of "bosses" whose names and power were unknown to the general public of their times—men "unsolicitous for fame," seeking power for its own sake. If these essays elicit more interest than usual, it will be because Americans have accepted one of Burr's rules of the game and discarded many of Hamilton's and Jefferson's. Despite the terrible spectacle of men who manipulate the political process with such skill and relish that they indulge in "dirty tricks" for sheer pleasure, the modern reader must still admit that what Burr knew one hundred and forty years ago is true—the practice and study of American politics is, if nothing else, "a great deal of fun."

NOTES

1. Paul L. Ford, ed., *The Writings of Thomas Jefferson* (10 vols.; New York, 1892–1899), I, 301–304.

2. Jefferson to Burr, 7 January 1797, in A. A. Lipscomb and A. E. Bergh, eds., *Writings of Thomas Jefferson* (20 vols.; Washington, 1903), XIX, 114–115; Jefferson to Burr, 20 May 1798, in Ford, *op. cit.*, VIII, 254–255; Jefferson to Burr, 26 May 1798, Conn. Hist. Soc.; Jefferson to Burr, 16 June 1798, Conn. Hist. Soc.

3. Dumas Malone, *Jefferson: The President* (Boston, 1970), pp. 88–89.

4. *Ibid.*

5. Burr to Pierce Butler, 16 September 1801, Library of Congress.

6. For political appointments in Massachusetts, see Burr to William Eustis, 29 March 1801, Mass Hist. Soc.; Elbridge Gerry to Burr, 18 September 1801, Am. Antiquarian Soc.; Burr to Gerry, Kans. Hist. Soc.; Benjamin Homans to Burr, no date [1801], Library of Congress. For Connecticut, see Burr to Samuel Smith, 10 April 1801, Huntington Library; Burr to Henry Dearborn, 2 May 1801, National Archives; Burr to Ephraim Kirby, 18 June 1801 (dealer's notice), Am. Antiquarian Soc. For New Jersey, see Burr to Gallatin, 21 April 1801, N. Y. Hist. Soc.; Burr to Gallatin, 10 August 1801, N. Y. Hist. Soc.; Burr to Samuel Smith, 6 June 1801, Univ. of Virginia; Joseph Bloomfield to Burr, 11 January 1802, Am. Antiquarian Soc. For Kentucky, see Burr to Madison, 27 April 1801, Princeton Library. For Rhode Island, see Jonathan Russell to Burr, 26 June 1801, Am. Antiquarian Soc. For the Northwest Territory, see Burr to Gallatin, 9 October 1801, N. Y. Hist. Soc.; For Delaware, see Burr to Rodney, 3 March 1801, Mo. Hist. Soc.; Burr to Rodney, 17 March 1801, N. Y. State Library.

7. Charles F. Adams, ed., *The Works of John Adams, with Life* (10 vols.; Boston, 1850–1856), IV, 43.

8. Adams to Jefferson, 15 November 1813, in Lester J. Cappon, ed., *The Adams-Jefferson Letters* (2 vols.; Chapel Hill, 1959), II, 401.

9. *The Idea of a Party System* (Berkeley, 1969), Chap. 2.

10. Hamilton to ?, 21 September 1792, in Harold C. Syrett *et al.*, eds., *The Papers of Alexander Hamilton* (24 vols. to date; New York, 1960–), XII, 408.

11. Hamilton to John Steele, 15 October 1792, in *ibid.*, 567–569.

12. Hamilton to Gouverneur Morris, 24 December 1800, in Henry

Cabot Lodge, ed., *The Works of Alexander Hamilton* (9 vols.; New York, 1885–1886), VIII, 570–572.

13. *Ibid.*

14. Hamilton to James Bayard, 16 January 1801, in *ibid.*, 581 ff.

15. *Ibid.*

16. Burr to Joseph Alston, 15 November–11 December 1815, Boston Public Library.

17. Cappon, *op. cit.*, II, 391.

18. Burr to Aaron Ward, 14 January 1832, Boston Public Library.

19. *The Price of Union* (Boston, 1950).

Edward Pessen

CORRUPTION AND THE POLITICS
OF PRAGMATISM: REFLECTIONS
ON THE JACKSONIAN ERA

The House of Politics is occupied entirely by human bein's.
If 'twas a vacant house, it could aisily be kept clean.

Mr. Dooley

In August, 1838, Samuel Swartwout, recently retired after two terms as the collector of the port of New York, sailed for England for what many people doubtless believed was a well-earned vacation. Information reported three months later by the Department of the Treasury indicated that the former customhouse chief was actually in flight. In what the contemporary diarist Philip Hone called "the most appalling account of delinquency ever exhibited in this country," it was revealed that Swartwout had stolen $1,225,705.69 during his nine years in office.[1] At the beginning of Andrew Jackson's first term as president nine years earlier, his secretary of state, Martin Van Buren, had tried unsuccessfully to dissuade Jackson from naming Swartwout, arguing that his appointment "would not be in ... the interests of the country or to the credit of the administration" and predicting that it "would in the end be deeply lamented by every sincere and intelligent friend of your administration throughout the Union."[2] Now himself the president, Van Buren, who had been so right about Swartwout, proved to be terribly wrong about the man he chose to replace him in the customhouse. For as Leonard D. White has observed, "Swartwout's successor, Jesse Hoyt, outdid his predecessor in everything but the amount embezzled."[3] When Hoyt fled the collector's office in 1841, his accounts were short by about $350,000. Nor did the bribery, embezzlement, graft, fraud and outright theft that had become characteristic of the nation's leading port cease with the resignation of these two prodigies of defalcation.[4]

As startling as was this rapid succession of corruptionists in high office was the fact that it was not the first time such a sequence had disfigured the public service of the Jacksonian era. Late in 1836 General Wiley P. Harris, receiver in the federal land office at Columbus, Mississippi, resigned from his post. Harris may have been the "true democrat" and "one of the main pillars of the democratic cause" that a Mississippi Jacksonian told the president he was but he left the land office with a shortage of $109,178.08. The administration nevertheless replaced Harris with the man he himself had recommended, his "warm personal friend" Col. Gordon D. Boyd. Boyd proved no slouch at misappropriating funds, falling more than $55,000 in arrears in a period of six months.[5] That the land examiner who investigated this misbehavior could recommend that Boyd continue in office, since "another receiver would probably follow in the footsteps of the two" defaulters, testifies as much to the Jacksonians' toleration for official corruption as to its pervasiveness. If not always manifested so strikingly as in the New York City customhouse and the Mississippi land office, public corruption was nonetheless remarkably widespread in antebellum America.

Political corruption, as Watergate has shown once more, can take at least two forms. There is the *corruption of venality*, what most scholars and laymen usually seem to have in mind when they speak of corruption.[6] Concerning misuse of government for the sake of personal enrichment or gain, it involves bribery, graft, embezzlement, theft, fraud, blackmail or nepotism. It may also be characterized by the use of political office in the interests not of the community by which the officeholder has been elected or appointed but in the interests rather of particular groups or individuals to whom the corrupt individual is beholden, often secretly.

Then there is the corruption typified by Watergate, involving the *abuse of power*. The essence of this form of corruption is the stretching or subversion of the law by powerful men in high office who seek to increase their power and are not fastidious about the means they use to do so. While this type of corruption may be more important because more dangerous to the community than the previous type, it is often ignored, particularly in its undramatic forms. This may be because of difficulty in establishing the existence of corrupt abuse of power. It involves the motives of men, is therefore enormously complex, can be manifested in subtle, unmeasurable ways rather than in obvious bribes or thefts, and with skillful demagogy can more easily be camouflaged, even denied, than the venal brand. The leaders of the Whig party in 1834 charged Andrew Jackson with this form of corruption. Scholars have typically dismissed the Whig charges as politically inspired. There is no doubt that they were so inspired, yet the politics of the Jacksonian years warrant examination for signs of corrupt abuse of power as well as the corruption of venality. To avoid awkward repetition of phrases, venal corruption will be referred to here as "corruption"; the other brand will be called "abuse of power."

Corruption is probably as old as government, certainly as old as money. As Carl Friedrich observed, it has been a ubiquitous phenomenon, flourishing in every kind of political environment, free and repressive.[7] Corrupt practices permeated the administration of England's North American colonies, particularly in the distribution of lavish land grants and lucrative political plums. In the era of the American Revolution some of the Founding Fathers were so heavily involved in questionable land speculations that the historian T. P. Abernethy wondered how their reputation for probity managed to remain intact for all the years that followed.[8] Independence hardly introduced politics free of moral taint. Men in national government were not above using inside information to enhance their speculations in public paper.[9] In the most notorious single act of corruption in the early national period, the Yazoo land fraud of the 1790s, the Georgia state legislature agreed to sell 35 million acres of valuable public land for 1½ cents per acre. With one exception every legislator who voted for the bill owned shares in a company that stood to make enormous profits from the sale.[10] John Quincy Adams, Andrew Jackson's predecessor in the White House, may have been a moralistic New Englander, hostile to the idea of profiting from political office. Yet the civil service during his administration was hardly spotless, with one collector helping himself to $88,000, another to $32,000, a third caught smuggling and a treasury auditor personally responsible for a shortage of thousands.[11] Quantitative evidence, to date ungathered, might in future modify judgments but the impression shared by most specialists in the early nineteenth century is that the volume of political corruption increased significantly during the years of Andrew Jackson's political ascendancy. There is no question that the incidence of corruption in the federal civil service became greater.[12] While no one has attempted a full-scale comparison of the degrees of corruption in other agencies and areas of politics during earlier eras and the Jackson years, what is clear enough is that corruption pervaded every facet of Jacksonian political life.

Collectorships, and not only in New York City, were a cesspool of iniquity before midcentury because neither the treasurer nor any other high official could systematically check or verify the accuracy of customhouse collections records. Appointing and presiding over thousands of clerks, inspectors, weighers, gaugers and measurers, collectors typically received fees on every entrance and clearance of vessels in their ports. They were permitted to keep a portion of fines and penalties for violations, thus by legitimate means commanding larger incomes than did cabinet members. The opportunity to tap their appointees for additional sums, extort money from captains, blackmail importing merchants, perform illegal seizures, keep fictitious records and simply pocket tariff proceeds proved irresistible to men who had been selected usually for political reasons rather than for their rectitude or administrative experience. Jackson brushed aside criticisms of Swartwout, intent on rewarding a political ally and old friend who not only hated Jackson's enemies but who, like Jackson himself, was ready to challenge them to a duel on slight pretext.[13] Discovering that the incumbent postmaster general, John McLean, would not make purely partisan appointments, Jackson in 1829 replaced him with William T. Barry, whose chief qualification seems to have been that he was a Kentuckian opposed to Henry Clay, whom Jackson hated. During Barry's six years' tenure, the Post Office became notorious for fraudulent contracts, favoritism, loans without interest, missing records, and the pressing of gifts on officials by private beneficiaries of its favors.[14] Andrew

Jackson's "reformation" of the administration of the public domain meant, according to the leading modern authority on the matter, that qualified men were replaced by unqualified, with the new appointees often participating actively with land company agents in illegal collusive bidding that brought huge profits to the speculators and land officials alike.[15] As for Indian affairs, whether involving the Indian Bureau, the imposition of one-sided treaties on southern tribes or the whole issue of Indian removal across the Mississippi, fraud and corruption were everywhere present, blandly overlooked if not actually perpetrated by government officials. In the understated language of the most recent comprehensive examination of this issue, the Jackson administration's "reaction to the orgy of speculation and fraud ... was inconsistent with the image that it sought to portray as the benefactor of the Southern Indians" in 1831 and 1832.[16] Congressmen rivaled federal civil servants in the number if not in the magnitude or dimension of their malfeasances, misrepresenting their use of travel allowances, abusing their franking privileges and misusing public funds.[17]

State and local politics were at least as low in tone as national, possibly even more unedifying. Congressmen and presidential administrations were concerned with great issues of national and foreign policy after all, even if the actual significance of these issues did not always measure up to the flamboyant rhetoric used in describing them. State governments focused on more prosaic matters. Studies of antebellum state politics reveal that in all geographical sections the regencies, juntos and cliques that controlled the parties in power were preoccupied with chartering banks, insurance and transportation companies, disposing of land, rewarding the party faithful, rearranging electoral units with an eye toward enlarging their representation and dispensing whatever legislative and political benefits were at their disposal not disinterestedly but almost always on the basis of partisan advantage.[18] It was no great leap for men engaged in such mundane matters to turn state legislation into a "matter of bargain and sale," influenced more by "pecuniary considerations than motives of a higher origin and character," as an unusually fastidious contemporary politician complained.[19] Party lines counted for little in the nation's cities, where the wealthy men of prestigious occupations who monopolized the mayor's office and the municipal legislature typically pursued legislative policies in the interests above all of the large property owners. At least this is the burden of modern research.[20] It did not always involve corruption, yet the history of most towns and cities contains numerous examples of the special sensitivity municipal governments showed their wealthiest constituents during the antebellum era. New York City's aldermen were not unusual in leasing on unusually favorable terms "water grants," wharves and other real estate to members of the Astor, Lorillard, Lenox, Schermerhorn, Goelet and similarly prestigious families or in granting special rights solicited by wealthy owners and lessees.[21] The point is not that every political actor and each of his political actions was tainted by corruption but rather that the level of political corruption was inordinately high during the Jacksonian era. The great question is why was this so?

In attempting to explain the causes of corruption in the federal service no scholar concerned with the issues has failed to mention the spoils system. While political considerations had sometimes played a part in earlier nominations to federal office, what is remarkable is how small a part they played during the first 40 years of our national history under the Constitution. At the very beginning of his first administration, George Washington advised a constituent that he planned "to nominate such persons alone to [public] office as shall be the best qualified to discharge its function."[22] From that time until the presidency of Andrew Jackson fitness or capacity remained the chief criterion of public appointment.[23] The Jacksonians initiated a system, imitated thereafter by their opponents, in which partisan political loyalty or affiliation rather than merit or past performance became the basic qualification for federal appointment.

In his first inaugural Jackson promised to select as public officers men of "diligence and talents," as well as "integrity and zeal." By December 8, 1829, when he delivered his first annual message, Jackson had retreated to a new position, which became the rationale for the spoils system. Hitting out at the "corruption" which ostensibly flourished in a civil service in which incumbents considered office "as a species of property," Jackson no longer stressed high ability or talent as the necessary qualities. He now told the country that "the duties of all public officers are, or at the least admit of being made, so plain and simple that men of intelligence may readily qualify themselves for their performance." He attempted to justify the removal of qualified men who had performed well with the argument that "more is lost by the long continuance of men in office than is generally to be gained by their experience."[24] This was the argument for "rotation in office." In practice "the men of intelligence" Jackson and his lieutenants had in mind for high office were men who were loyal supporters of Jackson's Democratic party. Using franker language than the president's, a Democrat told the Senate in 1832 that in politics as in warfare "to the victor belong the spoils."[25]

It used to be believed that a saving grace of the spoils system was its socially democratic implications. Ostensibly, commoners and plebeians replaced the "well-born and the well-to-do."[26] But as Sidney Aronson has shown, at least for what he calls the higher civil service, "at the time of appointment there was no important difference between Jacksonians and [previous] elites in the [unusually high] proportions of positions filled by men of high-ranking occupations."[27] The new men differed from the old less in social background than in their greater proclivity to corruptly misusing their positions. While the turnover in office may not have been as wholesale as used to be thought,[28] its significance does not appear to have been overestimated.

The spoils system fostered increased corruption. The chief function of top appointees came to be regarded as returning party majorities in their communities. Before long, lists were being posted on walls of federal offices, reminding each officeholder of the exact sum he was expected to contribute to the party. In the words of a congressional investigating committee, the effect of this practice was to "demoralize and prepare the mind of incumbents of office for acts of peculation and plunder upon the public revenues." Officeholders came to feel divided loyalties, with the needs and interests of the party assuming a higher priority than diligent performance of duty. (Interestingly, two of Swartwout's subordinates reported to Congress that they had known of his peculations years before they came to light: they had failed to report them because they "would not betray the secrets of [their] employer"—they "did not think it [their] duty," since "we clerks of the customhouse consider

ourselves as in the service of the collector, and not in the service
of the United States" [sic].)[29] Perhaps because he could not wait
to get his hands on a choice plum, the good New York Democrat
and corruptionist Jesse Hoyt wrote Van Buren early in 1829,
expressing his strong belief that federal office should thereafter be turned over to party stalwarts. It is hard to disagree
with Matthew Crenson's recent observation that the new atmosphere led appointees to regard federal offices "less as opportunities for public service than as sources of private profit."[30]
If, as Malcolm Rohrbough has noted, "opportunities for illicit
gains were virtually limitless" in field offices far removed from
supervision by Washington, the fact is that the new appointees,
unlike their predecessors in office, took full advantage of such
opportunities.[31]

The spoils system was not an accidental historical phenomenon. Like the political corruption that accompanied it, it was a
byproduct of a minor revolution in American politics and in
the American party system. Carl Russell Fish long ago and other
scholars more recently attributed the rise in corruption to the
democratization that transformed politics in the Jacksonian
era. I would attribute it rather to the commercialization, the
vulgarization and the growing pragmatism and opportunism of
antebellum politics.

Jacksonian no more than Whig administrations were prone to
appoint commoners without property to public office. In fact
Jackson, while ready to display massive patience toward public
defaulters in high office, early let it be known that there was
no room in the federal service for insolvent debtors.[32] Corruptionists in public office were hardly down-and-outs. They were
representative not of the rank and file of American society but
of the major parties that had come to monopolize politics in
that society. The constituencies of the Democrats and Whigs—
the major parties of the era—were a cross section of American
society, composed primarily of the small farmers who pre-
dominated in rural America and the artisans and working people
who were most numerous in the expanding towns and cities.
But the leadership of the major parties, ranging from aldermen
and county officials to senatorial and cabinet officers, were
socially most unrepresentative of the people at large. As study
of major-party leadership on every level and in each geographical

section has shown, they were inordinately wealthy men of high-prestige occupations.[33] It seems a canard against the common people of the time to attribute to them or to their influence acts of venality that were in fact committed by the uncommonly well-to-do men who ran, and were appointed by, the major parties.

That the people may have had an unusual tolerance for such misbehavior is another matter. Charles Dickens was one of many gifted visitors who was struck by an alleged American "love of 'smart' dealing, which gilds over many a swindle and gross breach of trust, many a defalcation, public and private, and enables many a knave to hold his head up with the best, who well deserves a halter."[34] Nevertheless, the fact remains that corruption was in bad popular repute, as politicians well knew. Henry Clay's opponents ruined forever his presidential chances by incessantly charging that he had become secretary of state in 1825 through a "corrupt bargain" he had struck with President John Quincy Adams. A minor treasury department official attracted favorable public notice in 1829 for formally advising clerks under his supervision that the government required "the practice of rigid morality by those engaged in public business." "Gambling, intemperance and extravagance" —let alone bribery, theft and embezzlement—"ought not to be tolerated in the agents of the people." The selfsame cabinet officer, who in practice subscribed to the interesting doctrine that the War Department had no authority to circumscribe the Indian's right to be defrauded, could pay lip service to the principle that a "public officer [ought] never to do an act, which he would not be willing should be disclosed to the whole world."[35] Numerous other testimonies to the popular antipathy toward flagrant corruption fill the record. To understand Jacksonian corruption, the student is better advised to examine the traits and values of the politicians than the traits and values of the people.

A thoughtful historian not long ago suggested that in choosing his political lieutenants Andrew Jackson showed a preference for men who could be described as "the practical, the shrewd, the opportunistic."[36] A subsequent study of Whig as well as Democratic leaders during the era discerned a remarkable degree of similarity in their backgrounds, values and behavior, both before and after they attained prominence. These

were thoroughgoing materialists, men who loved the good
things of life and were vastly ambitious to accumulate more of
them. While rarely very learned or betraying any affinity for the
intellectual life, they were unusually intelligent men. They
were masters of evasion and opportunism, pragmatists dedicated above all to the main chance, although their shrewdness
and their mastery of demagogy enabled them to proclaim their
love of justice and of the "sovereign people" most convincingly.[37]
It is precisely because they were men of this sort that they
came to assume leadership of the major parties of the era.

Any realistic interpretation of Jacksonian politics cannot deny
that the major parties differed sharply on a range of significant
issues.[38] It should be kept in mind, however, that in a democracy
even the most cynical of parties and leaders must identify themselves with some principle or other, since even the most gullible
of voters are unlikely to respond favorably to politicians frankly
proclaiming their preoccupation with pelf and plunder! It is
hard to avoid the conclusion that the parties that dominated
American politics in the antebellum decades were pragmatic
political coalitions dedicated primarily to winning and holding
office. Zealous concern for social justice, freeing slaves or for
less attractive goals was demonstrated not by Jacksonian Democrats and Whigs but by the Working Men's party, the Liberty
party, the Antimasonic party, and the various nativist or anti-
Irish Catholic political groups of the era. The thin and sometimes indistinct line between pragmatic and corrupt politics
was easily crossed by men whose chief interest in politics seems
to have been what they could get out of it in a broad sense or
who, in Crenson's words, regarded office "less as opportunities
for public service than as sources of private profit." As a correspondent told Martin Van Buren in 1836, to get rid of the
"bargain and sale" of political privileges that characterized the
New York state legislature, a "different class of men" would
have to be brought into it.[39]

Seeking to relate the prevalent political corruption to larger
forces operating in American society, a contemporary official
discerned an increasing "looseness in the code of morality," which
ostensibly explained the deterioration of political ethics.[40] Twentieth century political historians have also sought to connect
Jacksonian corruption to social changes that were supposedly

transforming American society and values during the era. Leonard White attributed the decline in "traditional standards of public morality" to "the decline of [both] the gentleman class" and the business morality of an earlier day. This decline was due to increased urbanization, the ascendancy of social upstarts, the new immigrants of the day and "new temptations" that, according to White, were besetting nineteenth century American society.[41] More recently Crenson, very much impressed with the surmises of Marvin Meyers and Stanley Elkins, has written that malfeasance in the Jacksonian period "reflected the deterioration of discipline" in law and business. "The old standards of honesty and propriety were no longer buttressed by the bar and the business community," he advises.[42]

There seems little doubt that the era's political phenomena were not unrelated to its social developments. The question of course is what precisely was that relationship? The problem with the explanations given hitherto is that they refer to developments, such as upward social mobility and the "decline of institutions" for which there is little or no supporting evidence.[43] American society during the Jacksonian decades was indeed changing, but until it has been demonstrated not only what these changes were but how they affected politics, it seems pointless to cite them as the explanation of political venality.

The American people no doubt had unique values. Contemporary visitors and natives alike insisted that the worship of the dollar was their true religion and that Americans admired material success no matter how achieved.[44] If these were indeed the reigning values, as Dickens, Alexis de Tocqueville, James Fenimore Cooper and Ralph Waldo Emerson insisted they were, the fact may throw light on the public's mild reaction to acts of surpassing corruption. Would anyone seriously suggest, however, that phenomena as complex, subtle and enduring as values changed from one political administration to another? If, as much evidence suggests, political venality did become more marked from the 1800s to the 1830s, it was due to a change not in values but in politics.

There had been major parties almost from the beginning of Washington's first administration. Electoral changes in the early nineteenth century, which rewarded presidential candidates and party congressional slates that won pluralities by assuring them either a state's entire electoral vote or all its congressional seats, buttressed the strength of major parties at the expense of minor. For the new rules of the political game catered to the interests of "likely winners" or the candidates offered by the major parties, those broad coalitions that came close to being all things to all men. These political "reforms" assured a near monopoly of office to the pragmatic parties that were alone capable of raising the money and organizing campaigns of the complexity necessary to persistent electoral success. The leaders of such parties introduced a spoils sytem, which further accentuated their nonideological tendencies and better explains the flourishing of corruption than does an unproven series of changes in the morals and practices of business and the professions.

Political venality was ultimately costly to the taxpayer and not only financially.[45] More significant was corruption in the form of abuse of power or the "corruption of power" that also became apparent during the era. _____

On March 28, 1834, the Senate voted to censure President Andrew Jackson for assuming "upon himself authority and power not conferred by the Constitution and laws, but in derogation of both.[46] As has been recently noted, the censure was politically inspired, "a transparent attack" by congressional Whig leaders, "with the end in view of influencing public opinion in their own favor."[47] Disposing of the probable motives of the men who attacked Jackson does not, however, dispose of a more important question: was the criticism of Jackson justified?

It goes without saying that scholars will give different answers to this question, depending upon their political philosophies and other subjective considerations. Having taken Jackson severely to task in a long essay published in 1969, I made the point that, had I thought better of the policies he and his followers pursued, I would perhaps have found less fault with their tactics and methods. Certainly the modern historians who think well of the Jacksonians' "programs," accepting at close to face value, for example, the Jacksonians' own explanation that the Bank War was a struggle for the common people against aristocracy, applaud Jackson's "vigorous measures," evaluating him as one of a handful of great presidents.[48] If the present generation has learned anything, it is the impossibility of separating ends and means. Yet perhaps an old-fashioned approach might be fruitful, one in which the worthiness or lack thereof of Jacksonian policies is put aside and the focus is trained entirely on the methods and procedures Jackson and other presidents used in trying to win acceptance of these policies. It is to be hoped that it is not too old-fashioned to continue to believe that ends do not justify means. In a discussion of abuse of political power, no subject is more substantive than the means used by the politically powerful.

During the Jacksonian era the constitutional balance of power between the legislative, executive and judicial branches of government was rudely upset by presidential acts. Brushing aside traditional restraints and usages, constitutional precedents, Supreme Court decisions, federal treaties and laws of Congress, Andrew Jackson transformed the executive office, in the process substituting what the constitutional historian Edward Corwin called presidential domination for the legislative authority that had prevailed earlier. Perhaps nothing the Jacksonians did was more arrogant than their action on January 16, 1837, when they "expunged" the censure resolution from the Senate record. "Never before and never since has the Senate so abased itself before a president," concluded Corwin of this action.[49] Never before and never since has a president so blown up the powers of his office and done so with such little historical justification.

Nor was Jackson's extraordinary inflation of executive power the reflection of a reasoned if arguable judgment. The extant evidence indicates that more often than not Jackson's most imperious actions were dictated by strong emotions rather than by philosophical considerations. He broke up his first cabinet after the women in the families of most of its members continued to snub socially the notorious wife of his intimate, John Eaton, his secretary of war. Without any warrant in law Jackson sent federal troops to break a strike against a canal company headed by this same crony. Disregarding the recommendations of Congress to the contrary, he jeopardized public monies by transferring them from a bank of high reputation, but a bank whose president he hated, to a number of banks of dubious reputation, but banks headed mainly by good Democrats. He kicked out one secretary of the treasury after another for upholding their rights under the law until he found one who would do his bidding and "remove the deposits," later rewarding this sycophant by naming him chief justice of the Supreme Court. He brought with him to the presidency the same contempt for Indian treaties and Indian rights under federal treaties as he had often expressed earlier as Indian fighter and speculator in Indian lands, permitting individuals and state governments to intrude where treaties and Supreme Court rulings explicitly barred them. When abolitionists in 1835 flooded the mails with their pamphlet literature, this substantial slaveowner acquiesced in his postmaster general's policy of permitting Southern postmasters to violate the actual law in behalf of an alleged "higher law," with the president himself urging that the names of those Southerners who wished to receive this "inflammatory" mail be publicly listed in order to "have them exposed." As for the "monsters" who composed the pamphlets, Jackson said they "ought to be made to attone [sic] . . . with their lives." Responding furiously to what he construed as insulting behavior, he brought the country to the brink of war with France, for reasons that were alarmingly similar to those that led him to hurl his many challenges to a duel over the slights, actual and fancied, to which he was so sensitive. (In 1846 his protégé President James Polk, having decided that the territorial fruits of an attack on Mexico were irresistible, declared his readiness to bring about a state of war with Mexico by means nowhere suggested in the Constitution.) Not the least significant of Jackson's innovations was his transformation of the veto power.

In vetoing more congressional bills than had all previous presidents combined, Jackson did not violate the Constitution. The American charter of government places no limits on the use of the presidential veto. What Jackson did repudiate was a tradition of presidential restraint that had bound chief executives from Washington through John Quincy Adams, a restraint heavily influenced by the clear intention of the Founding Fathers. As Alexander Hamilton recognized in *The Federalist,* the veto was a power associated with the British monarchy, an undemocratic and unpopular power that Hamilton assured the American people would be used only in those rare instances when congressional legislation either threatened to reduce the powers of the presidency or was flagrantly at odds with the Constitution. Unlike George Washington, who refused to invoke this power merely because he was presented with bills that, *were he a congressman,* he would have voted against, Jackson vetoed measures that for whatever reason he opposed. By that rhetorical alchemy of which they were masters, Jacksonian propagandists turned what two generations of Americans had considered a "monarchical power," the veto, into a "great expression of the popular will."[50] That Congress and public alike acquiesced in the creation of a swollen presidency says something interesting about their independence and the quality of their perceptions. It does not make the Jacksonian abuse of power any the less.

Finally it should be asked whether there was not a kind of corruption or a perversion of the democracy that Jacksonian politicians took so much credit for creating and expanding in the policies of these same politicians, who denied any role in the making and administration of policy to those very commoners whom they so exalted in their rhetoric. Democracy during the era was barely government of the people and to an even lesser extent government by and for the people.

A wealth of modern scholarly studies on early nineteenth century government at every level indicates that the men who ran it neither consulted nor showed any interest in consulting ordinary citizens in planning legislative policy. It is not for anyone to tell politicians long dead how they should have gone about their business. The historian's task is to try to understand history, not to tilt a lance at its actors for what they did or did not do. It may nonetheless contribute to such historical understanding to note that in county seats, city councils, mayors' offices and Statehouses throughout the nation, as in Washington city itself, men claiming to represent the common people created legislative systems that allowed the people neither voice nor, in modern parlance, input. It need not have been so.

As for the legislation that was enacted during the era, given its bulk and diversity, it inevitably brought benefits to varied elements in American society. One of the most striking features of this legislation, however, is how little it did—and was intended to do—for ordinary people. Major party politicians in effect agreed to confine themselves to issues the resolution of which one way or the other was likely to have little or no effect on the lives of most people, their opportunities or the things that mattered most to them. Again, it need not have been so. It may be argued that this was an age of laissez-faire. In response it should be noted that laissez-faire or a policy of inaction was only selectively followed by Jacksonian governments. When President Van Buren in 1837 told a special session of Congress, convened because of what was the nation's worst depression thitherto, that communities "are apt to look to government for too much" and "this ought not to be," he was only stating his own and other major party leaders' belief that government should leave rich and poor to their own devices "under its benign protection";[51] he was not stating a law of politics. As modern quantitative studies have shown, there were indeed many poor people in Jacksonian America, roughly half the population at midcentury, who suffered under that era's version of benign neglect.[52]

The two forms of political corruption were interrelated. Men and major parties as determinedly on the make as were those of the Jacksonian era had as little difficulty in ignoring the mass of their countrymen who lacked property and power as they did in ignoring traditional standards of political ethics and constitutional usages.

NOTES

1. The best and fullest published account of Swartwout's defalcation is Leonard D. White, *The Jacksonians: A Study in Administrative History 1829–1861* (New York 1954, 1965), pp. 424–28. White's version is based primarily on a series of House Documents and Reports emanating from the 25th Congress in 1838 and 1839.

2. John C. Fitzpatrick, ed., *The Autobiography of Martin Van Buren* (Washington, 1920), pp. 262–64.

3. White, *op. cit.*, p. 428.

4. *Ibid.*, pp. 171, 385; John R. Wennersten, "Parke Godwin, Utopian Socialism, and the Politics of Antislavery," *New-York Historical Society Quarterly*, LX (July/Oct. 1976), 117–18; and James A. Hamilton, *Reminiscences of Men and Events* (New York, 1869).

5. White, *op. cit.*, pp. 422–23. For a recent discussion that is interestingly charitable toward the Jacksonian defalcations, see Matthew A. Crenson, *The Federal Machine: Beginnings of Bureaucracy in Jacksonian America* (Baltimore, 1975). For corruption in the land offices, see Roy M. Robbins, *Our Landed Heritage: The Public Domain 1776–1936* (Princeton, 1942), and above all, Malcolm J. Rohrbough, *The Land Office Business: The Settlement and Administration of American Public Lands, 1789–1837* (New York, 1968).

6. Carl J. Friedrich defines corruption as "deviant behavior associated with a particular motivation, namely that of private gain at public expense";

The Pathology of Politics: Violence, Betrayal, Corruption, Secrecy, and Propaganda (New York, 1972), p. 127.

7. Friedrich, *op. cit.*, Chaps. 8–10.

8. T. P. Abernethy, *Western Lands and the American Revolution* (New York, 1937).

9. E. James Ferguson, *The Power of the Purse: A History of American Public Finance, 1776–1790* (Chapel Hill, 1961).

10. The Yazoo fraud is discussed in many texts on the early national period. A clear recent treatment is Donald DeBats, "Political Elites and the Structure of Ante-Bellum Georgia Politics," unpublished paper presented at the annual meeting of the Southern Historical Association, Nov. 12, 1976, in Atlanta.

11. Erik M. Eriksson, "The Federal Civil Service Under President Jackson, *Mississippi Valley Historical Review*, XIII (March 1927), 517–40.

12. This is a major theme of White's *The Jacksonians*. White's comparisons are based on his similarly thorough administrative studies of the Federalists and the Jeffersonians. See too Crenson, *op. cit.*, p. 131.

13. Hamilton, *op. cit.*, pp. 132–33, 173–74.

14. White, *op. cit.*, pp. 253–62.

15. Rohrbough, *op. cit.*, pp. 230, 293–94.

16. Ronald N. Satz, *American Indian Policy in the Jacksonian Era* (Lincoln, Neb., 1975), p. 85. For other indictments of the fraudulent aspects of Jacksonian Indian policy see Michael Paul Rogin, *Fathers and Children: Andrew Jackson and the Subjugation of the American Indian* (New York, 1975); and two essays by Mary E. Young: "The Creek Frauds: A Study in Conscience and Corruption," *Miss. Valley Hist. Rev.*, XLVII (Dec. 1955), 411–37, and "Indian Removal and Land Allotment: The Civilized Tribes and Jacksonian Justice," *American Historial Review* LXIV (Oct. 1958), 31–45. Rare for its positive appraisal of Jacksonian Indian policy is Francis Paul Prucha, "Andrew Jackson's Indian Policy: A Reassessment," *Journal of American History*, LVI (Dec. 1969), 527–39.

17. Edward Pessen, *Jacksonian America: Society, Personality, and Politics* (rev. ed.; Homewood, Ill., 1978), p. 168 *passim*, attempts to synthesize many studies of antebellum politics, which it also evaluates in a bibliographical essay.

18. Representative studies that make these points are Edwin A. Miles, *Jacksonian Democracy in Mississippi* (Chapel Hill, 1960); Arthur W. Thompson, *Jacksonian Democracy on the Florida Frontier* (Gainesville, Fla., 1961); John Vollmer Mering, *The Whig Party in Missouri* (Columbia, Mo., 1967); William B. Hoffman, *Andrew Jackson and North Carolina Politics* (Chapel Hill, 1958); Peter Levine, "State Legislative Parties in the Jacksonian Era: New Jersey, 1829–1844," *Journal of American History*, LXII (Dec. 1975), 591–608; and Rodney O. Davis, "Partisanship in Jacksonian State Politics: Party Division in the Illinois Legislature, 1838–1841," in Robert P. Swierenga, ed., *Quantification in American History* (New York, 1970), pp. 149–62.

19. The criticism was made by John A. Dix in a letter to Martin Van Buren, June 4, 1836, cited in White, *op. cit.*, p. 424.

20. For a synthesis of the literature, see Edward Pessen, "Who Governed the Nation's Cities in the 'Era of the Common Man'?" *Political Science Quarterly*, LXXXVII (Dec. 1972), 591–614, and Pessen, "The Social Configuration of the Antebellem City: An Historical and Theoretical Inquiry," *Journal of Urban History*, II (May 1976), 267–306.

21. *List of Real Estate Belonging to the Corporation of the City of New York* (New York, 1838); and *Proceedings of the Board of Aldermen, 1832–1833*, IV, 416–18.

22. Washington to Mary Wooster, May 21, 1789, cited in Carl R. Fish, *The Civil Service and the Patronage* (New York, 1905, 1963), p. 7.

23. Fish, *op. cit.*, White, *op. cit.*, and Crenson, *op. cit.*, all concur on this point.

24. James D. Richardson, ed., *A Compilation of the Messages and Papers of the Presidents, 1789–1897* (Washington, 1896), II, 438, 448–49.

25. The senator was the New York State Jacksonian leader William L. Marcy. The speech is cited in White, *op. cit.*, p. 320.

26. White, *op. cit.*, p. 566, and Fish, *op. cit.*, pp. 156–57.

27. Sidney H. Aronson, *Status and Kinship in the Higher Civil Service: Standards of Selection in the Administrations of John Adams, Thomas Jefferson, and Andrew Jackson* (Cambridge, 1964), pp. 192–99.

28. Eriksson, *op. cit.*, pp. 517–40.

29. Andrew Jackson was no friend to corruption, yet he showed amazing indifference, early in Swartwout's tenure, to a report sent the president directly by his supporter James A. Hamilton, who had observed at first hand a very questionable financial transaction by Swartwout in the New York Customhouse; Hamilton, *op. cit.*, pp. 173–74.

30. Crenson, *op. cit.*, p. 131.

31. Rohrbough, *op. cit.*, p. 290. The generalizations in this paragraph are based also on Gordon T. Chapell, "John Coffee: Land Speculator and Planter," *Alabama Review*, XXII (Jan. 1969), 24–25; White, *op. cit.*, pp. 334, 340, 387–88, 419–21, 566; John S. Bassett, ed., *The Correspondence of Andrew Jackson* (Washington, 1926–1935), V, 338–39; and Fish, *op. cit.*, p. 107.

32. Andrew Jackson to Edward Livingston, August 6, 1831, cited in Crenson, *op. cit.*, p. 79.

33. Detailed documentation of this point would amount to a catalog of every one of the by now many dozens of such studies that the author has examined. See Pessen, *Jacksonian America*, particularly Chaps. 9 and 11.

34. Charles Dickens, *American Notes* (London, 1842), p. 215.

35. White, *op. cit.*, pp. 431, 434; and Pessen, *Jacksonian America*, p. 321.

36. Lynn L. Marshall, "The Strange Stillbirth of the Whig Party," *Amer. Hist. Rev.*, LXXII (Jan. 1967), 445–68.

37. Pessen, *Jacksonian America*, Chap. 9.

38. For their voting differences on the national level, see Joel H. Silbey, *The Shrine of Party: Congressional Voting Behavior, 1841–1852* (Pitts-

burgh, 1967); and on the state level, Herbert Ershkowitz and William G. Shade, "Consensus or Conflict? Political Behavior in the State Legislatures During the Jacksonian Era," *Journal of American History*, LVIII (Dec. 1971), 591–621.

39. Cited in White, *op. cit.*, p. 414.

40. House Report 313, 25th Congress, 3rd sess., 189 (June 14, 1837), cited in *ibid.*, p. 423.

41. *Ibid.*, pp. 411, 420.

42. Crenson, *op. cit.*, pp. 45, 131–33.

43. For example see Elizabeth Caspar Brown, "The Bar on a Frontier: Wayne County, 1796–1836," *American Journal of Legal History*, 14 (April 1970), 136–56, which shows that the deterioration in the backgrounds and standards of lawyers that allegedly took place on the "frontier" did not occur, at least not in Michigan. Similarly, Maxwell Bloomfield ridicules "elaborated and often unwarranted inferences" about the law, based on "meager sources," in his *American Lawyers in a Changing Society, 1776–1876* (Cambridge, Mass., 1976). Marvin Meyers, *The Jacksonian Persuasion* (Stanford, 1957), like Stanley Elkins, *Slavery: A Problem in American Institutional Life* (Chicago, 1959), makes a case for the emergence of new values and the "decline of institutions" that rests on surmise rather than on historical evidence, let alone quantitative data. My own reading of the careers of hundreds of successful Northeastern businessmen and leaders in the professions is that continuity rather than change characterized their values as it characterized their social behavior during the entire first half of the 19th century; Pessen, *Riches, Class, and Power Before the Civil War* (Lexington, Mass., 1973).

44. Pessen, *Jacksonian America*, Chap. 2.

45. Fish, *op. cit.*, p. 140.

46. *Senate Journal*, 23rd Congress, 1st session, p. 197.

47. Edward Pessen, "Andrew Jackson and the Strong Presidency," in Philip C. Dolce and George H. Skau, eds., *Power and the Presidency* (New York, 1976), pp. 35–36.

48. The great influence of this evaluation is indicated in the high presidential rating most scholars continue to assign to Andrew Jackson. See Gary M. Maranell, "The Evaluation of Presidents: An Extension of the Schlesinger Polls," *Journal of American History*, LVII (June 1970), 104–13.

49. Edward S. Corwin, *The President: Office and Powers* (New York, 1940), p. 267.

50. For a fuller discussion of this issue, see Edward Pessen, "Flouting the Founders: The Arrogant Veto," *The Nation*, Aug. 1975, pp. 333–37.

51. Richardson, *op. cit.*, III, 344.

52. Edward Pessen, "The Egalitarian Myth and the American Social Reality: Wealth, Mobility, and Equality in the 'Era of the Common Man'," *Amer. Hist. Rev.*, LXXVI (Oct. 1971), 989–1034; Stuart Blumin, "Mobility and Change in Ante-Bellum Philadelphia," in Stefan Thernstrom and Richard Sennett, eds., *Nineteenth-Century Cities: Essays in the New Urban History* (New Haven, 1969), pp. 165–208; Gavin Wright,

" 'Economic Democracy' and the Concentration of Agricultural Wealth in the Cotton South, 1850–1860," *Agricultural History*, LXIV (Jan. 1970), 63–94; and Lee Soltow, *Men and Wealth in the United States, 1850–1870* (New Haven, 1975).

Hans L. Trefousse

CARL SCHURZ, THE SOUTH
AND THE POLITICS OF VIRTUE

It may seem strange that in a consideration of corruption excessive devotion to virtue may be questioned, but there are occasions when practical politics require that problems of corruption be viewed as less important than questions of national well-being. The period of Reconstruction was such a time. The integration of the freedmen into the mainstream of American life was the most portentous problem facing the nation; anything interfering with this objective was, in the long run, of secondary importance.

But not everybody realized this fundamental truth. From the very beginning many a convinced radical, many an old abolitionist, many a partisan Republican, was unable to see clearly that the period following Abraham Lincoln's assassination provided unparalleled opportunities for the reform of Southern society.[1] And as time moved on, some of those who had realized it forgot what they had once thought essential, especially when new problems began to engage their attention.

The career of Carl Schurz furnishes a good example of this trend. Singularly astute about the opportunities and necessities of Reconstruction during the immediate postwar years, he finally became so committed to civil-service reform that he significantly contributed to the defeat of the very ideas he had long cherished. For this reason, a closer examination of his course is warranted.

Perhaps the most famous nineteenth century American immigrant, Schurz arrived in the United States in 1852 after an adventurous career wholly unusual for a young man only twenty-three years old. As an ardent German nationalist and liberal, he

took an active part in the revolution of 1848, first on an in-
effective march from his home in Bonn to capture the nearby
Prussian armory at Siegburg, and then as a lieutenant in the
revolutionary armies of the Palatinate and Baden. Managing to
forestall capture and possible execution by fleeing through a
sewer from the besieged fortress of Rastatt and escaping across
the Rhine to France, he returned to Germany secretly in order
to rescue Professor Gottfried Kinkel, his teacher and friend,
who was serving a life sentence at Spandau prison. He succeeded
by bribing a guard and brought the professor safely to Great
Britain. The liberation of Kinkel brought him fame, and he
became a well-known member of the refugee community of
London and Paris, where he met the famous revolutionaries of
the day.

But life as an exile did not suit Schurz. Determined to take
an active part in politics, he came to the United States, a
country where foreign birth was no great obstacle to success
and where economic opportunity beckoned. After a brief stay in
Philadelphia, he moved to Watertown, Wisconsin, where he
became active as a journalist, lawyer, and "Latin farmer," as the
displaced German intellectuals were called.[2]

Before long, the promising young German was brought to the
attention of the leaders of the newly organized Republican party
then trying to break the Democrats' traditional hold on the
Germans. That Schurz was opposed to slavery was natural; he
had fought for human rights in Europe and believed the blacks
entitled to their freedom. Consequently, he sought to win over
as many of his German-American compatriots to the Republican
cause as possible.

The Republicans appreciated his efforts. Before he had even
been naturalized, he was nominated for lieutenant governor
of Wisconsin. Although he was not elected, he had made his mark
in politics, especially since he had a real gift of oratory, at first
in German, and after a while, in English as well. In 1860 he
performed so well for the Lincoln ticket that the new president
appointed him minister to Spain. But in the midst of civil war
a quiet diplomatic post did not please the ambitious German-
American, and after he complained that he ought to take part
in the conflict, the grateful president appointed him brigadier
and eventually major general of volunteers. And although

Schurz's military career was not especially distinguished, at the end of the war he was one of the best known German-American leaders and an intimate of such radicals as Charles Sumner and his associates.[3]

It was natural that an intellectual like Schurz had formed certain ideas about the South. Deeply nationalistic, he abhorred secession and excessive emphasis on states' rights, ideas which should have reminded him of what the Germans called "particularism," the tendency of the small states to interfere with national unification, even though he supported Wisconsin's insistence on states' rights in the struggle against the enforcement of the Fugitive Slave Law. Firmly liberal, he also detested slavery and the deprivation of human rights to which blacks had long been subjected. In fact, he had always hated prejudice. When the priest in Schurz's Roman Catholic native Rhenish village explained that only Catholics could hope for salvation, the young boy began to doubt this doctrine. Was not his father's Jewish friend, Aaron, a decent man who merited the Kingdom of Heaven? For the rest of his long life, he fought against prejudice and most definitely included Negroes among those to whom he believed justice ought to be done. The South did not measure up to his ideas of liberalism.[4]

Schurz's sojourn in the South during the war did not change these ideas. Appalled by the poverty he encountered in Tennessee, in 1863 he wrote to his daughter:

Actually, we soldiers live much better than the natives of the country. You have no conception of the poverty which prevails here. . . . Women and men are dressed in the most poverty-stricken way and live almost exclusively on corn bread and pork. . . . The difference between this population and that which we see in the North is tremendous.

As he explained it, slavery was the cause of this misery, and he thought the war would end the people's ignorance.[5] It was therefore with considerable hope that he turned to Reconstruction, fully aware that the time had come to do something for the devastated region and its newly freed blacks. And justice for the freedmen was essential for that purpose, as Schurz knew very well and sought to demonstrate to Andrew Johnson.[6]

The general's unfavorable opinion of the South did not extend to his personal relations with Southerners. Singularly free from feelings of personal hatred for the enemy, he treated captured officers with great consideration and extended personal courtesies to them.[7] Possibly this attitude was the prelude to his later interest in amnesty, although at first he did not differ from other radicals in demanding a thorough reformation of Southern society.

Schurz thought that the opportunity to accomplish this aim had arrived with the end of the war. With real appreciation of Lincoln's ability, he was genuinely distraught at the president's death, but he had met Johnson in Tennessee and believed he could work with him.[8] Establishing a temporary residence in Bethlehem, Pennsylvania—Mrs. Schurz never liked the West— the general traveled to Washington several times and offered advice to the president, both solicited and unsolicited. For example, he warned that the trial of Lincoln's assassins must be fair. If Jefferson Davis and other Confederate leaders were involved, the evidence against them must be proven in open court; a military trial would never do. He was anxious to take part in the trial of the Confederate president, and, never one to underestimate his own importance, he thought he had made some impression on the chief executive.[9]

Even more important than the trial of Jefferson Davis was the disposition of the Southern states. Convinced that black rights must be safeguarded, Schurz was at first optimistic about the prospects for a workable policy. But as Johnson's course began to unfold, the general became uneasy. Even before the president promulgated his proclamation of amnesty and his policy of reconstructing North Carolina and the other Southern states, Schurz warned Sumner to be on his guard. Though meaning well, Johnson was falling prey to the wrong influences. Anxious to maintain the administration's goodwill, the German-American still sought to give advice to the president, and although he was appalled at the revelation of Johnson's conservative tendencies after the publication of the amnesty and North Carolina proclamations, he nevertheless continued to hope that all was not lost. This was especially true because the president asked him to go south to investigate conditions and the effects of the administration's policy. Accepting with alacrity, Schurz prepared to take the trip, despite the inconvenience and his dismay at the prospect of spending the summer months in the South.

What Schurz found in the defunct Confederacy did not dispel his conviction that the former Confederate States must be totally revamped. Poverty, unwillingness to accept the end of slavery, and outrages against the blacks disturbed him. What was worst was the realization that prior to the publication of Johnson's proclamation most Southerners had been willing to accept almost any plan of reconstruction. They had been defeated and they knew it. But now, aware that the president favored a mild policy, they had become confident again, and the old Southern militancy began to reassert itself.

The conditions Schurz observed were much the same in all the states he visited. But when he arrived in Mississippi, he became involved in a quarrel between the local military commander and the governor. When Governor William L. Sharkey tried to call back the white militia, General Henry W. Slocum intervened to prevent it. Schurz immediately supported Slocum, only to discover that the president sided with Sharkey. From that time on, relations between Johnson and his emissary became more and more strained. Although Schurz still attempted to avert the worst effects of the president's policy by pointing out the likelihood of the old proslavery elements' success in Louisiana unless the administration supported their opponents, Johnson disregarded the warning. By the time the general returned, the break was complete. The president was barely civil. Granting Schurz a brief interview, he never discussed the trip with his visitor. The general immediately sought help from his radical allies, and Johnson, in order to counteract Schurz's influence, asked General Ulysses S. Grant to visit the South and to prepare a brief report on conditions there. The president then sent a message to Congress explaining that the former insurgent states were ready to return to their place in the Union, and although he appended Schurz's critical report, he based his conclusions on Grant's much shorter document, which he also submitted. Since Schurz's report was too long to be read in Congress, as Charles Sumner demanded, several thousand copies of the document were printed and distributed.

Schurz's report on conditions in the South became a radical campaign pamphlet. Well-written, incisive and supported by

many appropriate documents, it was a stinging indictment of
Johnson's policies and a strong pléa for justice to the freedmen.
The author's unfavorable opinion of the Southern whites had not
changed and the picture he conveyed was one of terror and stub-
born resistance to the changes brought about by the Civil War.
In the struggle between president and Congress which ensued,
Schurz unhesitatingly supported the radicals and Congress.[10]

In the meantime, the general was faced with the problem of
earning a livelihood. Fairly independent financially when he first
arrived in the United States because of an advantageous marriage
to a wealthy Hamburg heiress, he had lost much of the family's
money in land speculations which went sour after the panic of
1857. But now a newspaper career seemed to promise surcease
from financial woes. After working briefly as a Washington correspondent for the *New York Tribune*, he accepted the editor-
ship of the radical Detroit *Post* and a year later became one of
the coowners and editors of the *Westliche Post*, a German paper
in St. Louis. Accordingly, he moved to Missouri and became a
resident of St. Louis.[11]

Missouri with its large German population proved an excellent
location for Carl Schurz. With good connections in Washington,
a ready-made German-American constituency and an influential
newspaper mouthpiece, he naturally came to the attention of the
state's Republican leadership. Elected one of Missouri's delegates, he delivered the keynote address at the 1868 Republican
National Convention which nominated General Grant. In the
campaign that followed, he worked indefatigably, delivering
speeches in English and German throughout the country, and
once again rallied many of his countrymen to the support of the
Republican ticket.[12]

Schurz directed his special efforts to Missouri. In fact he devoted the entire month prior to the election to the state campaign, which was especially bitter because Francis P. Blair, Jr.,
representative of the state's most powerful family, was the Democratic candidate for vice-president. But the Republicans were successful, and Grant carried Missouri. The victory was in part due
to Schurz's efforts.[13]

The Missouri Republican party was badly divided. On the
one side, radicals wished to maintain the disfranchisement of former Confederates as long as possible; on the other, moderates

wanted to end at least some of these restrictions. If he desired political preferment, Schurz had to seek the support of one of these factions, and, ambitious as he had always been, he desired it very much. But the senior senator from the state was Charles D. Drake, an archradical from St. Louis. It was therefore impossible for the general to join the radical faction—Drake would never tolerate a second senator from his home city, since such a choice would give the western part of the state a claim to a seat at the next election. In addition, Drake was a protectionist, while Schurz favored a tariff for revenue only. Moreover he was on very good terms with Colonel William M. Grosvenor of the *Missouri Democrat*, the leading Republican newspaper of the city, who was a moderate himself. Thus it was not surprising that before long the moderates spoke of the general as a possible successor to Senator John B. Henderson, who had incurred heavy political liabilities when he voted for President Johnson's acquittal in the impeachment trial.[14]

Schurz's candidacy encountered Drake's bitter hostility. The senator's candidate was Benjamin F. Loan, a radical from the western part of the state, who prior to Schurz's entry into the contest had seemed a sure winner. Trying to prevent Loan's defeat, Drake came to Jefferson City in person. In a public debate before the Republican caucus, he made a number of unwise personal remarks and found himself totally routed by the German-American, who was an excellent debater. As a result the caucus nominated Schurz, and in January 1869 the legislature duly elected him. The former German revolutionary, who in 1853 had come to America as a complete stranger, had reached the highest political office within the gift of the nation to a naturalized citizen. He was immensely proud of his success.[15]

According to Schurz's *Reminiscences*, he had been interested in civil-service reform as early as 1854, when he visited Washington and was allegedly shocked at the journalist Francis Grund's revelation of the working of the spoils system. Whether these recollections are accurate, however, is questionable. The general's memoirs were written many years later, after he had long been the president of the National Civil Service Reform League and had made civil-service reform one of the principal efforts of his career. In his letters to his wife at the time of the visit to Washington, he failed to mention the spoils system, though to his European friends he admitted that not everything in a democracy was admirable.[16] As a matter of fact, it would appear that after his election to the Senate, he was not above engaging in the game of spoils politics himself. He had earlier conferred with Representative Elihu B. Washburne, asked Grant for patronage and been very much surprised when his requests were not entirely granted. The fact of the matter was that his opponent, Senator Drake, already had the president's ear and disposed of most of the appointments in Missouri.[17]

For Schurz this experience was sobering Although as early as October 1867 he had spoken of the necessity of cleaning the party of wire-pullers, a notion he repeated in the following spring,[18] he now decided that the spoils system was really one of the great evils afflicting American democracy. Almost as soon as he entered the Senate, he delivered a speech attacking the evil, and since civil-service reform had already been advocated for some time by Congressman Thomas A. Jenckes and others, he found many allies. As time went on, the crusade for a responsible civil service became an obsession with Schurz, and he never ceased to fight for it long after he himself might possibly have benefited from it. Probably his liberal tendencies as well as his familiarity with Prussia's excellent civil-service institutions predisposed him toward reform from the beginning, but his active participation in the fight for change came after he had personally become a victim of the spoils system.[19]

Schurz's disappointment with the administration because of its distribution of the patronage was soon reinforced by another frustrating issue. Shortly after he failed to obtain what he considered his due in appointments, his friend Charles Sumner became estranged from the president and his advisers. The ostensible cause was Grant's effort to annex the Dominican Republic, a policy Sumner opposed, but differences between two men with such contrasting personalities were probably bound to arise anyway. Schurz, a member of the Senate Committee on Foreign Relations, supported Sumner. It was not surprising that the general's access to patronage gradually dried up completely.[20]

But the advocacy of civil-service reform and the struggle for human equality did not necessarily complement each other. Because of the abnormal state of affairs in the South, the question in the former Confederate States was not one of good government by an educated elite, but simply one of government—government that would include and benefit the freedmen as well as the whites. For this reason many leading former Confederates had been temporarily disfranchised, and newly enfranchised blacks would hardly have been able to pass standard civil-service tests. And since corruption was rife throughout the country, in the North as well as in the South, glaring irregularities occurred in the reconstructed states. Naturally racists immediately accused the blacks of causing the demoralization in politics. That "Boss" William M. Tweed in New York and his counterparts in other Northern states took much more graft and debased the political process much more thoroughly was conveniently forgotten; the spectacle of former slaves, some still illiterate, sitting in the legislatures and conventions was too tempting a journalistic sensation to overlook. The civil-service reformers were shocked.[21]

Nor was the general problem of Reconstruction confined to the former Confederacy. The border states, too, experienced their share of postwar instability. With their many Confederate sympathizers, reenfranchisement of the former insurgents was bound to result in the restoration of Democratic party rule with its deep antiblack bias. The freedmen could not possibly reap any benefits from such a development, so that demands for amnesty and universal suffrage, no matter how well meant, tended to be destructive of black rights. But the advocates of "good government" were drawn to this solution.[22]

Missouri was a case in point. Stringent registration systems, stern test oaths for voters, officeholders and even professionals, as well as other measures, had kept the Republican party in office, even though the freedmen were still disfranchised and the voters rejected proposed black suffrage amendments. The moderate Republicans, however, favored the easing of voting restrictions. As leader of this group, Schurz naturally sympathized with these objectives, especially since they tended to coincide with his views on "good government." Idealistic as he was or fancied himself to be, he believed that the amnestied voters might endorse his ideas of reform and enfranchisement. But of course the Democrats of Missouri had other ideas.

The issue came to a head in 1870. The enfranchisement of freedmen tended to fade into the background as state after state ratified the Fifteenth Amendment and the Missouri legislature

passed resolutions authorizing a referendum on amendments easing voting restrictions. But the Republican party was still divided. The radical wing, controlled and marshaled by Drake and
his followers, did not wish to endorse the amendments, while the
moderates under Schurz and Grosvenor asked for explicit party
pledges supporting the changes. In addition, the moderates were
anxious to nominate B. Gratz Brown for governor, while the
radicals preferred to renominate the incumbent, Joseph W. Mc-
Clurg. When an attempt at compromise on the basis of acceptance
of the moderate platform with a different nominee failed, Schurz
and his followers walked out of the convention, reassembled in
a neighboring hall and founded the Liberal Republican party.
Nominating Brown for governor, the convention endorsed the
amendments as well as a liberal platform. At the same time, the
radicals renominated McClurg on a more restrictive platform.

The Democrats had long been observing the widening split
with pleasure. Knowing that they would be the beneficiaries, they
did everything possible to accentuate the rift. They formally
adopted a "possum" policy, one of not contesting the statewide
offices but running local candidates, and entered the campaign
with confidence. Let the hated Republicans tear each other to
pieces. The return of the disfranchised former Confederates would
ensure future Democratic control of the state.

Throughout the campaign, both Republican factions sought to
woo the freedmen but it was only natural that the radicals had
the edge. Frederick Douglass, though counseling the necessity for
amnesty, wrote a letter endorsing the radicals, and most blacks
heeded his advice. The national administration also supported
Drake and his followers. For the first time in his career, the former German revolutionary was not backed by the spokesmen for
the oppressed.

When the election returns were in, it became clear that the
moderates had won, and Brown had been successful. Nevertheless, the Democrats scored local and congressional victories, and
the doom of Republicanism in Missouri was in sight. Within one
year, Drake retired from the Senate to accept appointment to the
Court of Claims; Francis P. Blair, Jr., the recent Democratic
vice-presidential candidate, was elected to represent the state in
the United States Senate, and local Republican control withered
more and more.[23]

Perhaps this experience should have alerted Schurz to the danger. It was evident that his idea of attracting the bulk of the Democrats to a revitalized Liberal Republican party had failed, and that instead of good government the result was the reversal of Reconstruction with eventual reduction of the blacks to second-class citizenship. The institutions of the old South which he had always criticized would simply be restored as far as possible.

But the general did not see the situation in this light, or perhaps he was unwilling to see it. Increasingly devoted to civil-service reform, he grew ever more critical of the president. He professed to be nonplussed by Grant's strong endorsement of the radicals in 1870, while the president was incensed at the senator, whom he accused, correctly as it turned out, of wrecking the Republican party in Missouri. Schurz in turn became more and more convinced that Grantism was the exact opposite of civil-service reform, and, even though the administration was the principal supporter of the progressive forces in the South, he committed himself increasingly to Grant's displacement.[24]

These circumstances hastened the complete break with Grant. To be sure, relations had cooled considerably after Schurz supported Sumner's opposition to the annexation of the Dominican Republic, but as late as 1871 Secretary of State Hamilton Fish attempted to patch things up. Nevertheless Grant was not the sort of man to forget and forgive party disloyalty, and after Schurz split the Missouri Republican party, the President chose not to interpret the senator's action in any other way. Cutting off all personal relations and patronage from Schurz, he did not forgive the alleged lack of good faith until he lay on his death bed, when a last minute reconciliation was effected. But that lay years in the future, and in the meantime the senator began to woo the Southern wing of the Democratic party in earnest.[25]

Schurz's ostensible shift on the Southern question was gradual. In May 1868 he was still determined to fight against white prejudice. In August 1869 he warned Secretary of the Treasury George S. Boutwell against the hasty readmission of Texas to the Union. Conditions were not yet ripe for the step, he cautioned. He supported the Enforcement Act of 1870 as well as certain 1869 Reconstruction measures, but by 1871 he opposed all "force bills," even though these laws were designed to make a reality of the Fifteenth Amendment and to break the power of terrorist organizations browbeating the freedmen.[26]

In order to replace Grant with someone else in 1872, many reformers sought a rapprochement with the Southern Democrats, but it was Schurz who went furthest. As early as May 1868 he had been identified with a call for amnesty in the Republican platform. He spoke increasingly in favor of milder Reconstruction measures, opposed the extension of office for Georgia radicals and favored the speedy restoration of Virginia.[27] Thus he was already favorably known in the South when in 1871 he delivered a strong speech advocating reconciliation and opposing the Ku Klux Act.[28] Then he accepted ex-Senator Henry S. Foote's invitation to address a reform group in Nashville, where he repeated his constant theme: although Reconstruction had been necessary, it was time for an end to proscription and the excesses of radical regimes. The Negro, whose rights he still professed to cherish, would be much better off if he divided his political allegiance between two parties instead of remaining beholden to only one. General party realignment was needed and Missouri's example ought to show the way. Let Liberal Republicans and moderate Democrats fuse, and the abuses of the Grant administration—its corruption, disregard of civil-service reform and misgovernment of the South—would cease.[29] As he explained to Sumner, "You tell me . . . that the Republican party must be saved. I am convinced that it can be done only by making it the party of reform and by suppressing the bad influences governing it."[30]

Many Southerners responded with enthusiasm. Former Confederate soldiers sent him long letters of endorsement, individual ex-Confederates praised him and Foote expressed his utmost satisfaction. Sumner was somewhat more dubious,[31] and, in view of the evident failure of Schurz's strategy in Missouri, it is surprising that the old radical did not warn his friend of the probable consequences. While it was a good idea to attract the more progressive elements of the Democratic party and attach them to a reformed Liberal Republican organization, the exact opposite might happen in the nation at large as it was already happening in Missouri. Schurz does not seem to have considered this possibility.

To cement the new union and to give expression to his convictions, on January 30, 1872, the senator delivered a slashing attack against the pending amnesty bill. The measure did not go far enough, he declared; nothing but complete and total amnesty would do. At the same time, though one of Sumner's closest friends, Schurz refused to support the Massachusetts senator's civil-rights bill, not because he did not approve of equal rights but because he believed it would alienate his new allies in the fight against Grant's renomination. Southerners were again delighted. Letter after letter praised Schurz's stand in favor of full amnesty but made little reference to the rights of the freedmen.[32]

In preparation for the election of 1872, Schurz, Charles Francis Adams, Lyman Trumbull, Horace Greeley and others organized a national Liberal Republican convention to meet at Cincinnati. The gathering was supposed to nominate a Liberal for president; either the Republicans or the Democrats might then endorse him, so that the program of revenue, civil-service and Southern reform would become the Republican or Democratic platform as well. The new combination would defeat Grant and usher in a new era.

The miscalculations of the reformers at Cincinnati have often been described. How they arrived in high spirits, how they hoped for the nomination of Charles Francis Adams or someone of equal stature only to be disappointed because of a deal between Horace Greeley and B. Gratz Brown, who obtained the presidential and vice-presidential nominations respectively, is well known. Schurz, who served as permanent chairman, was generally thought to be in the position of a president-maker. But because of his foreign birth, a circumstance his detractors never permitted him to forget, he preferred to remain passive, so much so that the convention was taken away from him. Greatly discouraged by the result, he hastened to the home of his friend, Judge John B. Stallo, where he sought to console himself by playing the piano. It took several weeks and a series of letters between himself and Greeley, whose espousal of protection and temperance were anathema to Schurz, before the latter endorsed the ill-fated ticket. In July the Democrats also endorsed Greeley; they even accepted the equality of all citizens before the law, but as Schurz correctly realized, as soon as the Cincinnati nominations had been made, the Liberal ticket had been fatally weakened.[33]

The contest between Grant and Greeley further undermined the already endangered Reconstruction process. Southern blacks, seeing that their conservative enemies were flocking to Greeley's banner, could not detect much good in the new development. To be sure, some old abolitionists supported Greeley, but as James McPherson pointed out some years ago, three-quarters of all the old antislavery leaders remained loyal to Grant. The rift in the party caused by the Liberal movement weakened Republican resolve even more, facilitating the eventual return of conservatives to power in the South.[34]

As Schurz had predicted, in November Grant won without much trouble.[35] The Liberal Republican party was dead; the Democrats soon forgot all about their temporary commitment to human equality and the Republican bolters witnessed the failure of their dreams. The damage done to the cause of equal rights could not be undone.

Schurz's own actions following the debacle furnish an excellent example of the accelerating decline of Radicalism. Devoting himself more and more to civil-service reform, he paid less and less attention to the question of human rights in the South. To be sure, when Sumner died in 1874, it was Schurz who delivered the great egalitarian's eulogy, but not even his friendship for the departed champion of the freedmen could induce him to support the Civil Rights Bill of 1875, a measure for parts of which his friend had fought for so long. Characterizing an earlier proposal to integrate schools, which was not passed, as destructive of all public education because it would not be tolerated, he continued to preach the wisdom of inducing blacks to join both parties to enable them to exercise their political power by balancing Republicans against Democrats.[36] And when in 1874 disorders in Louisiana brought about federal intervention, he denounced the military interference in no uncertain terms.[37] The radical of 1865 had come a long way.

Schurz personally reaped the whirlwind he himself had sown. Instead of being gratefully reelected by the Democrats whom his policies had helped to victory in the Missouri legislature, he was cast aside in favor of a former Confederate general.[38] His policies had failed, failed utterly, but he was unwilling to admit it. On the contrary, when in 1877, after having campaigned for Rutherford B. Hayes, he was appointed Secretary of the Interior in the new administration, he became an enthusiastic supporter of President Hayes's Southern policy, the abandonment of the remaining Republican states in the region to the Democrats.[39] While it is true that he also introduced his cherished civil-service reform in his department,[40] the blacks did not recover from Hayes's policies for almost one hundred years. Schurz continued to sympathize with the blacks and wrote articles on their behalf, but his prescription remained the same: Negroes must join both political parties and obtain a good education.[41]

Thus the politics of virtue ended in disaster for the freedmen and the nation. The mistaken faith in mere administrative rather than thorough social reform resulted in misfortunes never foreseen by its advocates. But once they had convinced themselves of the importance of civil-service reform and the clean-up of the governmental structure, many of them, including Carl Schurz, tended to become blind to other issues. Sometimes they themselves, but more often the country, and especially the blacks, were the losers.

NOTES

1. For substantiation and further elaboration of this point, see Hans L. Trefousse, "Andrew Johnson and the Failure of Reconstruction" in *idem*, ed., *Towards a New View of America: Essays in Honor of Arthur C. Cole* (New York, 1977), pp. 135–49.

2. Carl Schurz, *The Reminiscences of Carl Schurz* (New York, 1907), Vol. I; Joseph Schafer, *Carl Schurz, Militant Liberal* (Evansville, Wis., 1930), pp. 92–93; *Watertown, Wisconsin Centennial, 1854–1954* (n.p., n.d.), p. 33; Charles W. Easum, *The Americanization of Carl Schurz* (Chicago, 1929), pp. 50–55.

3. Schurz, *op. cit.*, Vol. II.

4. *Ibid.*, I, 34-435; Frederick Bancroft and William A. Dunning, eds., *Speeches, Correspondence and Political Papers of Carl Schurz* (New York, 1913), I, 45, & IV, 368–400 [hereafter cited as Schurz, *Correspondence*]; J. G. Merrell to Schurz, January 8, 1904, Schurz Papers, Library of Congress.

5. Joseph Schafer, ed., *Intimate Letters of Carl Schurz, 1841–1869* (Madison, Wis., 1928), p. 291.

6. Schurz, *Reminiscences*, III, 221–27, 201; Schurz to Sumner, May 9, 1865, Schurz Papers.

7. Edmund Berkeley to Schurz, Dec. 17, 1895, Schurz Papers.

8. Schurz, *Reminiscences*, III, 94, 150.

9. Schurz to Johnson, May 13, 1865, Johnson Papers, Library of Congress; Schafer, *Intimate Letters*, pp. 336–37. On Mrs. Schurz's dislike of the West, see Schurz to Agatha Schurz, August 24, 1867, Arthur Hogue Collection, Bloomington, Ind. Cf. Michael Burlingame, "The Early Life of Carl Schurz, 1829–1865" (Ph.D. thesis, Johns Hopkins Univ., 1971).

10. Hans L. Trefousse, "Carl Schurz's 1865 Southern Tour: A Reassessment," *Prospects*, II (1976), 293–308.

11. Schafer, *Carl Schurz*, pp. 94–95; Burlingame, *op cit.*, pp. 149, 188; Schurz, *Reminiscences*, III, 210 ff., 256 ff.

12. *Ibid.*, 283 ff., 286–92.

13. Schurz to Mrs. Schurz, Sept. 30, Oct. 9 & 11, Nov. 17, 1868, Hogue Collection.

14. William P. Parrish, *Missouri under Radical Rule, 1865–1870* (Columbia, Mo., 1965), pp. 232 ff., 259–63; Earle Oudley Ross, *The Liberal Republican Movement* (New York, 1919), p. 14.

15. Schurz, *Reminiscences*, III, 292–301.

16. *Ibid.*, I, 25–26; Schurz to Mrs. Schurz, March 13, 1854; Hogue Collection; Schurz, *Correspondence*, I, 11–14, 15–18.

17. Schurz to E. B. Washburne, Nov. 13, 1868, Washburne Papers, Library of Congress; Schurz to Grant, April 14, 1869, Hogue Collection; Schurz to Hamilton Fish, April 16, 1869, Fish Papers, Library of Congress; Schurz to Emil Preetorius, March 12, 13, 1869, Hogue Collection.

18. Schafer, *Intimate Letters*, pp. 406–408; Schurz to Mrs. Schurz, April 12, 1868, Hogue Collection.

19. *Cong. Globe*, 41 Cong., 1 Ses., 155–56; 2 Ses., 236–38; Ari Hoogenboom, *Outlawing the Spoils: A History of the Civil Service Reform Movement, 1865–1883* (Urbana, Ill., 1968), pp. 56 ff. and *passim*; Claude M. Fuess, *Carl Schurz, Reformer (1829–1906)* (New York, 1932), pp. 2, 392. For a revealing insight into Schurz's disgust with his patronage problems, see Schurz to Mrs. Schurz, April 8, 1869, Hogue Collection. He wrote: "Nothing can be mentally and physically more debilitating than this constant running around and huckstering for that which is called by a most fitting expression 'the public plunder.' The absolute absurdity of the present system of filling offices has never appeared in a more glaring light than at this occasion, but at the same time the feeling that reform must come and that he who brings about this reform will be a public benefactor has never been so general. I have already written to you that I am going to make this my great task, and the more I reflect upon this task, the more overwhelming and attractive it appears to me."

20. Schurz to Emil Preetorius, Nov. 28, 1869, Hogue Collection; Hamilton Fish's Diary, May 14, 1870, Fish Papers; Horace Porter to Fish, Dec. 16, 1871, Fish Papers; David Donald, *Charles Sumner and the Rights of Man* (New York, 1970), pp. 368 ff.; Leon Burr Richardson, *William E. Chandler, Republican* (New York, 1940), pp. 125–26; Schurz, *Correspondence*, I, 520–21.

21. John Hope Franklin, *Reconstruction after the Civil War* (Chicago, 1961), pp. 144–51; Hoogenboom, *op. cit.*, p. 39.

22. Cf. Richard O. Curry, ed., *Radicalism, Racism and Party Realignment: The Border States during Reconstruction* (Baltimore, 1969).

23. Parrish, *op. cit.*, pp. 232 ff., 269–326.

24. *Cong. Globe*, 41 Cong., 2 Ses., 237–38; Schurz to Emil Preetorius, Dec. 27, 1869, Hogue Collection; *The New York Times*, Jan. 14, 1871; Schurz to Mrs. Schurz, Sept. 1 & 25, Oct. 9, 1870, Hogue Collection; Schurz, *Correspondence*, II, 2–69, 252; Hamilton Fish's Diary, June 29, 1870, Fish Papers; Charles Richard Williams, ed., *Diary and Letters of Rutherford Birchard Hayes* (Columbus, Ohio, 1924), III, 124.

25. Fish to Schurz, Jan. 23, 1871, Hamilton Fish Letterpress, II, 871–72, Fish Papers; Williams, *op. cit.*, III, 124; Schafer, *Carl Schurz*, pp. 194–95; Richardson, *op. cit.*, pp. 125–26; Schurz to his children, April 27, 1885, Hogue Collection.

26. Schafer, *Intimate Letters*, pp. 434–35; Schurz to Boutwell, Aug. 14, 1869, Schurz Papers; Schurz, *Correspondence*, I, 484–509; Edward McPherson, ed., *The Political History of the United States of America during the Period of Reconstruction, 1865–1870* (Washington, 1871), pp. 400, 611, Schurz, *Reminiscences*, III, 330–32. All the foregoing references maintain that he opposed all three Force Bills; he absented himself from the vote on each but spoke in favor of the first one. Cf. Schurz, *Correspondence*, II, 254, which shows his opposition to the Ku Klux Act; his attitude on amnesty must have been in conflict with the Second Enforcement Act.

27. *Proceedings of the National Union Republican Convention Held at Chicago, May 20 and 21, 1868* (Chicago, 1868), pp. 89–90; Schurz, *Reminiscences*, III, 319–20; *Cong. Globe*, 41 Cong., 2 Ses., 473–75.

28. *Evening Courier* (Newark), May 9, 1871.

29. Schurz, *Correspondence*, II, 257–306; Foote to Schurz, Aug. 10, 1871, Schurz Papers.

30. Schurz, *Correspondence*, III, 257.

31. Frank T. Reid to Schurz, Sept. 21, 1871; Henry S. Foote, Jr., to Schurz, Oct. 6, 1871; Foote to Schurz, Sept. 29, 1871; Sumner to Schurz, Sept. 25, 1871, Schurz Papers.

32. Schurz, *Correspondence*, II, 311–13, 320–52; Edward McPherson, ed., *Handbook of Politics, 1872–1876* (New York, 1972), pp. 74–82; James M. Nisbets to Schurz, Feb. 2, 1872; J. S. Rollins to Schurz, Feb. 4, 1872, Schurz Papers.

33. Ross, *op. cit.*, pp. 86 ff.; William Gillette, "The Election of 1872" in Arthur M. Schlesinger, Jr., ed., *History of American Presidential Elections, 1789–1968* (New York, 1971), II, 1303–30; Schurz to Godkin, Nov. 23, 1872, Schurz Papers; Schafer, *Carl Schurz*, pp. 199–200; *The New York Times*, May 9, 1872, 4–4.

34. Sambo Estelle to Sumner, Aug. 5, 1872; J. Braden to Sumner, Aug. 6, 1872, Sumner Papers, Harvard Univ.; Hans L. Trefousse, *The Radical Republicans: Lincoln's Vangard for Racial Justice* (New York, 1969),

pp. 454–63; James McPherson, "Grant or Greeley? The Abolitionist Dilemma in the Election of 1872," *Amer. Hist. Rev.*, LXXI (Oct. 1965), 43–61.

35. Schurz to Mrs. Schurz, Oct. 9, 1872, Hogue Collection.

36. Schurz, *Correspondence*, III, 2–72, 89 ff. & IV, 368–400; *Cong. Record*, 43 Cong., 2 Ses., 870.

37. *Ibid.*, 365–72.

38. Schurz to F. W. Bird, Nov. 25, 1874, Bird Papers, Harvard Univ.; Parrish, *op. cit.*, p. 324.

39. Schurz, *Correspondence*, III, 389 ff.; Schurz to W. G. Sherman, March 1, 1884, Schurz Papers.

40. *The New York Times*, April 12, 1877, 4–4; Circular, Dept. of the Interior, April 24, 1877, Schurz Misc. Papers, New York Public Library.

41. Schurz, *Correspondence*, IV, 368–400 & VI, 311–48; Schurz to W. G. Sherman, March 1, 1884; Booker T. Washington to Schurz, Nov. 6, 1897; Schurz to John Hay, June 16, 1903, Schurz Papers.

Melvin Williams

CORRUPTION AND THE END OF HOME RULE IN THE DISTRICT OF COLUMBIA

Corruption and antiblack feelings were principal factors leading to disfranchisement of white and black voters in the District of Columbia.[1] In 1867, the year Washington blacks received the franchise, the capital city was governed by a mayor and a city council consisting of a board of aldermen and a common council. In even years voters elected the mayor for a two-year term through citywide balloting. There were fourteen aldermen, two from each of the seven wards, half of whom were elected for two-year terms in even years and the other half in odd years. Annual elections filled the twenty-one seats on the common council. All city officials could run for reelection. Congress had created this type of government in 1847 and at that time it had won popular approval in the city.[2]

In 1866 when black suffrage seemed likely, Senator Lot Morrill of Maine proposed congressional takeover of the government of the district. Some white Washingtonians, willing to surrender their own rights rather than respect the rights of others, welcomed any alternative to a local government in which blacks would have a voice. The Morrill Bill failed in part because the House of Representatives and Senate objected to depriving free men of their rightful prerogatives. The more important reason, however, was that Radical Republicans felt that it was too soon to abandon their proposed experiment of black suffrage.[3] In 1870 when the Senate again considered the "resumption" scheme, some white citizens had second thoughts about the wisdom of letting congressional committees run the federal district. Senator Henry Davis of Kentucky

caused much consternation when he said that, during his
tenure in Washington, Senate and House District Committees
had never shown themselves to be friends of the capital. "These
committees," he exaggerated, "have been organized on the principle of elevating the negro, and when there was a conflict,
of subordinating the rights and interest and feelings of the
white man to those of the negro." Rather than risk that kind
of government, 150 influential white citizens begged Congress
to establish a territorial government for the entire district
with a popularly elected governor, legislature, and delegate to
the House of Representatives.[4]

Blacks and some whites labeled the plan a step backward.
Yet in January 1871, the House District Committee presented
a bill offering far less local autonomy than the petitioners had
asked for. Instead of a territorial government like that established for areas destined to become states, the House bill specified a presidentially appointed governor and an eleven-man
upper house, often referred to as the governor's council. Only
a lower chamber, the House of Delegates, and a nonvoting representative in Congress were to be elected by popular vote.
Appointed boards of health and education, the fire department
and the metropolitan police were to supervise matters in their
respective areas. More important than the governor, the two
houses and the other boards was a presidentially appointed
five-man board of public works which took charge of public improvements, fixed assessments and issued bonds to meet costs.
Enacted on February 21, 1871 the new law, creating a territorial government with greatly restricted popular participation,
went into effect in mid-May.[5]

Although some of the local population was dismayed at seeing so much authority vested in nonelective officials, few white
Washingtonians objected openly. No one, it seems, foresaw
that the board of public works, responsible neither to the local
electorate nor to Congress, would exercise despotic power.[6]

Black voters suspected that the new scheme was designed
to curtail their roles in municipal administration, but their
apprehensions subsided somewhat when President Ulysses S.
Grant announced his nominees for the governor's council. (The
provision that the governor and the members of his council must
have lived in the district for at least a year forestalled the pos-

sibility of the president using his appointive power to pay his
political debts.) Besides eight white men, he named Frederick
Douglass, the best-known black leader in the country, John Gray,
a caterer who occupied a secure place among Washington's
black upper class, and Adolphus Hall, a miller deeply respected
in the black community. Equally gratifying to blacks was the
president's selection for legal counsel of the board of health—
black, Ohio-born John Mercer Langston, who had served with
the Freedmen's Bureau and recently come to Washington to
head the Howard University Law School.[7]

In April 1871 voters qualifying by three months' residence
in any one of the eleven precincts into which the district was
divided elected two members each for a one-year term in the
house of delegates. Blacks were extremely disappointed when
returns showed only two of the twenty-two seats filled by fellow
blacks. As Douglass and J. Sella Martin, the charismatic black
minister of a Presbyterian church, had predicted, the new territorial government gave far less opportunity for black participation than had the former municipal government.[8]

In the spring of 1871 fewer white Washingtonians carped
about the "curse" of black suffrage and Washington's "black
government." A scant year later, unfortunately, the District
of Columbia was suffering the effects of corruption and imminent
bankruptcy and black leaders had to bear the brunt of the
blame for these conditions. Yet the burden of responsibility
for the tumultuous short life of the territorial government should
have been laid to the board of public works.[9]

The white five-man board of public works was empowered
to plan and contract for all public improvements, assessing a
third of the costs upon adjoining private property. The territorial legislature was to approve expenditures in advance by
appropriating the money or sanctioning bond issues to cover
costs not met by assessments. Prior territorial approval of expenditures and maintaining public indebtedness at less than
five percent of assessed property values unless sanctioned by
popular referendum were the only limitations placed on the
board of public works.[10] It was nonetheless quite easy for the
board to circumvent these restrictions, as later investigations
revealed. Unemployment, it is true, declined sharply during
1871 as the board of public works embarked on extensive proj-

ects—grading, paving and lighting the streets, laying sewer mains and planting trees. But the benefits of the sudden rush of activity quickly diminished. According to witnesses before an investigatory committee, workmen were coerced to vote for large public bond issues and the high wage scale announced by the board soon proved to be window dressing. For example, as soon as New York or Philadelphia firms were granted contracts, they imported groups of workers at cheaper rates. Local contractors, seeking to compete, also adopted lower pay scales. Of even greater agony, the special assessments levied on private property by the board very soon brought economic ruin to hundreds of owners, as houses, shops and land were sold at public auction for nonpayment of taxes. White as well as black families suffered, but fewer blacks than whites could withstand the financial strain.[11]

In testifying about the mismanagement of district affairs, witnesses at a congressional hearing estimated that expenses of the territorial government were 300 to 400 percent higher than the city's had been under the mayor-and-city-council government. Alexander Shepherd, head of the board of public works and on friendly terms with President Grant, successfully evaded specific answers to how the board spent the millions of tax dollars and borrowed funds allotted to it for improvement projects. The district treasurer testified that the board never submitted vouchers to him and never permitted him to see its books.[12]

In spite of these revelations, the committee ended four months of hearings with a majority report commending the achievements of the "high-minded, energetic" men who made up the board of public works. The report urged additional "generous appropriations from Congress" to aid the board's work. Such mistakes as the agency had made, the report declared, were honest errors and the public, while inconvenienced at times, had suffered no real injury and later would benefit.[13]

Financial disaster overtook the District of Columbia in early 1873 and by summer the nation's capital was bankrupt. Teachers, clerks in district government offices, police, firemen and laborers on the public-works projects went months without pay. Adding to the woes of the District of Columbia, in September a nation-wide panic ushered in a five-year depression that within a few months destroyed every hope of restoring the solvency of the district under its present form of government.

District affairs reached such a chaotic state that Congress conducted a second, more extensive investigation. It was discovered that the board of public works had exceeded by more than $8 million the $10 million debt limit authorized for public works and that the deficit for routine operating expenses was running to over $1 million a year.[14] These revelations sealed the fate of the territorial government. Drastic action was needed. The United States Treasury Department set auditors to work to unsnarl the tangle of the board of public works' contractual commitments.[15] Congress, with moderate Republicans and Democrats taking control, voted without debate to abolish the governorship, the governor's council, the house of delegates and the board of public works. The act, passed on June 18, 1874, abolished all elective offices and put three presidentially appointed commissioners in charge of local administrative matters. Congress authorized a bond issue backed by the credit of the United States to pay off over a period of fifty years the District's $20 million debt.[16]

Despite giving up a cherished American right—the vote— many Washingtonians, white and black, were relieved because they believed that reckless spending would cease, injured property owners would collect damages, and Congress would eventually return control of their own affairs to district citizens. Yet there were racial overtones as some white citizens saw an easing of their burdens because the new government would end what the Georgetown *Courier* labeled the "curse" of black suffrage.[17]

A scandalous incident, symptomatic of the times, silenced fair-minded citizens who understood the significance of what district residents were surrendering and knew it was ridiculous to blame the district's woes on black voters. Several members of the house of delegates, upon hearing of the territorial government's demise, rushed to the hall of the legislature and pocketed inkwells and other small objects. One culprit, caught walking out with a red feather duster protruding from his trouser leg, gave the label "feather duster legislature" to the entire assembly. Corruption, antiblack sentiments and ridicule killed representative government in the district even more thoroughly than congressional law. Nearly a century later whites opposed to the return of any local suffrage that included black voters were still speaking of "feather duster legislators." Anti-black bigots by implication held the eight blacks among the scores of officials of the territorial regime responsible for that government's collapse. They shut their eyes to the fact that the demise of representative government was due to the financial irresponsibility of the five white men President Grant had appointed to the board of public works.[18]

The end of home rule in the nation's capital had some far-reaching effects. Manhood suffrage in local elections, which came for blacks in 1867, had given blacks and whites a voice in municipal affairs through voting and officeholding. Of greater significance, suffrage had helped create wholesome daily black and white contacts. For example, during the first session in which blacks had served on the city council, it had passed a public accommodations act. The law made it illegal for any person who had obtained a license from the city "for the purpose of giving a lecture, concert, entertainment, or for conducting a place of public amusement of any kind, to make any distinction on account of race or color as regards the admission of persons" or in seating arrangements.[19] Clearly in this case there was enormous interracial cooperation, since at the time the law was passed there were only two blacks among thirty-five council members. Although desegregation in public places did not become widespread, an important precedent was established for a brief period. When the mayor-and-city-council government ended in 1871, local representative government became more restricted. In a like manner some of the social gains were lost, but limited opportunities for white and black interaction remained. The total loss of suffrage in 1874, however, severed the black and white contacts that local politics had created. It was to be years before former voters recognized the long-term consequences of that stoppage of interracial communication on a daily basis.

NOTES

1. Constance McLaughlin Green deals extensively with these ideas in *Washington: Village and Capital, 1800–1878* (Princeton, 1962), pp. 291–382.

2. *National Intelligencer* (Washington), Jan. 8, 9, 1867; *Cong. Globe,*

39 Cong., 1 Ses., 3191, 3431; 2 Ses., 304–14, App. p. 9; David Donald, *Charles Sumner and the Rights of Man* (New York, 1970), p. 181.

3. Green, *op. cit.*, p. 333; *Journal of the Sixty-third Council of the City of Washington, 1866–1867* (Washington, 1867), pp. 438, 482.

4. *Cong. Globe*, 41 Cong., 2 Ses., 847; Green, *op. cit.*, p. 335.

5. *Cong. Globe*, 41 Cong., 2 Ses., 3912–3914; 3 Ses., 639–47, 685–88; *New Era* (Washington), Jan. 27, 1870.

6. Green, *op. cit.*, p. 336.

7. *Ibid.*, pp. 340, 341.

8. *Evening Star* (Washington), April 21, 1871.

9. Investigations into the Affairs of the District of Columbia, 1874, Senate Report 453, 43 Cong., 1 Ses., Vol. I, pp. x, xi; Vol. II, pp. 396, 425.

10. *Cong. Globe*, 41 Cong., 3 Ses., 639–47, 685–88.

11. Investigations into the Affairs of the District of Columbia, House Report, 72, 1872, 42 Cong., 2 Ses., 9, 89, 170, 190, 442, 698.

12. Green, *op. cit.*, p. 350.

13. *Ibid.*, p. 351.

14. Investigations into the Affairs of the District of Columbia, Senate Report 453, 43 Cong., 1 Ses., I, 462–69; II, 12, 428.

15. Green, *op. cit.*, p. 361.

16. *Cong. Record*, 43 Cong., 1 Ses. 5116–24, 5154–56.

17. *Courier* (Georgetown), June 20, 21, 1874.

18. Green, *op. cit.*, p. 361.

19. *Laws of the Corporation of the City of Washington* (Washington, 1870), pp. 22–23; *Journal of the Sixty-seventh Council of the City of Washington* (Washington, 1870), I, 782.

Ari Hoogenboom

DID GILDED AGE SCANDALS BRING REFORM?

Gilded Age corruption is well documented. Reformers, whether journalists, administrators or legislators, exposed the sordid details of numerous scandals. Yet the steps that Gilded Age Americans took to prevent corruption have been less publicized. In many instances exposure of corruption produced more lasting results than satisfying a fleeting desire to "turn the rascals out." The age of reform began in the corrupt Gilded Age. Yet while Gilded Age scandals prompted lasting political reforms, Gilded Age enterprise, by provoking government intervention in the economy, enlarged opportunities for corruption. Conflict of interest baffled the Gilded Age as much as it has baffled succeeding generations.

*   *   *

Gilded Age corruption brought fundamental changes to the municipal governments of New York, Philadelphia and Washington. These cities, however, did not recast their own governments. Their charters were restructured by legislative bodies, most or all of whose members did not represent the cities. Had these legislators had a larger political stake in the cities, they might have been less willing to alter their governments.

The spectacular career of New York's William M. Tweed—whom contemporaries regarded as both a boss and a crook—produced two revisions of New York's charter. Tweed in 1870 expended $600,000 to procure from the state legislature a charter creating a powerful mayor, defining lines of responsibility clearly, increasing the city's control over its debt and taxes, and generally giving it a measure of home rule. With Tweed's downfall,

the legislature in 1873 passed a new charter—a compromise between the wishes of New York City reformers and New York
State Republicans—that increased minority representation, divided power and responsibility among the mayor, the comptrol-
ler, several boards and department heads, and reasserted the
state legislature's power to direct New York City's development.
Ironically, the Tweed charter was a reform charter—and in 1870
it had reform support—but reformers and Republicans designed
the 1873 charter to curtail home rule and to impede future
programs.[1]

Although New York and Philadelphia differed politically, they
were similar in corruption. In the 1870s Republican James Mc-
Manes, the head of the corrupt Gas ring, ruled Philadelphia.
Righteous Philadelphians revolted in the 1880s, overthrew the
Gas ring and in 1885 secured from the state legislature the
reform-backed Bullitt Charter. State Republican leader Matthew
S. Quay—hardly a symbol of Gilded Age virtue—favored the charter to check McManes, who, with his Philadelphia power base,
was Quay's political enemy. Going into effect in 1887, the Bullitt
Charter concentrated power and responsibility in the mayor,
but this arrangement—similar to Tweed's charter—seemed in en-
suing years merely to simplify machine corruption. Despite reformer and legislator intent, the charter gave McManes and his
successors little trouble in Philadelphia.[2]

Unlike Philadelphia and New York, Washington had no voice
in selecting the legislative body (the United States Congress)
that controlled it, but all congressmen lived—at least part of the
time—in Washington. Yet, as in New York and Philadelphia, corruption accompanied efforts to modernize Washington. With
its unpaved and badly lit streets, open sewers and contaminated
drinking water, Washington failed to provide the amenities
expected in a growing metropolis and capital city. To facilitate
modernization, Congress in 1871 enhanced its own role, reduced
home rule, made the District of Columbia a territory, centralized
its government and created a powerful board of public works.
Over the next few years Boss Alexander R. Shepherd, whom
President Ulysses S. Grant appointed first to the board of public
works and later as governor, dominated the District of Columbia.
While transforming Washington, Shepherd recklessly spent
enormous sums ($17 million) beyond appropriations and dis-

tributed among his friends lucrative contracts, which had not been subjected to competitive bidding. Though Shepherd apparently did not profit personally, a congressional investigation confirmed charges of corruption. Concerned over Shepherd's dubious methods and exorbitant expenditures, Congress in 1874 scrapped the District of Columbia's territorial status, gave the city a commission form of government, and further reduced home rule. Although Grant, still loyal to Shepherd, named him a commissioner, the Senate refused to confirm him.[3]

The point is not the success or failure of contradictory legislative moves granting or depriving cities of home rule, but that legislative response to municipal corruption was swift and sweeping. Turning the rascals out was not enough. Legislators groped for machinery to transform the desire to end corruption into the reality of reform. Machinery, however, did not necessarily bring reform, which could be guaranteed best by an alert, powerful political opposition.

*   *   *

Ironically, the New York and Pennsylvania legislatures and the United States Congress were also corrupt during the Gilded Age. Despite their eagerness to cure municipal ills, these bodies were reluctant to heed the injunction: "Physician, heal thyself." *The Nation*—which tended to exaggerate, but did not fabricate, stories of corruption—reported in the spring of 1867 that the votes of New York legislators were bought and sold like "meat in the market." To pass bills legislators—renowned as the Black Horse Cavalry—were bought with agents openly facilitating their purchase. Jay Gould's enormous "legal" expenses ($500,000) in 1868 to secure legislation in Albany during the Erie War is merely the best known among many such transactions. Besides accepting bribes, the New York legislature practiced blackmail. Legislators introduced "strike" bills harmful to wealthy interests, such as building a railroad on Broadway. These bills were then withdrawn upon payment. *The Nation* noted that the "knaves" representing New York City's Irish did not "drive this trade. . . . The main body of the corrupt drove are lawyers, farmers, and what not from the interior of the State, Republicans in politics, and sound enough on all the great issues of the day to please Thaddeus Stevens himself."[4]

The Pennsylvania legislature was scarcely an improvement. Dominated by Republican boss Simon Cameron (who earlier had bribed Democratic legislators to name him to the United States Senate), the legislature was notoriously corrupt. The absence of a general incorporation law and the prevalence of special and local legislation made corruption easy. Legislators sold their votes to grant corporations privileges and then blackmailed these corporations by threatening to pass strike bills that would rescind their privileges. Out of 9,230 acts passed between 1866 and 1873, 8,700 were special and local acts, passed with little study or debate.[5]

The *New York Sun's* headline on September 4, 1872, proclaimed "The King of Frauds: How the Crédit Mobilier Bought Its Way into Congress." Congressman Oakes Ames in early 1868 had distributed between 160 and 343 Crédit Mobilier shares among colleagues, where they would "produce most good to us." Though Ames offered the stock at par, which was a fraction of its worth, he generously gave credit and allowed congressmen to purchase the stock from the large dividends it earned. This arrangement amounted to an outright gift. Ames's quick work prevented a congressional investigation and exposure of the fact that the Crédit Mobilier, which was constructing the Union Pacific Railroad, was reaping exorbitant profits and was owned largely by Union Pacific directors.

In these instances of corruption involving colleagues, legislators appeared reluctant to strike at the roots of corruption. Although congressional investigations concluded that the Crédit Mobilier had cheated the federal government and the Union Pacific and that Ames, another representative and a senator (both of whom he had bribed) should be expelled from Congress, there was no expulsion. Since the terms of all three culprits were about to expire anyway, the senator was not reprimanded and the representatives were simply censured. The widely publicized investigations destroyed some congressmen, wounded others and revealed yet more to be either naïve fools or opportunistic scoundrels. While these investigations clearly defined and condemned bribe-giving, bribe-taking and fraud, they did not produce constructive legislation to prevent similar scandals.

The clear definition and condemnation were both important and

necessary. Although most involved congressmen realized that they
had committed improper or corrupt acts, one insisted that his purchase was "both honest and honorable, and consistent with my
position as a member of Congress," and Ames claimed that his
acts were the "same thing as going into a business community
and interesting the leading businessmen by giving them shares."
Besides defining bribes and frauds for morally obtuse congressmen, the Crédit Mobilier investigations made them aware that
there was a conflict-of-interest problem. As Ames himself indicated, his object was to create a conflict of interest through
his gifts. "I have found," he observed, "there is no difficulty
in inducing men to look after their own property." Congress,
however, neither outlawed gifts from lobbyists nor required the
disclosure of assets to heighten an awareness of conflict of interest. Indeed Congress saw nothing wrong in Ames voting to
preserve his Crédit Mobilier interests, but it did see evil in
bribing others to preserve them.[6]

Growing more sophisticated, Gilded Age lobbyists abandoned
simple bribery to dispense among legislators expert information
mixed with opportunities to earn money through investments,
loans and retainers. By 1886 conflicts of interest became so
numerous that Senator James Beck of Kentucky moved to forbid
senators from accepting employment or fees from land-grant or
federally chartered railroads. The Senate rejected Beck's proposal, complaining that it singled out railroad interests while
ignoring similar conflicts and maintaining that a legislator with
interest in an enterprise would also have knowledge to legislate
more intelligently concerning it. Conflict of interest was a complicated problem. The following year, California Senator Leland
Stanford of the Southern Pacific Railroad joined with four
other past and present railroad presidents to vote against the
Interstate Commerce Act, apparently without troubled con-
sciences; while innumerable shippers, seemingly equally free of
remorse, voted for the measure, which in varying degrees involved everyone's personal interests. The Senate continued
to be troubled by conflict of interest, though it adopted no new
moral code. As the Gilded Age ended, public aversion to a
close connection between an economic interest and a legislative
responsibility was apparent.[7]

The New York and Pennsylvania legislatures in the 1860s

and 1870s were even more reluctant than Congress to rid
themselves of the virus of corruption. Their inability, or refusal, to heal themselves brought public demand for constitutional revision in both states. Following a stipulation in their
1846 state constitution, New Yorkers voted in 1866 to revise it.
A constitutional convention deliberated from June 1867 to
February 1868 and set up a committee on the "suppression of
official corruption," which took extensive testimony on bribery
in the legislature. The proposed constitution defined bribery
of public officers, prescribed a three-year jail sentence for those
convicted of that offense, and prevented pardons or commuted
sentences for the guilty unless they could prove their innocence.
Moving to destroy a particularly virulent form of strike bill and
to control railroads, the constitution required railroad companies
to obtain the consent of those owning at least half the real
estate abutting their proposed routes. The constitution also
forbade certain private and local bills—notorious sources of corruption—and required that those that were permissible should
be published twenty days before the legislative session began
and introduced in the first 60 days of that session. Although determined Democratic opposition—particularly by the Tweed ring
—and sporadic Republican criticism defeated the constitution,
in 1874 New Yorkers adopted the proposed article on bribery
and on local and special bills.[8]

Constitutional revision was more successful in Pennsylvania.
By the early 1870s reformers demanding a new constitution were
joined by Democratic and Republican political outs who objected
to the power of the Cameron machine and by businessmen who
objected both to legislative blackmail and to favors given powerful corporations. With diverse groups ranging from the Union
League of Philadelphia to the Allegheny County Republican
organization backing constitutional revision, the Cameron machine, bowing to the inevitable, did not offer serious opposition.
After voters approved revision by a five-to-one margin, the
constitutional convention began its work in November 1872.
Reasoning—with dubious validity—that it is more difficult to
bribe a large group, architects of the new constitution nearly
doubled the size of the legislature, specifically defined bribery,
and prescribed that state officials should swear that they had
contributed nothing illegal to secure their nomination and

election. By preventing amendments altering the purpose of bills, by limiting all but appropriation bills to a single, clearly titled subject, by requiring that bills be read on three separate days and by insisting that a bill's amendments be printed and distributed before its passage, the convention hoped to prevent treachery in passing legislation. The new constitution forbade special and local legislation on twenty-eight subjects and required thirty days' notice in the locality affected before the introduction of permitted local legislation. Taxation was equalized on similar property, and to eliminate a future "Crédit Mobilier," charters under which no bona fide corporation existed when the constitution went into effect were voided. In December 1873, by a margin of five to two, Pennsylvanians approved the new reform constitution. With legislative reform thus imposed by a higher authority and following the example of other industrial states, the Pennsylvania legislature approved in 1873 an incorporation law for the iron and steel industry and in 1874 as a consequence of the constitution—a general act of incorporation.[9]

Since railroads were among the leading corrupters of Gilded Age legislatures, the creation of railroad commissions was in part a reaction to that corruption. Without doubt the shippers, particularly farmers and merchants, forced railroad regulation on state legislatures and Congress primarily to eliminate rate discrimination. It is clear, however, that to gain advantages and to forestall moves against their questionable practices, railroads corrupted legislatures—with bribes in the form of free passes, retainers for lawyer legislators, stock options and outright gifts. Reformers hoped that energetic and capable railroad commissioners, enjoying a longer tenure of office than legislators, would be able either through publicity or regulation to eliminate railroads' corrupt political and business practices. The main objective was to end rate discrimination, but the desire to stop railroads from corrupting legislatures was real.[10]

*　　*　　*

Corrupt elections supported municipal and legislative corruption. Gilded Age political machines frequently prevented voters from freely expressing their preferences by intimidating, purchasing and creating voters and falsifying returns. Techniques made highly effective by the absence of the secret ballot included distributing free booze, employers transporting employees to the polls to vote for the bosses' candidate, repeaters touring polling places, allowing residents of graveyards—including the Founding Fathers—to register and vote, and when these heroics proved inadequate, delaying returns to stuff ballot boxes with fraudulent votes. Though the Gilded Age refined election fraud into an art form, widespread corruption produced demands for reform.

In Pennsylvania the constitution of 1873 tried to solve the problem of corrupt elections. Prior to its adoption, anyone whom election judges permitted could mark and cast a ballot, and at many polling places election judges—either Republican machine members or paid-off Democrats—were cooperative. The new constitution instituted statewide voter registration, required that ballots be numbered, defined bribery and prescribed its punishment, insisted on minority representation at the polls, and provided that contested elections be settled in the courts. When the Uniform Elections Act of 1874, implementing these provisions, failed to eliminate fraud, demands increased for greater reform, particularly the secret ballot. In 1888 Massachusetts adopted it, in 1891 Pennsylvania, by 1892 thirty-two states used it and by 1896 citizens of thirty-nine states voted in secret. The secret ballot did not eliminate fradulent voting—one Philadelphian voted Republican thirty-six times in 1899—but it curtailed the intimidation and purchase of voters and made cheating more difficult by depriving the machine of the accurate count of votes it needed while the election was in progress. The surest guard against fraud at the polls, however, is a strong two-party system.[11]

From 1870 to 1871 Congress, dominated by Radical Republicans, passed three Enforcement Acts ("force bills") to combat corrupt elections in the South and in Northern cities. The first act (30 May 1870) provided heavy fines and imprisonment for attempting to hinder citizens from voting, placed such cases in federal courts, authorized use of the army to enforce the court's decision and provided federal regulations for congressional elections. Since Ku Klux Klan atrocities continued, the third act (20 April 1871), also known as the Ku Klux Act, enumerated Klan activities that intimidated black voters, specified them as crimes and authorized federal intervention in troubled areas without local invitation. The Second Enforcement Act (28 February 1871), which should really be called the Federal Elections Law, was rooted in the Tweed election frauds of 1868 that threw New York to the Democrats. This law provided for federal poll supervisors during congressional elections in cities with populations over 20,000. In effect for eleven campaigns, it was used primarily in Northern cities and particularly in New York, where in 1890 an army of 10,000 federal officers effectively guarded the polls.

The year 1890 proved a turning point. In that year Congressman Henry Cabot Lodge sponsored a strong federal elections bill to enlarge federal supervision of congressional elections to ensure that Southern black Republicans could vote and have their votes counted. The House approved the bill by a strict party vote but it never passed the Republican Senate. To gain Democratic support for the McKinley Tariff and the Sherman Silver Purchase Act, Republican senators representing commercial, industrial and Western silver interests combined with Democrats to defeat the Lodge force bill. Though Republicans endorsed the bill in the 1892 campaign, the Democratic slogan "No Force Bill: No Negro Domination in the South" helped elect Grover Cleveland and Democrats soon repealed the enforcement acts. This move coupled with the Electoral Count Act of 1887, which made law the 1877 decision not to investigate state returns in the disputed Hayes-Tilden election, signaled congressional abdication of responsibility for combating corrupt elections.[12]

Election corruption also helped inspire the civil-service reform movement. Reformers, it is true, wished to increase public-service efficiency by using competitive examinations to select competent officers but their chief aim was to divorce politics from the civil service. Since Andrew Jackson's time, the public service had become an arm of the party in power and the reformers aimed to eliminate the civil service's influence in elections. While civil servants who used their time and money to perpetuate their party's power could hardly be called corrupt, the political opposition thought that their contributions were political assessments rather than voluntary offerings, that their campaign activities were detrimental to the public service, that the money and manpower derived from the civil service gave incumbents an enormous advantage in elections and that such

an advantage was corrupt. Apart from the many honest civil
servants whom politicians used to corrupt the electoral process,
some civil servants were themselves corrupt and helped perpetuate their party's power with their ill-gotten gains. By making
public servants no longer beholden to political patrons and by
barring political assessments, civil-service reform would break
the alliance between the political party and the civil service, and
would free elections from the influence of that alliance, which
political outs labeled corrupt. In 1883 congressmen who were
outs (or, since it was a lame duck Congress, shortly would be
outs) and wished to curtail civil-service activity in future campaigns combined with reform-influenced congressmen to pass the
Pendleton Civil Service Reform Act.[13]

*   *   *

Though Gilded Age scandal can be exaggerated, it did touch
all executive departments of the federal government. The dubious
financial schemes of United States ministers to Britain and
Brazil, the Whiskey Ring and the Sanborn contract in the
Treasury Department, the sale of post traderships by Secretary
of War William W. Belknap, the silent connection of Secretary
of the Navy George M. Robeson with a firm supplying the navy,
the payment of household bills out of Justice Department funds
by Attorney General George H. Williams, the perpetration of
land frauds by Secretary of the Interior Columbus Delano and
the Star Route frauds in the Post Office Department illustrate
that no department was immune and that the Grant administration was particularly vulnerable to scandal. Corrupt actions
produced reform reactions and, as time went on, improvement.
Many Republicans rejected Grant and his Stalwart cohorts,
espoused civil-service reform and ultimately in 1883 helped
push the Pendleton Act through Congress. That salutary law
would not have directly affected the officers responsible for the
aforementioned scandals, but in developing honesty, ability,
and *esprit de corps* in the public service, it made future frauds
more difficult to commit.[14]

Although turning the rascals out and appointing good people
to office would obviously combat administrative corruption, the
Gilded Age response to specific scandals varied from constructive
legislation to mere changes in personnel. As with municipal,

legislative and electoral corruption, the reform of administrative corruption was also imposed by the higher authority of public opinion working either directly on the executive or through Congress. A political opposition is essential to expose corruption, to arouse public opinion and to root out evils. Usually the reform response is in proportion to the degree of corruption or the reprehensibility of the scandal. The effectiveness of reform, however, depends more on the reform program adopted than on the heat generated by the corruption and, since wise regulations discourage but do not prevent corruption, reform requires the continuing existence of a strong political opposition.

Perhaps the most effective reform response to administrative scandal in the Gilded Age was to the Sanborn contracts and the Phelps, Dodge case, both of which involved the ancient and rather dishonorable moiety system. To encourage customs officials and to discourage smugglers, the first Congress in 1789 provided that confiscated smuggled goods were to be divided among the government (50 percent), the informer (25 percent) and the local customhouse officials (25 percent). High protective tariffs beginning in the 1860s increased both smuggling and the proceeds from forfeitures, known as moieties, which customhouse officials collected. Clearly open to abuse, the moiety system fostered "fishing expeditions," which used general search warrants to look not for designated proof but to see if proof existed, and it allowed compromise settlements which increased the potential for extortion by customs officials. By 1872 the collector, naval officer and surveyor of the port of New York received about $50,000 a year each from moieties, twice President Grant's salary. Such funds made these officers politically important; they contributed heavily to their party's treasury and controlled lesser customhouse posts and assessments.

Although the moiety system had been periodically attacked, it took the Phelps, Dodge case in early 1873 to bring it under heavy fire. A disgruntled clerk, who had been fired for dishonesty, accused Phelps, Dodge and Company of undervaluing certain imported items. A special treasury agent investigated the charge (aided by broad powers enabling him to search the company's books) and concluded—or at least alleged—that the charge was true. Since the law demanded that the entire shipment, worth $1.75 million, be forfeited, Phelps, Dodge readily settled out of court for $271,017, the value of the imports on the invoices in question. The actual undervaluation was $6,000 and the duty Phelps, Dodge avoided paying was about $2,000. Blaming "knavish politicians" searching for personal and party funds for bringing the case, merchants and reformers complained that the seizure of books and papers was outrageous and that the moiety system drove treasury agents to excess.[15]

The Sanborn contracts involved moieties in the Internal Revenue Service rather than the Customs Service. Because of criticism, Congress in June 1872 had abolished the moiety system for collecting delinquent internal revenue taxes, but the preceding month in a seemingly innocent rider to an appropriation bill it enabled the secretary of the treasury to appoint three agents to assist in "discovering and collecting" money due the federal government. Secretary of the Treasury William A. Richardson in 1872 and 1873 awarded contracts to John D. Sanborn, an associate of Radical Representative Benjamin F. Butler, to collect delinquent taxes from railroads, distillers and others for a 50 percent moiety. Swearing that he had personal knowledge that 592 railroads (which he found listed in a railroad guide) owed back taxes, Sanborn collected $427,000, pocketed $213,500 as his share, and paid $156,000 in expenses to others (probably including Butler), whose names he refused to reveal. Since in the normal course of its operations the Internal Revenue Service would have collected most of these delinquent taxes, it was demoralized by the Sanborn contracts.

Outraged public opinion compelled the House Ways and Means Committee to investigate in early 1874 both the Phelps, Dodge case and the Sanborn contracts. While the committee refused to say that either Sanborn or Secretary of the Treasury Richardson was corrupt, it condemned the contracts and recommended that Richardson be censured. Though Phelps, Dodge had technically violated customs law, the public concluded that the enormous penalty it paid amounted to extortion. Congress in June 1874 abolished the moiety system, required a court proceeding to determine intent to defraud and made that intent a prerequisite for confiscation, limited confiscation to smuggled items rather than the entire shipment and restricted the right of search. Presumably influenced by Butler, Grant determined not to sign the bill, which he claimed would aid

smugglers and cost the country $20 million, but Hamilton Fish
and Benjamin H. Bristow convinced him to approve it. Although
the act raised the official salaries of collectors, those in larger
ports suffered a decline in income. New York Collector Chester
A. Arthur's salary dropped from approximately $56,000 a year
to $12,000. Ending the moiety system was a significant reform
demanded by citizens enraged by official greed so blatant that
it appeared synonymous with corruption.[16]

Secretary of War William W. Belknap scandalously used his
power to sell trading posts, established at remote frontier military installations to accommodate soldiers, travelers and Indians.
His misdeeds not only led to an investigation but also to changes
in the administration of the army. In February 1876 Charles
Nordhoff, Washington correspondent of the New York Herald, in
an excellent early example of investigative reporting, wrote that
those favored with traderships collectively paid $100,000 a year
for their posts. These funds were received by Belknap, his wives
and other Washington insiders, including the president's brother
Orvil Grant. Earlier exposures had been ignored but in early
1876 Democrats controlling the House of Representatives were
eager to expose the sins of Republican administrators. Further
investigation by the House revealed that the first Mrs. Belknap
offered a post tradership to her friend Caleb P. Marsh, who
applied for the one at Fort Sill. Since the incumbent trader
John S. Evans was in Washington seeking renewal of his post,
he, Marsh and Mrs. Belknap hit upon a satisfactory arrangement.
Evans would remain post trader at Fort Sill but would pay
Marsh $12,000 annually, which Marsh would halve with Mrs.
Belknap. Though Mrs. Belknap died, her share went to her
sister and successor as Belknap's wife. With the secretary of
war himself at times collecting this kickback, the Belknaps from
1870 to 1876 received $24,450 from the Fort Sill business. Other
posts brought in similar amounts. Although Belknap hastily
resigned, the House impeached him. The Senate, however,
doubting its jurisdiction with Belknap no longer in office, failed
to convict him.[17]

Curiously, Belknap's kickback opportunity resulted from Congress' attempt to resolve the power struggle between the commander in chief of the army, General William T. Sherman, and
the civilian secretary of war. When Belknap removed the pop-

ular post trader at Fort Laramie, Sherman promptly restored him, whereupon Belknap's ally and Sherman's enemy, Senator John A. Logan, pushed through a law taking the appointment of post traders away from the commanding general. Having moved his headquarters from Washington to St. Louis to prevent further inroads on his authority, Sherman was delighted that Belknap's corruption confirmed the view that the commanding general rather than the secretary of war should appoint post traders. Influenced by the Belknap scandal, Congress in July 1876 insisted that the secretary of war appoint only post traders recommended by local army officers. Belknap's successor Alphonso Taft successfully wooed Sherman back to Washington and neither he nor his successors, James Donald Cameron, George Washington McCrary and Robert Todd Lincoln, interfered with the general. When Philip Henry Sheridan succeeded Sherman in 1883 and attempted to secure even more power for the commander in chief, he was rebuffed by Secretary Lincoln.[18] By destroying an aggressive secretary of war and by discrediting civilian army administration, the Belknap scandal helped reverse the long-term trend of increased civilian control over the army.

The aftermath of the Star Route frauds provides another example of Gilded Age response to administrative corruption. These post office frauds during the Rutherford B. Hayes administration resemble post office corruption during the Jackson era. Both sets of scandals involved unscrupulous public servants and unscrupulous contractors splitting exorbitant rewards for transporting the mail. Amos Kendall reformed the Jacksonian post office not only through zealous attention to detail but also by instituting new accounting, auditing and inspection systems and by reorganizing the department. Congress likewise responded to postal corruption by enumerating contract procedures in the 1836 Postal Act. These combined efforts did not prevent the Star Route frauds forty years later.[19] By the 1870s railroads and steamboats usually transported mail but in sparsely settled Western areas the mail still traveled by stage and horseback. Marking these routes with three stars—standing for certainty, celerity and security—the Post Office Department awarded to the lowest bidder four-year contracts to move the mail in these remote areas. If in the course of the four years better service on a Star Route proved necessary, Congress allowed the post office to secure improved service by increasing the contractor's compensation. The second assistant postmaster general—who from 1876 to 1881 was Thomas J. Brady, a Grant appointee— was responsible for contract changes. Uneasy over repeated requests for funds to meet post office deficiencies, the House Committee on Appropriations questioned Brady's extravagance. Although both Rutherford Hayes and his postmaster general did not suspect corruption but thought the issue was whether the West deserved legitimately expensive mail service, Hayes was sufficiently concerned over runaway expenses to insist that future increases be considered by the president and the cabinet and approved by the postmaster general.

In 1881 James A. Garfield's postmaster general, a suspicious reformer, investigated the Star Route business and found fraud. Firing Brady, Garfield ordered further investigation and prosecution. Corrupt contractors, it was discovered, eliminated competition by submitting low bids and then with Brady's approval improved service on 135 routes at a cost of hundreds of thousands annually. Among the crooked contractors was former Senator Stephen W. Dorsey of Arkansas, who, as secretary of the Republican National Committee during the 1880 campaign, presumably helped finance Garfield's victory with returns from Star Route contracts. Brady raised one of Dorsey's routes from $2,350 to $72,350 and another from $6,330 to $150,592. Despite the confession of Dorsey's clerk, the government in civil and criminal proceedings was able neither to recover the money nor to convict Brady or Dorsey for conspiracy to defraud.[20]

Unlike Kendall who found administrative machinery totally wanting in Jackson's post office, Gilded Age reformers blamed the Star Route frauds on dishonest people. Although Congress made some minor legislative changes, particularly for Star Route subcontractors, it did not try to overhaul the department. J. Martin Klotsche concludes, however, that the unsuccessful prosecutions exposed "gross carelessness and incapacity," paving the way for a "thoroughgoing reform" that transformed the post office into "a more efficient administrative body." Since political partisanship was closely identified with the frauds, their exposure helped make the postal service nonpartisan. Spurred by the Pendleton Civil Service Reform Act of 1883, loyalty to the service itself began taking precedence over loyalty to a political patron, an *esprit de corps* developed and morale improved. Perhaps the best indication of the impact of the Star Route prosecutions was the $2.5 million decrease in the annual cost of Star Route service and the fact that post office receipts in 1882 exceeded expenditures for the first time since 1865.[21]

❈   ❈   ❈

These various examples demonstrate that it was outsiders who exposed corruption, published scandals and initiated reform. Indeed superior outside forces—a legislature, a constitutional convention or public opinion—usually forced a reform program. An alert, powerful political opposition enjoying press support was the crucial element in the process. Although reform programs differed and some were even contradictory, most programs aimed to create machinery to eliminate future corruption. Yet despite their efforts to create reform machinery— the civil-service reform law is the best example—reformers realized that the system could be no more honest than the people who operated it. And these people have not always been honest—as the Harding and Nixon administrations, the Vare brothers' Philadelphia, James Curley's Boston and contemporary Arizona all attest. Accompanying Gilded Age reform was a shift from intimidating and buying votes, from frauds and theft, from bribery and blackmail, from naked, easily identifiable corruption toward the subtleties involved in the phrase conflict of interest. As government became more involved in the economy, the range of corrupt activities became larger. Wider opportunities for corruption have been offset by more sophisticated accounting and information storage and retrieval systems, creating an eternal tug-of-war or equilibrium. These sophisticated systems, like Gilded Age reform programs, are only as effective as the people who operate them. Outside forces, particularly a responsible political opposition and press, remain the essential components of the ongoing, never-ending process of reform.

NOTES

1. Seymour J. Mandelbaum, *Boss Tweed's New York* (New York, 1965), pp. 71–72, 105–107; Alexander B. Callow, Jr., *The Tweed Ring* (New York, 1966), pp. 225–28.

2. Lincoln Steffens, *The Shame of the Cities* (New York, 1957), pp. 136–38, 142–44.

3. John Garraty and Edward James, eds., *Dictionary of American Biography* (10 vols.; New York, 1974), *s.v.* "Shepherd, Alexander Robey."

4. *The Nation*, IV (April 11 and 25, 1867), 286, 325; Ari Hoogenboom, *Outlawing the Spoils: A History of the Civil Service Reform Movement, 1867–1883* (Urbana, Ill., 1961), p. 36; Homer Adolph Stebbins, *A Political History of the State of New York, 1865–1869* (New York, 1913), pp. 267–302.

5. Philip S. Klein and Ari Hoogenboom, *A History of Pennsylvania* (New York, 1973), pp. 155, 257, 318.

6. James Ford Rhodes, *A History of the United States from the Compromise of 1850 to the End of the Roosevelt Administration* (9 vols.; New York, 1928), VII, 65–137; Garaty and James, *op. cit.*, *s.v.* "Ames, Oakes"; Vivian Shurkin Wein, "The Crédit Mobilier Scandal" (Seminar paper, Brooklyn College, 1977). Congress did pass a rider to a March 1873 appropriation bill requiring the Attorney General to sue the Union Pacific and all persons who obtained stock without paying for it and received dividends, profits or remuneration against the government's interests. The Attorney General sued the Union Pacific to recover fraudulent profits from the Crédit Mobilier but the railroad contended—and in October 1878 the Supreme Court agreed—that the suit was invalid since it made the Union Pacific both a plaintiff and a codefendant. The suit was a farce in any case since the Crédit Mobilier had ceased to function. The rider achieved nothing and those who had profited from the Crédit Mobilier had nothing further to fear. *Ibid.*

7. David J. Rothman, *Politics and Power: The United States Senate, 1869–1901* (Cambridge, Mass., 1966), pp. 191–220.

8. Alexander Clarence Flick, *Samuel Jones Tilden: A Study in Political Sagacity* (New York, 1939), pp. 160–61; Stebbins, *op. cit.*, pp. 241 n., 245–46; J. Hampden Dougherty, *Constitutional History of the State of New York* (2nd. ed.; New York, 1914), p. 220.

9. Frank B. Evans, *Pennsylvania Politics, 1872–1877: A Study in Leadership* (Harrisburg, Pa., 1966), pp. 74–95; Klein and Hoogenboom, *op. cit.*, pp. 273, 319–20.

10. Edward C. Kirkland, *Industry Comes of Age: Business, Labor, and Public Policy, 1860–1897* (New York, 1961), pp. 116–24. See pp. 116–17 for the idea that commissions would eliminate a source of legislative corruption.

11. Klein and Hoogenboom, *op. cit.*, pp. 320, 322–23; Leonard D. White, *The Republican Era, 1869–1901: A Study in Administrative History* (New York, 1958), p. 382; Stebbins, *op. cit.*, pp. 249, 253.

12. Hans L. Trefousse, *The Radical Republicans: Lincoln's Vanguard for Racial Justice* (New York, 1969), pp. 432–35; Everette Swinney, "Enforcing the Fifteenth Amendment, 1870–1877," *Journal of Southern History*, XXVIII (1962), 202–18; Stanley P. Hirshson, *Farewell to the Bloody Shirt: Northern Republicans & the Southern Negro, 1877–1893* (Bloomington, Ind., 1962), pp. 202–35, 238–50; Albie Burke, "Federal Regulation of Congressional Elections in Northern Cities, 1871–1894"

(Ph.D. dissertation, Univ. of Chicago, 1968); Rosalind Kaye, "The Effect of the Enforcement Act of February 28, 1871, on the Presidential Election of 1876 in New York City" (Seminar paper, Brooklyn College, 1977).

13. The theme that the outs used civil-service reform to counteract the corruption of the electoral process by a politicized civil service is developed at length in Hoogenboom, *Outlawing the Spoils*.

14. The most convenient catalog of scandals can be found in Allan Nevins, *Hamilton Fish: The Inner History of the Grant Administration* (New York, 1937).

15. Richard Lowitt, *A Merchant Prince of the Nineteenth Century* (New York, 1954), pp. 275–83; White, *op. cit.*, pp. 123–26; Hoogenboom, *op. cit.*, pp. 130–31. See also an indignant but excellent article, "The Extraordinary Element in the Case of Phelps, Dodge & Co.," *The Nation*, XVI (May 1, 1873), 297–99.

16. White, *op. cit.*, pp. 370–72; Nevins, *op. cit.*, pp. 708–10, 714, 725–26; Hoogenboom, *op. cit.*, pp. 131–32.

17. Nevins, *op. cit.*, pp. 804–16; White, *op. cit.*, pp. 368–69; Garraty and James, *op. cit.*, *s.v.*, "Belknap, William Worth"; U. S., Congress, House, *The Management of the War Department*, 44 Cong., 1 Ses., Aug. 5, 1876, p. ii; Barbara de Zorzi, "Belknap's Anaconda: The Post Tradership Scandal of Grant's Secretary of War William Worth Belknap" (Seminar paper, Brooklyn College, 1977).

18. Russell F. Weigley, *History of the United States Army* (New York, 1967), pp. 286–87; de Zorzi, *op. cit.*

19. Leonard D. White, *The Jacksonians: A Study in Administrative History, 1829–1861* (New York, 1954), pp. 251–83; Matthew A. Crenson, *The Federal Machine: Beginnings of Bureaucracy in Jacksonian America* (Baltimore, 1975), pp. 104–15.

20. White, *op. cit.*, pp. 376–78; Thomas C. Reeves, *Gentleman Boss: The Life of Chester Alan Arthur* (New York, 1975), pp. 213–16; 297–305.

21. J. Martin Klotsche, "The Star Route Cases," *Mississippi Valley Historical Review*, XXII (1935–36), 407–18; U. S., Post Office Department, *Report of the Postmaster General, 1882*, 47 Cong., 2 Ses., 1882, H. Ex. Doc. 1, Pt. 4: 66.

Jerome L. Sternstein

THE PROBLEM OF CORRUPTION
IN THE GILDED AGE: THE CASE OF
NELSON W. ALDRICH AND THE SUGAR TRUST

Early in 1881, Senator William Windom of Minnesota announced the sale of his mansion in Washington, D.C., to Senator Thomas Collier Platt of New York and unveiled plans to
construct a larger, more elaborate edifice to take its place. Shortly
afterwards Senator Henry L. Dawes of Massachusetts, noting
the ability of many of his colleagues to afford such extravagances
when he himself was finding it increasingly difficult to meet his
grocery bills, wrote his wife in disgust: "What a miserable faculty
we have to have been here so long and be able to keep ourselves
so poor."[1]
Had contemporary critics of the Washington political scene
known that the senatorial profession had not made Dawes rich,
they would have been genuinely surprised, especially in view
of his more than twenty-five years of service on Capitol Hill
and his well-earned reputation as a dedicated champion of New
England's banking and manufacturing interests. As Americans
from all walks of life explained to Beatrice Webb when she
toured the United States during the 1890s, "Senators do not go
to Washington . . . 'for their health.' "[2] What senators supposedly
went to Washington for, so most citizens agreed, was either to
accumulate a fortune by looking after the needs of big business
in return for campaign contributions, unsecured loans, legal
retainers, stock participations and other beneficences, or to
protect their investments and satisfy their egos by capping off
previously remunerative careers in business with a seat alongside
others of similar outlook and ambitions in the most exclusive

gentlemen's club in the world. An eminent Midwestern newspaper cogently expressed this popular belief when it editorialized
in 1884:

Behind every one ... of the portly and well dressed members of the
Senate can be seen the outlines of some corporation interested in getting
or preventing legislation, or of some syndicate that has invaluable contracts
or patents to defend or push. ... Once, great men went to the Senate
to work for their principles and ideas; now rich men go there to work
for their interests or to air their purses.[3]

And not surprisingly, considering what her hosts told her over
and over about the "Millionaires' Club" and her own tendency
to assume the worst about the capitalist system, when Mrs.
Webb went to Washington to observe those portly and well-
dressed men among their cuspidors and soft leather chairs, she
discovered them to be exactly as described. "Who can watch
the proceedings of the Senate," she wondered, "without notic-
ing . . . the presence of a subterranean government carried on
in the interests of small groups of profitmakers and without
consideration of the interests of the whole people?"[4]

Until comparatively recently most historians of post-Civil-War
America have, like Mrs. Webb, found the contemporary estimate
of the Senate to be substantially in accord with their perception
of the facts. From Charles Beard through Matthew Josephson
to Richard Hofstadter and Ray Ginger, the standard treatment
of the men who prowled the corridors and cloakrooms of the
Upper House between the administrations of Ulysses S. Grant
and Theodore Roosevelt has often read like an extended, though
obviously refined, paraphrase of such celebrated muckraking
tracts as David Graham Phillips's *The Treason of the Senate*,
which originally appeared in 1906, but which echoed themes and
allegations first heard in the 1880s. Ray Ginger's description of
the quid-pro-quo relationship which James G. Blaine supposedly
pioneered with the business community in the 1870s encapsulates
the traditional historical interpretation and its assumptions in
two sentences: "He would watch out for their interests, day in
and day out. They in turn would let him in on a few stock deals
and would finance his campaigns for re-election."[5]

Today, however, this view of the politicos is rapidly being
revised, as indeed much of it deserves to be. Its underlying prem-

ise, that the senators and representatives of the era were nothing more than kept functionaries or self-serving millionaires
without a political will or role of their own apart from the aims
of big business, is no longer tenable. New biographies and mono-
graphs have demonstrated that the majority were seasoned
politicians possessed of a highly developed professional self-
consciousness which reinforced their partisan commitments and
bent them firmly in the direction of order and system.[6] A number of these studies have also suggested that the most important
development on Capitol Hill during the Gilded Age and the
Progressive Era was not the capture of the congressional machinery by Wall Street but the transformation of Congress from
loosely structured bodies in which significant legislative influence was dispersed among several competing factions in both
parties into partisan and disciplined chambers in which principal
legislative control rested in the hands of a few leaders who held
dominent positions on key committees as well as homogeneous
opinions on public policy.[7] To underscore these findings, fresh
examinations of the economic and political issues of the period
have found that conflict was often just as characteristic of American enterprise as consensus, thereby shattering the conventional
concept of a monolithic, overweening business community.[8]

This revisionist assault has much to commend it. It is solidly
researched, sophisticated and logical. Few will quarrel with its
conclusion that commentaries emphasizing venality and domination by the Robber Barons as the chief determinants of how and
why the politicos cast their yeas and nays can no longer suffice
to explain congressional behavior during the Gilded Age and
after. But before historians replace the unfavorable references
to the Blaines and Nelson W. Aldriches in their textbooks and
lectures with testimonials extolling their virtues, a word of cau-
tion is necessary. For if the revisionists have established that
they were accomplished politicians who were never as subservient
to big business as their critics claimed, it does not follow that
they were as resistant to corporate blandishments and as con-
strained about exploiting their positions for personal gain as
many of the recent reevaluations would have readers believe.

In his study of the Senate, for example, David Rothman rightly
disposes of the notion that big businessmen had anything like
the overwhelming leverage over decision-making which the

stereotype accorded them. But it is something else to contend that, because the Senate leaders controlled the legislative process, it was an untainted process, rendered so by the professionalism of the participants, their general political competence, their willingness to subordinate themselves to the needs of their party, and the electorate's growing intolerance of conflicts of interest.[9] There is some basis for Rothman's claim that, as the Gilded Age Senate was professionalized and its parliamentary functions, particularly in the area of the economy, became more complex, the public demands for stricter standards of congressional ethics increased. It also seems beyond argument that, as the capacity of the Senate leadership to control the parliamentary machinery became greater and party solidarity strengthened, the influence of their constituents on the behavior of legislators grew progressively weaker. But to claim, as Rothman does, that the emergence of party government on Capitol Hill during the Gilded Age established an environment in which "corporations could not expect to affiliate public officials, through bonds and retainers, . . . Senators . . . could no longer dare accept such offers, and companies, anticipating rebuff or scandal, feared to initiate them" is to posit an inverse correlation between political consolidation and political morality which is as misleading as anything Josephson or Hofstadter ever wrote about senators giving aid and comfort to corporations and being in their employ.[10]

Political scientists examining modernizing societies today argue that, when parties become strong and cohesive, interest groups tend to become ineffectual and that, when legislative bodies centralize and institutionalize, corruption generally declines.[11] Theoretically, it is easy to understand how a party that can enforce adherence to its policies can enfeeble otherwise powerful private interests and thus provide a formidable barrier to corruption. But if a disciplined party organization can more effectively repulse interest groups than an undisciplined one, the reverse of this proposition is equally true: legislative bodies characterized by a high degree of political organization can, if their leaders are so inclined, effectively enact legislation sought by those with money and connections and foster corruption rather than inhibit it. What a centralized party machine does depends on the purposes and ambitions of those who control it. The mere development of a cohesive party does not automatically reduce corruption or make public policy "less vulnerable" to assertive private interests. It may, depending on the predilections and attitudes of its leaders, provide a parliamentary setting which is highly conducive to both.[12] There is considerable evidence that the circumstances surrounding the progressive strengthening of the senatorial parties in the 1880s and 1890s did just that. These years saw the expansion of the power of such senators as Nelson W. Aldrich, William Boyd Allison and Arthur Pue Gorman, all of whom enjoyed close personal and ideological ties with industrial capitalism, and a corresponding constriction in the policy-making role played by the whole membership, many of whom were fervid opponents of "Wall Street." Far from insulating the legislative process from big business and reducing the incentives for corruption, the concentration of institutional authority in the hands of senators like Aldrich had precisely the opposite effect.

To prove this point, the remaining part of this essay will focus on the mutually beneficial relationship that evolved during the last two decades of the nineteenth century between the American Sugar Refining Company, better known as the Sugar Trust, a corporation whose name was a code word among contemporaries for fix and privilege, and Senator Nelson W. Aldrich, the Rhode Island lawmaker who grew rich as the trust's most successful fixer. An exploration of the interplay between the sugar industry and the senator will illustrate concretely how personal financial benefit accrued to those who spent long years acquiring a power base in Congress and also identify the components of legislative corruption and clarify the role played by important private interests in helping to shape public policy.

The process by which Nelson Aldrich became the Sugar Trust's "man in Washington" began in 1882, when, shortly after entering the Senate, he was appointed to the Finance Committee. Though sugar refining was not a Rhode Island industry, Aldrich nevertheless had a deep and abiding concern for its welfare. As a wholesale grocer who for years had bought sugar in New York and Boston in carloads lots, he was well acquainted with the esoteric language of the trade and knew on a first-name basis many of the men connected with it. He could discuss intelligently the uses of bone black and filtering pans, the distinctions between muscovado and centrifugal sugars, the shades of color that differentiated number 13 Dutch Standard from number 16 Dutch Standard, the relative merits of sugars measuring 75 degrees of saccharine strength on the polariscope and sugars measuring 90 degrees—a subject "so inextricably confounded," Senator John J. Ingalls of Kansas once stormed in debate, "that . . . nobody in the Senate understands it."[13] Thus it was not surprising that when the Eastern refiners sought a spokesman on the Finance Committee for their views they went straight to Aldrich and that he accepted them as his clients without the slightest hesitation.

In 1882 the Eastern refining industry was fighting for survival. As was the case in other branches of manufacturing, following the panic of 1873 and the subsequent depression, the sugar-refining business had fallen on hard times. The basic problem was overproduction. Large profits in the years after the Civil War, low start-up costs and wages, improved transportation and technological breakthroughs had promoted the rapid growth of the industry. But demand for refined sugar began to lag well behind the ever-increasing supply. Consumption had slowed down in the early 1870s and the depression brought further decline. The effect was cutthroat competition—plummeting prices, desperate efforts to slash costs, rapidly shrinking profit margins and numerous bankruptcies. Moreover, adding to the industry's distress, beginning in the late 1870s, it encountered a growing threat from the San Francisco sugar tycoon Claus Spreckels. Capitalizing on the Hawaiian Reciprocity Treaty of 1875, which permitted raw sugar from the islands to enter the United States duty-free, he had managed to gain almost monopoly control of the refining business on the Pacific slope. Until then the Eastern refiners had dominated the sugar market in the Midwest, but after Spreckels succeeded in driving his competitors to the wall in California, he began to do the same thing along the Missouri River where, a spokesman for the hardpressed Eastern refiners complained, his untaxed Hawaiian sugars "came into competition with the [taxed] eastern coast importations on a basis that is entirely unfair."[14] Consequently, with their share of the Midwest market shrinking every day, the Eastern refiners commenced a fierce, no-holds-barred campaign to destroy this advantage. Specifically, they brought intense pressure on Congress to abrogate the Hawaiian treaty and reduce the high duties on the raw sugar they imported from the Caribbean.

Of the two objectives the Eastern refiners considered essential for their corporate well-being, a lowering of the raw-sugar duties seemed more likely of quick attainment, since the reciprocity treaty had some years to run before it came up for renewal. There was, however, a barrier to tariff reduction: an alliance between Louisiana sugar planters, Midwestern glucose manufacturers and Spreckels which consistently marshaled enough votes in Congress to block their efforts. To breach that barrier, the Eastern refiners placed great reliance on Aldrich and he did not disappoint them.[15]

Breaking with tradition which held that freshman senators should be seen and not heard, he worked tenaciously to frame the sugar schedule in the so-called Mongrel tariff of 1883 to the industry's satisfaction. He made it a personal crusade to reduce the raw-sugar duties in the bill reported out by the Finance Committee, not only in the face of opposition from the Democrats, but also contrary to the desires of many Republicans, including his two venerable colleagues on the committee, Senators John Sherman of Ohio and Justin Smith Morrill of Vermont. At first he found very little backing for his position in the Senate chamber and might well have faltered but for the invaluable assistance he received outside it from a business acquaintance of his "for a great many years," John E. Searles, Jr., then the managing partner of the Havemeyer Sugar Refining Company, a leading small firm. Searles, who would shortly achieve national prominence and notoriety as one of the top organizers and operating officers of the Sugar Trust, had been a fixture in Washington since the 1870s, lobbying for lower rates on raw sugar as well as masterminding the drive against the reciprocity treaty. Often, however, he found himself pleading his cause to deaf ears. In Aldrich he now had a skilled and highly accessible sympathizer and he made the most of it. He helped mobilize a petition and letter-writing campaign, fed Aldrich reams of statistics and information, furnished technical assistance and haunted the cloakrooms and corridors buttonholing senators. Typically, after sending Aldrich a proposal for possible submission to the Senate, Searles asked: "If you think it is best for me to come over and see some members . . . before the sugar schedule is reached I will do so. . . . Telegraph me on receipt of this your views as to when sugar will be reached and if you so desire I will come on at once."[16]

Eventually, after weeks of energetic industry lobbying and wearying floor debate, Aldrich succeeded in persuading the Senate to cut the rates on raw sugar about one-half cent per pound, the first reduction in such duties in decades. He confirmed his virtuoso command of the situation when he persuaded his fellow members of the conference committee of the two houses to ignore their instructions and raise the rates on refined sugar to substantially above their former level.[17] But more important than this legislative victory, his labors on behalf of the beleaguered Eastern refiners established the pattern of his future relations with Searles. If, at its inception, the formal pattern of this relationship did not show the slightest trace of money changing hands, things were quite different ten years later.

Reasons for this difference rest in part on how Aldrich functioned as a senator. Like other men of affairs who entered the Upper House during the Gilded Age, he was ardently wedded to the concept that legislation affecting businessmen should be drawn up in close collaboration with businessmen. He assumed that only successful business leaders possessed the skills, experience and knowledge that legislators had to have if they were to deal intelligently with the multitudinous and complex problems of a modern industrializing society. In his role as senator, he saw himself as a broker, as an intermediary between the parliamentary arena and the magnates of Wall Street or the cotton barons of Rhode Island. This role dovetailed beautifully with one of the dominant motifs of his life history: his search for power and position. In pursuing personal power few men were more dedicated, and no one had a more sensitive feeling for drawing it from other men's self-interest. As soon as he entered the Senate, he employed the tariff as a primary means to achieve this end. From the mahogany-paneled rooms of the Finance Committee, he put his remarkable political talents and technical expertise to work allocating privileges and distributing rewards, always conscious that the favor-seeker was beholden to the favor-doer, and that the essence of influence and power consisted in having something valuable to give. To businessmen, especially those with Eastern banking and manufacturing credentials, he was always accessible, treating them with the utmost respect and as valued counselors rather than, as they often were, persistent special pleaders. "Somehow I find myself writing to you rather than to Senators from my own State," a Philadelphia chemical manufacturer once told him. "You must accept . . . as my excuse . . . your cordial and frank reception of me when in Washington."[18]

But besides providing businessmen with a sympathetic and engaging audience, Aldrich invariably impressed them with his ability to understand their problems and to act decisively in formulating legislative remedies. So successful was he in tailoring tariff schedules to fit the profiles of Eastern corporations that his correspondence bulged with warm, unsolicited testimonials from grateful clients. "We need no assurance that you will do all that lies in your power to further our interests in Washington," purred one industrialist in 1883. "They have never before been so well cared for."[19] Similarly, some years later, the secretary of the National Association of Wool Manufacturers gushed like a teenage groupie when he wrote Aldrich requesting his photograph. "I should like to frame it," he said, "and hang it in the office of the National Association where the wool manufacturers can look upon the features of the man who has done more service, in a more effective way, in their behalf, than any other man, living or dead."[20]

Probably no businessman had better cause to appreciate Aldrich's legislative "service" than did John E. Searles, Jr. In one way or another following the enactment of the Mongrel tariff, Aldrich continued to put his parliamentary talents at his disposal. One such occasion involved the hotly disputed Hawaiian Reciprocity Treaty. In 1884, the Arthur administration had renegotiated the agreement and submitted it to the Senate for approval. But Senate opponents, led by Aldrich and the Democratic senators from Louisiana, kept it bottled up in the Foreign Relations Committee while Searles, coordinating his actions with them, intensified the industry's campaign to defeat it. When the Cleveland administration entered office in 1885, Secretary of State Thomas F. Bayard exerted great pressure on the committee to bring the treaty to the floor. Again, nothing happened. Then suddenly, on April 14, 1886, without Bayard's knowledge and to the immense consternation of the Hawaiian minister to the United States, H. A. P. Carter, the committee reported the treaty to an executive session of the Senate with a provision calling for Hawaii to cede Pearl Harbor to the United States. And although Bayard, warning that the Hawaiian government would reject the treaty rather than relinquish any of its territory, joined Carter in strenuously objecting to the amendment, the Senate ignored their protests and on January 20, 1887, ratified the committee's action.[21]

Since the origins of the Pearl Harbor amendment have long been somewhat obscure, the standard interpretation simply assumes that Senate expansionists designed it with the specific objective of gaining a territorial foothold in the Pacific for the United States.[22] Recently discovered evidence, however, suggests that the amendment owed its existence to other, more mundane motives; namely, that it was an audacious scheme concocted by Searles and executed by Aldrich to sabotage the treaty and thereby destroy the competitive advantage it had afforded Claus Spreckels. Searles laid bare some of the considerations behind the amendment in a letter to Aldrich two days after the Senate's vote sustaining the treaty:

I tried to see you yesterday in order to tell you how well satisfied I am with the action of the Senate . . . concerning the Hawaiian Treaty. From information which I have from the Islands I am satisfied that the second article, interpolated by the Senate, is impossible: that the Kanakas will not allow His Majesty to make the concession even if he were so disposed, and that should they show any disposition to make such concession the existing treaty with England and other nations would stand in the way. Hence I think they must reject this proposition, and that the rejection will give us a majority in the Senate for abrogation of the existing treaty.[23]

But Searles's optimism was premature. Unaccountably, both he and his informants had neglected to reckon with the long-smoldering hostility of many American sugar planters in Hawaii toward the regime of King Kalakaua and his ministers, a hostility that flared into open rebellion with the king's threatened refusal to accept the amended treaty and culminated in the installation of a new government and the cession of Pearl Harbor to the United States.[24]

Although the campaign to terminate the reciprocity treaty was thus aborted, neither the American cane growers in Hawaii

nor Claus Spreckels were destined to remain the exclusive beneficiaries of free sugar for very much longer. In 1890 the Sugar
Trust, organized three years earlier under the aegis of Searles
and Henry O. Havemeyer, reached absolute competitive parity
with the Californian. Once more Aldrich provided his clients
with crucial legislative assistance. He was largely responsible
for the sugar bounty in the McKinley tariff which proved extremely beneficial to the trust by giving domestic sugar producers a subsidy of two cents per pound for their crop in order
to gain their support for the admission of raw Caribbean sugars
duty-free. And despite widespread criticism of his actions both
within and without the Senate, he saw to it that the bill also conferred a protective duty of one-half cent per pound on refined
sugar, even though free sugar reduced the trust's operating costs
dramatically. Partly as a result of these provisions, less than two
years after the enactment of the McKinley tariff Searles and
Henry O. Havemeyer entered into an agreement with Spreckels
giving them a virtual monopoly over the industry, a monopoly
that generated earnings estimated at from twelve to twenty
million dollars per annum during the 1890s.[25]

"Aldrich is looking out for the Sugar Trust's interests." So
wrote E. W. Halford, President Benjamin Harrison's personal
secretary, in his diary shortly after the enactment of the McKinley tariff.[26] So thought a lot of other people. The intense concern
Aldrich exhibited in the development of public policy toward
the sugar industry could not help but cause many to suspect
there was much more to his efforts than met the eye. Washington
gossips knew that Aldrich was "very good friends" with Searles
and Henry O. Havemeyer, and as the years passed and he
became noticeably wealthy, spending well beyond his $5,000
salary, buying art, yachts, hundred-room mansions and annual
European vacations, "the question was naturally asked, 'Where
did he get it?'" As his former secretary and Washington news-
paperman David S. Barry recalled, "Men would smile when they
spoke of Senator Aldrich's wealth, and raise their eyebrows,
but no one of them ever openly accused him of wrong-doing.
They were afraid to do so because, as they said, he was too
smooth for them to catch and while they claimed to know they
openly confessed their inability to prove anything."[27]

Barry's memory must have been failing him when he made this

statement to the senator's friendly biographer in the 1920s, for he had obviously forgotten that *The New York Times* had created a sensation by leveling allegations of corruption at Aldrich in the spring of 1894. The immediate occasion was Aldrich's leadership of the Republican effort in the Senate that year to defeat the Democratic-sponsored Wilson-Gorman tariff. Once again controversy erupted over the sugar schedule, but this time the Democrats were under fire for supposedly selling out to the trust. Vivid newspaper accounts claimed that Searles and Henry O. Havemeyer had colluded with certain Democratic members of the Senate Finance Committee to jack up the rates recommended in the House bill and had then speculated in the resulting rise in sugar stocks, an accusation that triggered an immediate Senate investigation as well as sharp Republican attacks on the sugar schedule's alleged corrupt paternity.[28] The strategy was to try to build up public revulsion by emphasizing the influence of the American Sugar Refining Company, thereby causing the bill to be amended downwards and the fragile Democratic coalition supporting it to collapse. In that event, the higher McKinley rates would remain in force. As Republican Senator Redfield Proctor of Vermont explained, "We are all hoping that the whole tariff legislation may fail. . . . If the one-eighth on sugar can be stricken off, it seems as though the bill will be defeated."[29]

Aldrich orchestrated the assault on the sugar schedule expertly. Invoking all his powers of analysis and obfuscation, he took to the floor repeatedly to charge that it gave far more protection to the trust than the McKinley tariff, not less, as the Democrats correctly contended.[30] He assailed its mixture of ad valorem and specific duties as a "contemptible juggle," deliberately written "at the dictation of the American Sugar Refining Company" to confuse and exploit the American consumer. It was, he said, a horrible spectacle to see "a great party . . . hopelessly and helplessly under the control of influence outside of this Chamber, . . . not known to the Constitution or the laws, not recognized as any part of the National Government, . . . cravenly submit" without a whimper to the demands of the trust.[31]

While Aldrich was thus hammering away at the integrity of the Democrats, *The New York Times* published its charges on June 20, 1894, in a lengthy story headlined on page one: "Senator

Aldrich and Sugar: The Republican Tariff Leader Owned by the Trust, Indebted to It for Financial Aid." Terming Aldrich a "disgusting hypocrite," it arraigned him for posing as a critic of the trust when he was actually on its payroll. According to *The New York Times*, in 1892 the Sugar Trust, in the person of John E. Searles, "grateful for the favors which it had received at his hands, . . . came to the rescue of Senator Nelson W. Aldrich with substantial aid at a time when he needed backing for the consummation of a great business enterprise." It gave him, said the article, $1,500,000 which he used in conjunction with several other investors to purchase all the extant stock in the Union Railway Company, a Providence traction line. "Mr. Aldrich conceived the idea that there was money in extending this railway company" but he did not have the cash to put his ideas into effect. So he "appealed to such capitalists as were his friends" and the Sugar Trust responded with the necessary funds as payment for what Aldrich did for it in the writing of the McKinley tariff. "It was a pleasing exhibition," *The New York Times* concluded, "of how a great corporation which was under no legal obligation might be counted on not to forget a friend who had helped it. . . . This, at any rate, is the kindest view of the situation."[32]

As a rule Aldrich never replied to public criticism. He believed strongly, he wrote a constituent, that "to try to create or correct current opinion in regard to any of my political opinions or actions . . . would be to unduly magnify their importance . . . without any compensating benefit."[33] The axiom "Explain nothing, deny nothing" was firmly embedded in his political creed, but he could not remain silent in the face of *The New York Times*'s accusations. They were the topic of widespread conversation, not only in political and business circles but also among many middle-class families and other people outside politics. When the newspapers appeared in Rhode Island, newsdealers were sold out within minutes and secondhand copies went for fifty cents apiece.[34] Aldrich was thus forced to confront his accusers for the first and only time in his career. On June 21, he issued a denial of "this article . . . so false and villainous in its insinuations. . . ." There was only one statement in the account that contained "even the semblance of truth," he said. Searles did indeed have "an interest in a street railway company in which

I also have an interest," but he paid for his interest as others paid for theirs; Searles was a partner in a business venture as others also were partners. "He did not," Aldrich asserted categorically, "nor did any other person, at any time, advance any money to or for me on this or any other account, and I am not and never have been under the slightest possible financial or other obligations, directly or indirectly, immediate or contingent, to him or to any other person who is or ever has been connected with the sugar refining company or the company itself."[35]

Aldrich's disclaimer sounded very convincing. *The New York Times* had offered no documentation to support its charges, relied heavily on innuendo and hearsay, and presented its case in a strident, prosecutorial tone. The *New York Tribune* probably spoke for many Republicans when, comparing Aldrich's cool, precise, lawyerlike refutation with *The New York Times* impassioned rhetoric, it maintained that he was being deliberately vilified in order to draw attention away from the corrupt dealings of the Democrats. "To misrepresent innocent men for the purpose of diverting public censure from the guilty," the *New York Tribune* editorialized, "is a performance not worthy of any respectable newspaper."[36]

It is true that *The New York Times* was then a partisan organ but, if its motives were questionable, most of its allegations were not. Those allegations, in fact, are backed up by a considerable body of evidence, including two remarkable legal documents signed by the parties involved. The first, an agreement in principle dated January 7, 1893, acknowledges Aldrich's receipt of $100,000 in cash from Searles for the purchase of stock in the Union Railroad Company and commits Searles "to furnish the money necessary to carry through . . . the purchases thereby contemplated, and such other purchase of other Street Railroad stocks and charters as may hereafter [be] mutually agreed upon by us. . . ."[37] The second, a contract signed on February 2, 1893, formalized the agreement in principle and established the terms and conditions which eventually enabled the senator to become a multimillionaire.[38]

Under its provisions, Searles and his associates, F. P. Olcutt of the Central Trust Company of New York, a firm closely allied with the American Sugar Refining Company, and Anthony M. Brady, a New York traction promotor, agreed to provide

Aldrich and his partners, Marsden J. Perry, president of the Narragansett Electric Company, and William G. Roelker, a Providence lawyer and state senator, with at least $5,500,000 and up to $7,000,000 in cash to be used to buy, and later to electrify, modernize and extend, four profitable but inefficient horse-drawn traction lines servicing the area in and around Providence. On the completion of the purchase of these lines—which cost less than $3,000,000—the syndicate formed a New Jersey holding company, the United Traction and Electric Company (UTE), with Aldrich as president and Searles as a director, and transferred ownership of the various companies to it. UTE then issued $8,000,000 in forty-year, five-percent first mortgage bonds as collateral to Searles and his partners as well as $8,000,000 in stock, half of it going to the Aldrich group and half to the Searles group. In the next few years the company electrified and expanded the system and, through Aldrich's control over the state's political machine, led nominally by "Boss" Brayton, also obtained extremely favorable tax and franchise legislation from the Rhode Island General Assembly. By 1896 UTE's $100 par-value shares sold for $40; by 1900 they had reached $110. In seven years, and without investing a penny of his own money, Aldrich had acquired properties worth many millions. He and his partners sold the properties in 1902, partly for cash (about $1,000,000 apiece), and partly for a large block of new stock, to the United Gas and Improvement Company, a holding company controlled by the Philadelphia traction magnates William L. Elkins and Peter A. B. Widener.[39] They in turn, in a deal Aldrich helped to set up and negotiate, sold out to the New York, New Haven and Hartford Railroad in 1906 for $21,000,000, a sum which even its president, Charles S. Mellen, conceded was "an unconscionable price," and one Aldrich's partner, Marsden J. Perry, proudly called "a very profitable figure."[40] Years later Mellen explained to a body investigating the railroad's management why he had overpaid for the Rhode Island traction lines. "I was dealing with Nelson W. Aldrich," he said plaintively. "Do you think I got the stock of these railroads at par?"[41]

How much money did Aldrich make from all these transactions? No accurate assessment is possible. His wealth at his death in 1915 was valued for tax purposes at $5,700,000 and a good esti-

mate would be that the great bulk of it flowed from the contract
he signed with Searles in 1893.[42]

Such then are some of the observable facts necessary to understand why muckrakers like Ida Tarbell dubbed Aldrich's mag-
nificent two-hundred-acre estate on Narragansett Bay "The House
that Sugar Built," and why *The Nation* described him upon his
retirement from the Senate as "the living embodiment of that
sordid and corrupt system which has left its ineffaceable brand
on the history of the Republican party for three decades."[43] Still
the question remains: why did Aldrich's relationship with the
Sugar Trust turn into a corrupt one? Certainly, no material incentives were needed to secure his loyalty to the sugar refiners
in the 1880s, nor is there any evidence that he ever required or
demanded, either tacitly or explicitly, a specified compensation
from them or any other businessmen before agreeing to undertake or forgo a particular legislative action in their behalf. Indeed,
on those rare occasions when the Senate debated what the ethical
standards of its members should be when faced with possible
conflicts of interest, Aldrich staked out an impressively high
moral position. For example, he agreed when Senator Thomas F.
Bayard assailed "the proposition that a man has a right to
stand in either Hall of Congress and advocate his personal
interests" so long as they comported with the interests of his
constituents. He asserted that "whenever a question arises in
this body in which I have a personal interest, either directly or
indirectly, I trust I may be found as sensitive as the Senator from
Delaware in attempting to influence the action of the Senate
either by my voice or my vote."[44] And although his ethical code
never proved to be as sensitive in practice as it was in theory,
at no time did he ever publicly repudiate the principles embodied
in this statement or seek to justify a less lofty conception of
political morality. Why therefore did Searles find it necessary to
take care of Aldrich financially? What prompted Aldrich to
accept what was essentially a political payoff?

The main reason, apparently, was a very practical one on the
part of both parties: each needed what the other possessed. By
1890 Aldrich had "long since determined to retire" from the Senate on the completion of his term in 1892.[45] Much of the joy seems
to have gone out of public life for him. Reelection in Rhode
Island, virtually a certainty for any Republican after the Civil

War, had become chancier as immigrants swelled the ranks of
the Democrats and growing factionalism weakened the G.O.P.
Although the psychic rewards of having reached a position of
power and prestige in the Senate were considerable, he found
the material strains of trying to run two households, in Providence and Washington, and support a family of eight school-age
children becoming increasingly burdensome. Other than his
Senate salary, his income in 1890, so he confided to Marsden J.
Perry, amounted to $3,600 from his partnership in the grocery
business. This was not adequate, he said, to meet his needs.[46] As
a young man he had experienced poverty, leading him once to
exclaim in anguish what he wanted most from life: "Willingly
or forcibly wrested from a selfish world, *Success!* Counted as
the mass counts it by dollars and cents!"[47] He had a certain
amount of money but he wanted more. Obviously, he no longer
intended to sacrifice his business affairs on the altar of his
political ambitions. Thus when Perry broached his plan of con-
solidating Providence's street railways to him and offered to
take him in as a partner, Perry recalled years later, Aldrich
jumped at the opportunity.[48] What Perry neglected to say in
recounting this incident is that neither he, nor William G.
Roelker, nor the senator had the capital required to carry it off
successfully. Searles did. The evidence indicates that he decided
to back the scheme as a courtesy to Aldrich, partly because it
was potentially a money-making proposition but mainly because
this was a way of ensuring his friend's continued service in the
Senate. Aldrich's retirement would have dealt the Sugar Trust
a severe blow. The power he wielded over tariff policy was already immense and was bound to increase as he accumulated
seniority and, eventually, the chairmanship of the Finance Committee and the informal leadership of the Senate Republican
power structure. In countless ways in the past Aldrich had promoted the well-being of the trust and there was every reason
to expect that he would continue to do so in the future.

As it was, reelected in 1892 with the monetary assistance of
the Trust, Aldrich would demonstrate his special solicitude repeatedly throughout the 1890s, particularly in the framing of
the sugar schedule to the Dingley tariff of 1897. Once more
conflict over sugar duties brought the Senate to a virtual stand-
still and once more Aldrich placed his unrivaled expertise and

influence at the disposal of the corporation he was now financially indebted to.[49] The result, after weeks of jockeying and
debate, was a sugar schedule highly favorable to the American
Sugar Refining Company but also one which deepened the already pervasive "feeling on the part of the people," one com-
mentator noted, "that the Sugar Trust controls the Senate. . . ."
To former Minnesota Senator William D. Washburn, the ability
of the American Sugar Refining Company to get its way in the
Upper House looked all too familiar. "As in 1890," he wrote
Senator William Boyd Allison, "I fear you have too many speculators in sugar in the Senate . . . or rather the friends of the
sugar monstrosity."[50]

In sum, Searles had made an investment in Aldrich for the
benefit of his company; Aldrich in turn had capitalized his power
for the benefit of himself and his family. The form their relationship took in the 1890s was in many respects a logical consequence
of Aldrich's business-oriented approach to legislation and the
growth of his leverage and influence over economic policy-
making. Actuated as he was by a political vision that identified
the national interest with the values, goals and needs of business, and increasingly capable of putting it into a legislative
framework desired by a variety of corporate interests, Aldrich
found money and favors flowing to him naturally. Businessmen
did not bribe him, they did not dominate him—they simply rewarded and supported him. Only influential "business-minded"
senators like Aldrich, for example, could expect to receive investment opportunities exemplified by the following proffered
him by Henry P. Davison, a partner in J. P. Morgan & Company:

The enclosed refers to the stock of the Bankers Trust Company, of which
you have been allotted one hundred shares. You will be called upon for
payment of $40,000. . . . It will be a pleasure for me to arrange this for
you if you would like to have me do so.
I am particularly pleased to have you have this stock, as I believe it
will give a good account of itself. It is selling today on the basis of a little
more than $500 a share. I hope, however, you will see fit to put it away,
as it should improve with seasoning. Do not bother to read through
the enclosed, unless you desire to do so. Just sign your name and
return to me.[51]

On top of this letter there is a simple notation which reads:
"Signed and returned, Aug. '09." Perhaps these few words cap-

ture better than anything else the ethical perspective of a whole generation of politicians.

In the final analysis the alliance between Aldrich and the Sugar Trust became a mutually beneficial and corrupt one because it originally began as an alliance of the mind and heart. It was this aspect of Aldrich's behavior that no less a critic of his than Lincoln Steffens felt overshadowed everything else. "What I really object to in him," Steffens wrote Theodore Roosevelt, "is something he probably does honestly, out of general conviction. . . . He represents Wall Street; corrupt and corrupting business; men and Trusts that are forever seeking help, subsidies, privileges from government."[52] Whether political corruption always thrives best, as Steffens seemed to think, in an atmosphere where the leading power brokers and businessmen agree on fundamentals is, of course, debatable. But a conclusion that must be drawn from this examination of Aldrich's relationship with the sugar industry is that legislative organization and bureaucratization tended to increase the scale of corruption and to channel it in certain directions rather than inhibit it. The environment responsible for making Aldrich rich was not distinguished by the suffusion of parliamentary power but its concentration and structuring. The development of strong parties may, at times, weaken pressure groups and political consolidation often does act as an enemy of graft. But in the Gilded Age Senate, at least, just the opposite proved to be true.

NOTES

1. Henry L. Dawes to Electa Dawes, May 2, 1881, box 14, Henry L. Dawes Papers, Library of Congress (hereafter LC).

2. Beatrice Webb, *Beatrice Webb's American Diary, 1898*, ed., David A. Shannon (Madison, Wis., 1963), p. 151.

3. *Chicago Tribune*, January 10, 1884.

4. Webb, *op. cit.*, p. 150.

5. Charles A. Beard and Mary R. Beard, *The Rise of American Civilization* (1-vol. ed.; New York, 1930), pp. 285–343; Matthew Josephson, *The Politicos: 1865–1896* (New York, 1938); Richard Hofstadter, *The American Political Tradition and the Men Who Made It* (New York, 1948), pp. 164–79; Ray Ginger, *Age of Excess: The United States from 1877 to 1914* (New York, 1965), p. 100.

6. These views are best represented in the following works: David J. Rothman, *Politics and Power: The United States Senate, 1869–1901* (Cambridge, Mass., 1966); John A. Garraty, *The New Commonwealth,*

1877–1890 (New York, 1968), pp. 220–58; Leland L. Sage, *William Boyd Allison: A Study in Practical Politics* (Iowa City, 1956); John R. Lambert, *Arthur Pue Gorman* (Baton Rouge, La., 1953); Richard E. Welch, Jr., *George Frisbie Hoar and the Half-Breed Republicans* (Cambridge, Mass., 1971); Lewis L. Gould, "The Republican Search for a National Majority" in H. Wayne Morgan, ed., *The Gilded Age* (rev. ed.; Syracuse, N. Y., 1970), pp. 171–87; Lewis L. Gould, "New Perspectives on the Republican Party, 1877–1913," *American Historical Review*, LXXVII (1972), 1074–82; Morton Keller, "The Politicos Reconsidered" in Donald Fleming and Bernard Bailyn, eds., *Perspectives in American History*, (Cambridge, Mass., 1967), I, 401–408.

7. Rothman, *op. cit.*, pp. 4–5, 73–108, *passim*; Randall B. Ripley, *Power in the Senate* (New York, 1969), pp. 21–50; *idem, Party Leaders in the House of Representatives* (Washington, 1967), pp. 12–53; George B. Galloway, *History of the House of Representatives* (New York, 1969), pp. 131–36.

8. Lee Benson, *Merchants, Farmers, and Railroads* (Cambridge, Mass., 1955); Irwin Unger, *The Greenback Era: A Social and Political History of American Finance, 1865–1879* (Princeton, N. J., 1964); Robert P. Sharkey, *Money, Class, and Party* (Baltimore, 1959); Stanley Coban, "Northeastern Business and Radical Reconstruction: A Re-Examination," *Mississippi Valley Historical Review*, XLVI (1959), 69–90.

9. Rothman, *op. cit.*, pp. 191–220.

10. *Ibid.*, 219.

11. Samuel P. Huntington, "Modernization and Corruption," *Political Order in Changing Societies* (New Haven, Conn., 1968), pp. 59–71.

12. Rothman, *op. cit.*, p. 6.

13. *Cong. Record*, 47 Cong., 2 Ses., 2553 (Feb. 13, 1883).

14. Alfred S. Eichner, *The Emergence of Oligopoly: Sugar Refining as a Case Study* (Baltimore, 1969), pp. 42–50, 87–89; David M. Pletcher, *The Awkward Years: American Foreign Relations Under Garfield and Arthur* (Columbia, Mo., 1961), pp. 146–47; Jacob Adler, *Claus Spreckels: The Sugar King of Hawaii* (Honolulu, 1966), pp. 10–15; Ralph S. Kuykendall, *The Hawaiian Kingdom: The Kalakaua Dynasty, 1874–1893* (3 vols.; Honolulu, 1967), III, 374–75; National Board of Trade, *Proceedings of the Thirteenth Annual Meeting of the Board of Trade . . . January 1883* (Boston, 1883), p. 136. The speaker was John E. Searles, Jr.

15. Edwin F. Atkins to Nelson W. Aldrich, Dec. 27, 1882, Nelson W. Aldrich Papers, LC; Atkins to Messrs. L. W. & P. Armstrong, Dec. 27, 1882, Atkins Family Papers, Massachusetts Historical Society, Boston (hereafter MHS).

16. *Cong. Record*, 47 Cong., 2 Ses., 1794–1802 (Jan. 30, 1883); 1843–1845, 1849 (Jan. 31, 1883); Aldrich to Thomas F. Bayard, March 14, 1886, Thomas F. Bayard Papers, LC; James A. Garfield, diary, Jan. 27, 1880, James A. Garfield Papers, LC; Eichner, *op. cit.*, pp. 60–62; John E. Searles Jr. to Aldrich, Feb. 7, Jan. 27, 1883, Aldrich Papers.

17. *Cong. Record*, 47 Cong. 2 Ses., 2551–55 (Feb. 13, 1883); 3579 (March 2, 1883).

18. Thomas S. Harrison to Aldrich, Feb. 20, 1883, Aldrich Papers.

19. E. P. Taft to Aldrich, Feb. 14, 1883, Aldrich Papers.

20. S. N. D. North to Aldrich, Sept. 18, 1897, Aldrich Papers.

21. Merz Tate, *Hawaii: Reciprocity or Annexation?* (East Lansing, Mich., 1968), pp. 139–77; Donald M. Dozer, "The Opposition to Hawaiian Reciprocity, 1876–1888," *Pacific Historical Review*, XIV (1945), 157–83; John E. Searles Jr. to Aldrich, Jan. 25, 1884, Aldrich Papers; Aldrich to Thomas F. Bayard, March 18, 1886, Vol. LXXXVI, Thomas F. Bayard Papers, LC; Edwin F. Atkins to Searles, Dec. 16, 22, 1886, Atkins Family Papers; Charles C. Tansill, *The Foreign Policy of Thomas F. Bayard, 1885–1887* (New York, 1940), pp. 372–81.

22. Tate, *op. cit.*, pp. 185–86, 190–91, 206.

23. John E. Searles Jr. to Aldrich, Jan. 22, 1887, Aldrich Papers.

24. Tate, *op. cit.*, pp. 197–205; Kuykendall, *op. cit.*, III, 391–97.

25. Eichner, *op. cit.*, pp. 70–84, 91–92, 152–73, 211–13. For Aldrich's role in framing the McKinley tariff, see Jerome L. Sternstein, *Nelson W. Aldrich: The "General Manager of the United States"* (forthcoming).

26. E. W. Halford, diary, Dec. 1, 1891, E. W. Halford Papers, notes of J. P. Nichols, Aldrich Papers.

27. Interview with General Edwards, "Aldrich and Havemeyer," Oct. 16, 18, 1926, notes of J. P. Nichols, Aldrich Papers; David S. Barry, "General Outline of Senator Aldrich's Career Prepared by Mr. Barry," n.d., Aldrich Papers.

28. Allan Nevins, *Grover Cleveland: A Study in Courage* (New York, 1933), pp. 577–78; Lambert, *op. cit.*, pp. 224–26.

29. *Philadelphia Public Ledger*, May 15, 17, 1894; Henry Cabot Lodge to [Charles A.?] Dana, May 21, 1894, Henry Cabot Lodge Papers, MHS; Redfield Proctor to Justin Smith Morrill, July 23, 1894, Justin Smith Morrill Papers, LC.

30. *Cong. Record*, 53 Cong., 2 Ses., 5641–44, 5659–60 (June 2, 1894), 5726–27 (June 4, 1894), 5755–58 (June 5, 1894). Compare Aldrich's assessment of the Wilson-Gorman sugar schedule with that of Edwin F. Atkins, the Boston sugar refiner: "The new tariff will . . . work harm in every way to the sugar interest. The protection on refined sugar is reduced . . . which will admit refined sugar from Europe. . . ." Atkins to Don Esteban Caciedo, Sept. 4, 1894, Atkins Family Papers.

31. *Cong. Record*, 53 Cong., 2 Ses., 5643 (June 2, 1894); 5758, 5775 (June 5, 1894).

32. *The New York Times*, June 20, 21, 1894.

33. Aldrich to Henry Metcalf, May 29, 1889, Aldrich Papers.

34. *The New York Times*, June 21, 1894; *Providence Journal*, June 24, 1894.

35. *The New York Times*, June 21, 1894.

36. *New York Tribune*, June 21, 1894.

37. Statement of Nelson W. Aldrich to John E. Searles Jr., Marsden J. Perry and William G. Roelker, Jan. 7, 1893, Aldrich Papers.

38. Contract, "IN CONSIDERATION of the mutual promises hereinafter contained, it is AGREED By and Between . . ." Feb. 2, 1893, Aldrich Papers.

39. *Ibid.*; Robert E. Falb, "Marsden J. Perry: 'The Man Who Owned Rhode Island'," (Honors Thesis, Brown Univ., 1964), pp. 16–31; Charles R. Brayton to Aldrich, April 5, 1902, Aldrich Papers; *Providence Journal*, April 18, 1895, March 8, 1902, Nov. 25, 1906.

40. Charles S. Mellen to Howard Stockton, Oct 10, 1907, Charles S. Mellen Papers, New Hampshire Historical Society, Concord, N.H.; Interview with Marsden J. Perry, n.d., notes of J.P. Nichols, *loc. cit.*

41. *New York American,* April 17, 1915.

42. For the value of Aldrich's estate at probate, see clipping, n.d., n.p., in *Scrapbook,* S. S. Rider Collection, Rhode Island Historical Society, Providence, R.I. Most likely the estate was worth three or four times its probated value.

43. Ida M. Tarbell, *The Tariff in Our Times* (New York, 1911), p. 243; *The Nation,* XC (April 21, 1910), 393.

44. *Cong. Record,* 47 Cong. 2 Ses., 2028–29 (Feb. 3, 1883).

45. Aldrich to Edward Atkinson, Jan. 6, 1890, Edward Atkinson Papers, MHS.

46. Interview with Marsden J. Perry, Aldrich Papers. See also Interview with Judge Matteson, "Senatorship in 1892," n.d., notes of J. P. Nichols, *loc. cit.*

47. Aldrich to Abby Greene, Aug.[?], 1866, Aldrich Papers.

48. Interview with Marsden J. Perry, *loc. cit.*

49. *Providence Journal,* May 5, 6, 13, June 9, 10, 1897; *New York Tribune,* May 26, 30, June 9, 1897; John Coit Spooner to H. A. Taylor, June 15, 1897, Spooner to S. M. Booth, June 22, 1897, box 124, John Coit Spooner Papers, LC. See also Frank W. Taussig, *The Tariff History of the United States* (8th ed.; New York, 1931), pp. 350–51.

50. Thomas K. Cree to William Boyd Allison, July 17, 1897; William D. Washburn to Allison, June 18, 1897, William Boyd Allison Papers, Iowa State Department of History and Archives, Des Moines, Iowa.

51. Henry P. Davison to Aldrich, Aug. 6, 1909, Aldrich Papers. For other business deals which came the senator's way, see Jerome L. Sternstein, "King Leopold II, Senator Nelson W. Aldrich, and the Strange Beginnings of American Economic Penetration of the Congo," *African Historical Studies,* II (1969), 189–204.

52. Lincoln Steffens to Theodore Roosevelt, June 9, 1908, Theodore Roosevelt Papers, LC.

Robert Muccigrosso

CORRUPTION AND THE ALIENATION
OF THE INTELLECTUALS

That corruption cut deeply into the body of post-Civil-War American life could surprise only the most untutored. The sad spectacle of Grantism, the unseemly rush and jostle to gobble at the "Great Barbecue," the raping of the land, resources, and small entrepreneurships by all too skilled robber barons and captains of industry are the given to any primary understanding of the age. Apart from its more blatant political and economic manifestations, moreover, corruption assumed another form, one which if less striking than the aforementioned nevertheless carried enough force to affect the nation's contours in subtle but important ways. Beyond simple disgust and the impulse to reform generated in the mugwumps, corruption sowed the seeds of alienation for a generation of writers and artists to reap.

To portray the last quarter or so of the nineteenth century as intellectually and culturally feckless would seriously distort reality. Van Wyck Brooks caught the colors of a bright if rapidly fading Indian summer among the New England literati and spoke of "confident years"; Lewis Mumford has argued impressively for the artistic and architectural *succès d'estime* that moved the nation far along the path of modernism.[1] But to permit these achievements, solid though they were, to obscure the genuine deracination that was the fate of a number of intellectuals would constitute a misrepresentation of commensurate magnitude.

One of the first and certainly most perceptive critics to discern a disturbing milieu for the artist in postbellum America was Walt Whitman. Though the war for union had been won and the scars of internecine strife had begun slowly to heal, he warned in *Democratic Vistas*:

I say we had best look our times and lands searchingly in the face, like a physician diagnosing some deep disease. Never was there, perhaps, more hollowness at heart than at present, and here in the United States. Genuine belief seems to have left us. . . . I say that our New World democracy, however a great success in uplifting the masses out of their sloughs, in materialistic development, products, and in a certain highly-deceptive superficial popular intellectuality, is, so far, an almost complete failure in its social aspects, and in really grand religious, moral, literary, and esthetic results.[2]

The element perhaps most responsible for this condition, according to the poet, was the materialism of national life:

I say of all this tremendous and dominant play of solely materialistic bearings upon current life in the United States, with the results as already seen, accumulating, and reaching far into the future, that they must either be confronted and met by at least an equally subtle and tremendous force-infusion for purposes of spiritualization, for the pure conscience, for genuine esthetics, and for absolute and primal manliness and womanliness—or else our modern civilization, with all its improvements, is in vain, and we are on the road to a destiny, a status, equivalent, in its real world, to that of the fabled damned.[3]

More than any single act of business piracy or political corruption, it was this sense of pervasive, corrosive materialism that contributed most to the alienation of the man of culture and intellect. The whole was indeed greater than the sum of its parts. In this sense, corruption, true to its etymological origins, caused a breaking in pieces of the general hopes for a rejuvenated, healthy republic that were expressed after the war. Whitman, ever sanguine of democratic prospects, had responded to the problem in a positive manner, urging fellow artists to eschew a slavish imitation of Old World creations and to fashion instead indigenous art forms in the name of a vital national culture. His words rang strong—and equally unheeded. Purveyors of the Genteel Tradition continued overwhelmingly to follow (and usually lag far behind) artistic lines well demarcated by Europeans, though they, too, lamented with Whitman the nation's strident materialism. There were, however, other writers and artists—a minority—who revolted not only against this materialism but also against the Genteel Tradition as well. *Outré* in the eyes of the philistine businessman, scornful politician and defender of genteel culture alike, these figures experienced intense alienation. While more often than not continuing to take cues from their European confreres, the fact remains that, both in numbers and seriousness of enterprise, they attest to that late nineteenth century corruption which had debased the ideals and values of an Edenic republic. Three of the most significant manifestations of this intellectual and artistic protest were estheticism, exoticism and expatriation.

There is a time, perceived V. S. Pritchett, "when a culture reaches a sunset in which private relationships are given supreme importance and when there is leisure for wit and perspective and an intense sensibility to the arts for their own sake."[4] Though its devotees could not or would not perceive that it was already hedged by gathering shadows, genteel culture began to chip, if only slightly, under the blows dealt by the esthetic and decadent movements in *fin de siècle* America.

Crucial to the flowering of these movements was Oscar Wilde's celebrated visit to the United States in 1881. Sent to America as a publicist for Gilbert and Sullivan's *Patience*, Wilde immediately set the tone for his extended sojourn by announcing to the custom's officer that he had nothing to declare but his genius. Though Harvard students would mock him by donning wigs and ostentatiously carrying sunflowers, and Thomas Wentworth Higginson irascibly would propose that Boston society ostracize him socially for his "immoral" poems, countless others with serious and not so serious artistic pretensions and who lived both in large cities and the hinterlands would hail that genius.[5] Touting *Patience* soon became a secondary consideration for the visitor, who turned his considerable talents to publicizing art for art's sake, a movement of which the tone and tenets had been set in England largely by himself and James McNeill Whistler. Wilde, initially hopeful, wrote to Archibald Forbes: "I have something to say to the American people, something that I know will be the beginning of a great movement here, and all foolish ridicule does a great deal of harm to the cause of art and refinement and civilization."[6] Nearly a year later, having toured and lectured in thirty-six states, a chastened Wilde delivered his final salvo aboard the "Bothnia," which was to take him homeward: "They say that when good Americans die they go to Paris. I would add that when bad Americans die, they stay in America.... For you, Art has no marvel, Beauty no meaning, and the Past no message."[7]

It is not difficult to fathom why the gospel of art as preached by Wilde largely fell on deaf ears. The prevailing climate of harsh materialism in the United States had provided little nutriment for the growth of an estheticism which was both novel and dandified. Yet the pollen of the esthetic movement and, even more so, of its offshoot, decadence, proved too plentiful and powerful in its European setting not to drift across the Atlantic. The lure of Whistler and Wilde, Walter Pater, Algernon Swinburne and Aubrey Beardsley in England, of Joris Huysmans, Émile Zola, Henrik Ibsen, Arthur Schopenhauer, Friedrich Nietzsche, Gabriele d'Annunzio and the Symbolist poets on the Continent—in short, the avant-garde—provided siren songs too compelling for some American artists to ignore. If the latter ran the risk of being labeled "degenerate," as defined by Max Nordau,[8] it was a risk that usually elicited positive delight, coming, as it did, from a society they scorned.

Unlike its European counterpart, the decadent movement in the United States produced little of lasting artistic merit. Its poets and novelists, such as Bliss Carman, Richard Hovey, Percival Pollard, Walter Blackburn Harte, Vance Thompson, Edgar Saltus and James Huneker, never wrote what would be considered more than period pieces for limited audiences. Nor did the spate of avant-garde journals, commonly referred to as "little magazines," that erupted in the 1890s fare much better. Deriving from England's famous decadent magazine, *The Yellow Book* (edited, ironically enough, by the American expatriate Henry Harland), they sprang to life in major cities throughout the country beginning in 1894, glowed with bright incandescence and then burned out with remarkable speed. Part of the reason for their hasty demise can be attributed to the failure to uncover new talent, but mostly it seems to have resulted from their inability to attract a sufficient audience. When Gelett Burgess, poet of "The Purple Cow" quatrain fame and himself a founder of one of these magazines (*The Lark*), quipped

I am an Idiot, awful result
Of reading the rot of the *Yellow Book* cult[9]

many may have construed the playful jesting as a serious pro-
nouncement and ultimate verdict on the movement.

Much of the meaning of American decadence, like its
European cousin, was an attempt simply to shock and scandalize
conventional tastes and mores, to *épater les bourgeois*. This accounts in large measure for such lurid sensationalism as the
female character in Edgar Saltus's *A Transaction in Hearts* who
beheads both her husband and lover and then for years keeps the
decaying fruits of her violence. In contradistinction to the exciting
swirl of late nineteenth century events and ideas, decadence also
assumed a pose of contemptuous boredom. More than one writer
of the movement lamented, as had Stendhal and Charles Baude-
laire earlier in the century, that ennui had made modern life all
but insufferable. Thus Saltus could sense an urgent need "to
deliver us from boredom" and, along with others, create fictional
characters modeled on Des Esseintes, Huysmans's prototype
of the disaffected esthete.[10] Even young Ralph Adams Cram, a
decade away from fame as a Gothic architect, breathed the fumes
of decadence and fictionalized a young man with exquisite
tastes and ennui mixed in nearly equal proportion which resulted in a "despair which kills all effort."[11] Pessimism merged
with boredom and the bizarre for a number of the decadents.
Brooks might speak of the "confident years" and popular expression of the "gay nineties," but Saltus, more attuned to the
darker elements of the age, became a serious popularizer of
that brooding negativist, Schopenhauer, and predicted that pessimism would prove the "religion of the future."[12]

As devotion to art for art's sake, ennui, pessimism and a
desire to shock were forming the farrago of decadence, a few,
like Gelett Burgess, watched with amusement; more remained
indifferent or avowedly hostile. With the exposure of Oscar
Wilde's homosexuality in 1895 an increasing number came to
see the movement as less harmlessly naughty and more wickedly
perverse. Decadence, in sum, had become decadent.

But was it decadent? To turn one's back on a dominant culture holding fast to the exiguous structure of gentility and on
a society filled with industrial strife and agrarian discontent,

and heading for an appointment with imperialism, as America was during the 1890s, scarcely seems a sign of degradation and decay. As one critic has noted of the larger *fin de siècle* revolt against Western society: "One might ask, in any case, whether it is not the civilization itself that has become decadent rather than those creative individuals within it who struggle to rediscover the wellsprings of human vitality."[13] The American decadents were only in a limited sense "creative individuals." Their most constructive literary value was to call attention to contemporary talent, particularly French. As Claire Sprague has observed of Saltus, who typified this small group of craftsmen: "He helped to make literary insularity impossible. The 1920's completed his job."[14] Meanwhile the movement served to underscore the growing malaise of the waning century, and if society at large deemed the decadents corrupt, the sentiment was fully reciprocated.

Another group of alienated figures, akin to and sometimes overlapping with the esthetes, were the exotics. These individuals who turned to a different religion, an earlier historical epoch or a foreign culture were too motley in their tastes to form a distinct movement. Only in their estrangement did they share common cause.

Homo oeconomicus might well conceive that Providence had guided the destiny of the United States, for it was clear that, despite signs of growing inequality, stress and dislocation, its inhabitants were, to use David Potter's phrase, a "people of plenty." Put another way, the GNP, that "tribal God of the Western world," as it has been called, continued to soar. Given the religious complexion of the population, that Providence assuredly must have been Protestant. It therefore comes as no great surprise that Roman Catholicism, the bane of their forebears and religion of the despised Irish and various contingents of the New Immigration, generated a strong attraction for not a few *désengagé* intellectuals. Moreover, had not Huysmans, high priest of Satanism for the esthetes and decadents, become an apostate to Catholicism? Whatever the prime motivation, young Van Wyck Brooks and his fellow students, all scions of staunch Protestants, conspicuously flaunted crucifixes and altars in their rooms at Harvard.[15]

The example of Brooks and his classmates might and perhaps

should largely be dismissed as a case of faddishness or generational rebellion or both. But what is to be made of the more complex figure, Henry Adams? The quintessential avatar of late nineteenth century alienation in America, Adams relentlessly pursued his education in search of salvation from the horrors of modernity and the shock of his wife's suicide. A self-confessed child of Quincy and the relative simplicity of eighteenth century life, he brooded upon the centrifugal disorders of the nineteenth century, unable to accept with equanimity the meaning of change. Visiting the Far East in 1891, Adams sat beneath Buddha's bo tree in Anuradhapura in a symbolic attempt to attain nirvana.[16] More seriously, he later turned toward Roman Catholicism, supplicating the Virgin to reverse the triumph of the Dynamo and restore the order and purpose of the High Middle Ages, when "all experience, human and divine, assured man . . . that the lines of the universe converged."[17] Adams never completed the journey to Rome. Perhaps the coils of modern science against which he writhed proved too ensnaring. Or perhaps the spectral tradition of familial Protestantism proved too strong. Still, at the time of his death a copy of his "Prayer to the Virgin of Chartres" was found in a wallet of special papers he kept.[18]

The call of a different religion beckoned other disaffected individuals, too. Some Boston Brahmins did follow the road to Rome to its completion. Others—probably more numerous—turned to Anglo-Catholicism in an effort to buttress their culture and position against inroads made by their Irish neighbors.[19] Conversion to High Church Episcopalianism also befell non-Brahmins like Ralph Adams Cram, who was born to a free-thinking mother and to a father who was a Unitarian minister. Any mention of Cram leads to an association with Gothic architecture, which in turn is intimately linked with yet another manifestation of alienation from the dominant culture of the period: the resuscitation of medievalism.

Medievalism provided an unusually exotic transplant for a nation so markedly lacking in a feudal past. Yet it was able to command a certain number of the faithful because for some "it fitted in with the dominant pattern of the age" and "provided the most relevant answer that the past could offer to the problems of a new society."[20] The esthetic appeal of the medieval seemed undeniable. Since the early 1800s generations of young readers had thrilled to the "Waverley Novels" of Sir Walter Scott, while, at a more sophisticated level, Charles Eliot Norton had inspired educated laymen, as well as his late nineteenth century students at Harvard, with a love for Dante and the art of the Middle Ages.[21] Paralleling the European, especially the English experience, nineteenth century America had witnessed no fewer than three distinct revivals in Gothic architecture, culminating in the churches, colleges, businesses and occasional private homes designed by Cram and fellow enthusiasts. The fact that there was more than a hint of the derivative in these enterprises did little to deter their widespread acceptance.

For some intellectuals, however, the pull of the medieval went far beyond the literary or artistic. Responding both to the widening chasm that separated capital from labor and to the dehumanization of work wrought by the machine, several English reformers, following the path of Thomas Carlyle, turned to medievalism as a heuristic example. As John Ruskin, whose influence in the United States was pronounced, indicated: "The things that actually happened were of small consequence—the thoughts that were developed are of infinite consequence."[22] Those thoughts "of infinite consequence" included the concept of an organic society in which each member experienced the salutary effects of communal interdependence and the restoration of what Thorstein Veblen was to call the "instant of workmanship." Concerned, as was Karl Marx, with the worker's loss of craftsmanship and its attendant misery, William Morris became the age's chief polemist for and practitioner of a revivified medieval artisanship, arguing that "the pleasurable exercise of our energies is at once the source of all art and the cause of all happiness: that is to say, it is the end of life."[23]

The reformist preachings of the medievalists drew a mixed response from American audiences. Many applauded the esthetic doctrines but drew back from the far-reaching social and economic changes advocated.[24] Not all shied away, however. Social gospelers were impressed, as was Cram, who, refusing to restrict himself to the confines of his art, steadfastly championed the establishment of a Christian Commonwealth to replace the materialistic, secular society he found so odious.[25] Following Morris's lead, Cram, Elbert Hubbard and others strove to revive the art of craftsmanship in the United States, precisely at the time when technology was enthroning itself as an arbiter of national destiny. Despite the seeming hopelessness of its cause, an arts and crafts movement did thrive in thin soil for a brief period, to the extent that even a Ruskin Co-operative Association, both socialist and utopian in its dimensions, could survive for five years in Tennessee. For all the failure of his vision to achieve reality, perhaps Ruskin was right: to judge by twentieth century lamentations against automation, the facts of medievalism were less important than the ideas bequeathed.

Differing forms of Christianity and medievalism had given expression to the alienation of various individuals and groups. So, too, would the still more exotic attraction of the Orient. Just as eighteenth century Westerners had become enamored of chinoiserie, their later nineteenth century descendants were to turn to *japonisme* with dazzling results. One need only consider the influence of Japanese art forms on the French Impressionists and Art Nouveau, architecture, gardening, interior decoration and exquisite bric-a-brac. Yet only have historical perspective and the modern preference for cultural pluralism accorded the Japanese influence deep-rooted acceptance. Many in the *fin de siècle* West heartily agreed with Gilbert and Sullivan's self-scoffing Bunthorne when he confessed: "I do *not* long for all one sees / That's Japanese." For them, *japonisme* was the quaint preserve of the avant-garde and those torn from traditional moorings.

The Centennial Exposition held in Philadelphia in 1876 was responsible both for initially introducing appreciable numbers of Americans to Japanese art and for effecting the craze for that art which quickly ensued. However, it fell to a handful of scholars, mostly New Englanders, to explore the culture more fully and critically and to insure that it progressed beyond the state of a vogue. The naturalist Edward S. Morse visited Japan for the purpose of scientific research in 1877 and while there accepted a position to teach zoology at the Imperial University in Tokyo. Four years later he delivered the Lowell Lectures at Harvard, drawing the attention of many, including Henry Adams, John La Farge, Isabella Stewart Gardner and William Sturgis Bigelow, to the rich culture he had surveyed.[26] Shortly thereafter, Morse, Bigelow and Ernest Fenollosa were in Japan, where, according to Clay Lancaster, they "were not only instrumental in opening American eyes to the beauties of Japanese art; they also helped establish a renewed appreciation among the Japanese."[27] The relationship between the visitors and the visited was indeed to be symbiotic. One Japanese scholar, for example, believed it was Fenollosa, the adept connoisseur, who "taught us how to admire the unique beauty of our art"; Morse, it is claimed, was of extreme importance in encouraging the study of science among Japanese students.[28] On the other hand, these men sent back to Boston a rich collection of Japanese art which Morse hoped would be the "greatest" in the world.[29] It was Fenollosa, moreover, who brought the Noh plays to the attention of the West. Even as this small group performed its labors of two-way cultural transmission, others were also contributing to the understanding of Japan, notably Percival Lowell, brother of Amy Lowell and Brahmin astronomer, who published *The Soul of the Far East*, the most rigorous and successful attempt at that time to explain Japanese ideas, values and institutions to Americans.[30]

But there was also a darker or at least less fruitful side to this encounter. The more congenial Japanese culture became, the more painful for some seemed the flaws and maladies of the Occident. Before Commodore Matthew Perry had forcibly ended its isolation in the mid nineteenth century, Japan, argued Cram, "was still artistically intact," with a civilization that "might still serve as the cherished flame for the rekindling of the dead fires of the West." Having hastened to adopt foreign cultural influences, it stood at the edge of moral and artistic bankruptcy by the century's turn.[31] Traveling to Japan with his good friend Henry Adams in 1886, John La Farge, an appreciator of Japanese art a full decade before the Centennial, wrote: "If there is anything good here, it must resemble some of the good that we have with us. But here at least I am freer, delivered from a world of canting phrases, of perverted thought, which I am obliged to breathe in at home so as to be stained by them."[32] But the East ultimately could not bind either of the travelers. "If only we had found Nirvana," wrote La Farge in dedicating a book to Adams, "but he was right who warned us that we were late in this season of the world."[33]

For other travelers disillusioned with the West, Japan provided a more compelling experience. In the 1880s both Fenollosa and Bigelow converted to Buddhism. They were to die in Japan and be buried close to each other along the shores of Lake Biwa. A similar fate awaited their contemporary, Lafcadio Hearn, one of the foremost Western experts on Japanese literature, culture and traditions. Alienated from family, friends and society from early childhood, Hearn wandered rootlessly from a lonely Ionian island to the United Kingdom, to the United States, to the West Indies, back to the United States and finally in the 1890s to Japan, where, after marrying and begetting children, he became a citizen, taught at various schools and devoted himself to his writing. A figure much too complex to hold consistent views, Hearn wavered in his allegiance to the two worlds, torn between the magnetism of Buddhism on one side and that of Herbert Spencer on the other. Despising the crass materialism of the familiar Occident, he also lashed out against the bureaucratic officiousness and growing militarism of his adopted country. Though he had at last established roots, he could still cry out: "Another day, and I was in touch with England again. How small my little Japan became!—how lonesome! What a joy to feel the West! What a great thing is the West!"[34] Yet ultimately Hearn rejected the West on moral grounds. Foreseeing repeated instances of the Boxer rebellion, he concluded that "Western civilization will have to pay, sooner or later, the full penalty of its deeds of oppression."[35] Unable, as it were, to go home again, he voiced the hope that his expected first child would "never have to face life in the West."[36]

As expatriates, Hearn, Fenollosa and Bigelow exemplify perhaps the most extreme form taken by alienation. Though not numerous, other artists also absented themselves permanently or for extended periods of time from the United States. James Whistler and John Singer Sargent found the country too inhospitable for their work, as eventually did Edith Wharton, for whom wealth and social prominence could neither stave off the ill effects of a disastrous marriage nor provide a sufficiently rich and variegated culture to sustain artistic creation. Then, too, there was the example of the period's most famous expatriate, Henry James.

Like Nathaniel Hawthorne whom he much admired, James found America severely lacking in the shadows and mystery that Europe offered artists and so in the early 1880s he went into self-imposed exile. Never having lost interest in his homeland, however, he wrote a French friend in 1903: "Europe has ceased to be romantic to me, and my country, in the evening of my days, has become so."[37] The following year the "passionate pilgrim" returned to examine first-hand, as one critic put it, "the internal implications of American prosperity."[38] For James, the America of his younger years had changed—but not improved. Fascinated as he was by the energy and vitality of the nation, he could not accept its many defects: the corroding materialism, the grating accents of its people, the informality of its manners and ways, the presence of immigrant hordes who had swarmed from southern and eastern Europe. Van Wyck Brooks was probably correct in observing that the fastidious fictionist was "destined to make certain exactions of America which America could not fulfil."[39] In any case, when James left the country after a visit of nearly a year, he found his English home and garden "better and sweeter than they ever were."[40]

In a sense, all were homeless—esthetes, exotics and expatriates alike. Some, like Hearn and Bigelow, led lives that were tortured from childhood and so may have been doomed inescapably to alienation, irrespective of cultural environment. None remained unscathed by that general corruption of the late nineteenth century which had undermined the values of a simpler age and was rapidly transforming the nation into an imperial republic. Whitman had been right to fear the effects that the smothering embrace of materialism would produce. Yet these alienated figures rejected Whitman's plea to form a viable national culture, opting instead for escape in one form or another. Americans speak today of the "lost generation" of the 1920s, but rarely of the previous generation, which in its own terms may have been fully as lost. Ironically, by saying "no" to a changing America and by emphasizing the richness of foreign cultures, the latter helped make possible the achievements of the former. Relatively few in number though they were, the alienated of the late nineteenth century had correctly foreseen the end of the nation's innocence.

NOTES

1. Van Wyck Brooks, *New England Indian Summer* (New York, 1940) and *The Confident Years, 1885–1915* (New York, 1952); Lewis Mumford, *Sticks and Stones: A Study of American Architecture & Civilization* (New York, 1924) and *The Brown Decades: A Study of the Arts in America, 1865–1895* (New York, 1931).

2. Walt Whitman, *Specimen Days, Democratic Vistas, and Other Prose,* ed. Louise Pound (Garden City, N.Y., 1935), pp. 269–71.

3. *Ibid.,* p. 328.

4. V. S. Pritchett, review of Murasaki Shikibu's *The Tale of Genji,* trans. Edward G. Seidensticker, in *The New York Review of Books,* XXIV (February 3, 1977), 3.

5. Philippe Jullian, *Oscar Wilde* (New York, 1969), p. 99; Rupert Hart-Davis, ed., *The Letters of Oscar Wilde* (London, 1962), p. 98, n. 3.

6. Wilde to Forbes, January 20, 1882, Hart-Davis, *op. cit.,* p. 88. Though Wilde did smirk in a letter to Whistler a few weeks later that Americans took his views too seriously, this was probably the affectation of one poseur to another. February[?], 1882, *ibid.,* p. 96.

7. Jullian, *op. cit.,* pp. 104–105.

8. Appearing in English translation in 1895, Max Nordau's *Degeneration* suggested that a number of contemporary artists, as apostles of rampant individualism, mysticism and instinctualism, possessed a psychological makeup similar to that of criminals, lunatics and other undesirables. His book enjoyed a fairly extensive popularity.

9. Larzer Ziff, *The American 1890s: Life and Times of a Lost Generation* (New York, 1966), p. 140.

10. Claire Sprague, *Edgar Saltus* (New York, 1968), p. 39. Oswald Quain, "hero" of *Enthralled* (1894), seems to have been modeled, at least in part, on Des Esseintes.

11. Ralph Adams Cram, *The Decadent* (n.p., 1893), p. 36.

12. Sprague, *op. cit.,* pp. 32–36, 40.

13. William Barrett, *Irrational Man: A Study in Existential Philosophy* (Garden City, N. Y., 1962), p. 132.

14. Sprague, *op. cit.,* p. 121.

15. Claire Spague, ed., *Van Wyck Brooks: The Early Years* (New York, 1968), p. x. Malcolm Cowley saw the same lure of Catholicism for his classmates at Harvard at the time of World War One. Malcolm Cowley, *Exile's Return: A Literary Odyssey of the 1920s* (New York, 1963), p. 35.

16. Henry Adams, *Letters to a Niece* (Boston, 1920), p. 62.

17. Henry Adams, *Mont-Saint-Michel and Chartres* (Boston, 1936), p. 375.

18. Adams, *Letters,* pp. 26–27.

19. Barbara Solomon, *Ancestors and Immigrants: A Changing New England Tradition* (Cambridge, Mass., 1956), p. 49; Arthur Mann, *Yankee Reformers in the Urban Age: Social Reform in Boston, 1880–1900* (Cambridge, Mass., 1954), p. 7.

20. Alice Chandler, *A Dream of Order: The Medieval Ideal in Nineteenth-Century English Literature* (Lincoln, Neb., 1970), p. 11.

21. See Kermit Vanderbilt, *Charles Eliot Norton: Apostle of Culture in a Democracy* (Cambridge, Mass., 1959).

22. Chandler, *op. cit.*, p. 206.

23. William Morris, "The Socialist Ideal," in *idem, On Art and Socialism: Essays and Lectures,* (London, 1947), p. 321.

24. Roger B. Stein, *John Ruskin and Aesthetic Thought in America, 1840–1900* (Cambridge, Mass., 1967), pp. 257–58.

25. Robert Muccigrosso, "Ralph Adams Cram: The Architect as Communitarian," *Prospects: An Annual Journal of American Cultural Studies,* I (1975), 165–78. Ruskin's social ideas also influenced such progressives as Charles Beard, Herbert Croly, Vernon Louis Parrington and Vida Scudder. Stein, *op. cit.*, pp. 259–60.

26. Van Wyck Brooks, *Fenollosa and His Circle: With Other Essays in Biography* (New York, 1962), pp. 26–27.

27. Clay Lancaster, *The Japanese Influence in America* (New York, 1963), p. 66.

28. Brooks, *Fenollosa*, pp. 9, 26.

29. *Ibid.*, p. 27.

30. Moving beyond his preferred Gothic, Ralph Adams Cram also sought to enlighten Americans on the subject of Japanese culture with his highly praised *Impressions of Japanese Architecture and the Allied Arts* (New York, 1905).

31. *Ibid.* (rev. ed.; Boston, 1930), p. 208.

32. John La Farge, *An Artist's Letters from Japan* (New York, 1897), p. 109.

33. *Ibid.*, p. vii.

34. Hearn to Basil Hall Chamberlain, July 15, 1894, Elizabeth Bisland, ed., *Life and Letters of Lafcadio Hearn,* IV (Boston, 1923), p. 217.

35. Lafcadio Hearn, *Japan: An Attempt at Interpretation* (New York, 1904), pp. 522, 524.

36. Hearn to Ellwood Hendrick, April[?], 1893, Bisland, *op. cit.*, II, pp. 222–23.

37. Carl Van Doren, "Henry James," in Dumas Malone, ed., *Dictionary of American Biography,* V (New York, 1961), p. 584.

38. F. W. Dupee, *Henry James* (New York, 1956), p. 296. For an account of his observations, see Henry James, *The American Scene* (New York, 1907).

39. Van Wyck Brooks, *The Pilgrimage of Henry James* (Folcroft, Pa., 1969), p. 41.

40. Leon Edel, *Henry James: The Master* (Philadelphia, 1972), p. 305.

James P. Johnson

CO-OPTION, CONFLICT OF INTEREST
OR COOPERATION: THE U.S. FUEL
ADMINISTRATION OF WORLD WAR I*

Students of relations between business and government in the United States have detailed how industrialists time and again have used government power for their own objectives. Repeatedly, business spokesmen have shaped legislation to suit their industry, or worked out ententes with government regulators, or co-opted agencies regulating their area of industrial activity.[1] But must regulatory agencies tolerate conflict of interest or be co-opted by business agents?

Government's need for business expertise and information during war, of course, increases the possibility of conflicts of interest for businessmen involved in government work.[2] Modern American governments have relied on businessmen during war. Woodrow Wilson's administration created over one hundred advisory committees staffed by businessmen. As America entered the Second World War, Franklin D. Roosevelt replaced New Deal reformers with industrialists. *Business Week* gloated that the amateurism of "braintrusters and theoreticians" was being exchanged for valuable "business talents."[3] Eventually, dollar-a-year businessmen comprised three-fourths of Roosevelt's War Production Board.[4]

Wilson's use of businessmen led to many instances where a particular industry wielded power and influence to "shape federal policy to meet its own desires."[5] Indeed, until the conflict-

* Thanks are due to my colleague Jerome L. Sternstein for his critical suggestions on an earlier draft.

of-interest amendment to the Lever Act was passed in 1917, businessmen helped make decisions about purchases from their own industries. Afterward, under the War Industries Board (WIB), the government paid high prices for steel, copper, hides, skins, aluminum and cotton goods, prices that had been negotiated in friendly, cooperative bargaining.[6] Even after the reorganization of the WIB under the Overman Act, according to one historian, "contracts were virtually in industry's hand." Only "ceremonial distinctions between government and business operations were preserved."[7]

To coordinate and regulate the fuel supplies of the nation for the First World War, Congress created a U. S. Fuel Administration (FA), and Wilson appointed his old friend and fellow professor, Harry A. Garfield, to head it. The FA faced the usual conflict-of-interest problems. Coming from the presidency of Williams College to the war administration, Garfield needed the industrialists' help. Many thought the coal men would co-opt his bureau and dominate him.

Then as now liberals and large portions of the general public feared the power of those who control fuel supplies. Today the target is "Big Oil" or the "Seven Sisters." Then it was the "Coal Trust." Hostility toward the "coal operators" soared during the anthracite strike of 1902. Their self-righteous refusal to arbitrate their differences with the United Mine Workers of America (UMWA) made the railroad presidents and their anthracite-mine managers caricatures of selfish capitalists. Indeed, Reading Railroad President George Baer's gibe that the managers of capital were "the Christian men to whom God in his infinite wisdom has given the control of property interests in this country" is quoted in most history books as an outrageous example of turn-of-the-century business autocracy.[8] During the Progressive Era, South Carolina Democrat Benjamin "Pitchfork Ben" Tillman and others sought to investigate the "power and influence of the so-called Coal Trust."[9] Just before the war, the Wilson administration brought antitrust suits against a number of coal industrialists and corporations for conspiring to increase prices.[10]

Against this background, it is not remarkable that Postmaster General Joseph P. Tumulty was aghast when he found out in the fall of 1918 that Garfield had "dollar-a-year-men" valued at over $1.5 million annually working in the Fuel Administration. Although his informant told Tumulty that Garfield had initially kept the coal producers "in their place" and had given them "no special favors," "in due time things changed."[11]

Tumulty's concern deepened when he learned that Wilson's foe, Massachusetts Senator Henry Cabot Lodge, knew of the apparent conflict of interest and planned to attack Wilson with it in the November, 1918, elections. The postmaster general wrote Wilson that Garfield's use of coal personnel in the FA would make an "unfortunate impression" on the country "for the coal operators, whether they are justly entitled to the reputation or not, are looked upon by the public at large, especially the consuming public, with grave suspicion, just as the packers of America are despised by the ordinary man on the street."[12]

But Tumulty's fears proved unfounded. Lodge never raised the issue. A lengthy congressional investigation of the Fuel Administration after the war found no conflict of interest. Garfield proudly defended his practice.[13]

Despite public and administrative fears, the FA had not allowed conflict of interest to develop, nor did the industrialists co-opt the fuel bureau. Rather, the Fuel Administration co-opted the industry for the government's objectives. A college professor had kept the infamous "Coal Trust" on a tight leash.

Garfield could keep the coal men in check for several reasons. First, the "Coal Trust" was a myth. Down to the war, the coal operators had proved themselves incapable of cooperating for any purpose. Next, the administration destroyed the initial attempts by the operators under the leadership of Interior Secretary Franklin K. Lane to form a wartime fuel committee that could set policy or prices. In addition, Garfield refused to allow operators any positions of power or consequence in the early months of government regulation. When a winter distribution crisis prompted him to turn to the industry for help, he accepted some costly services from trade association personnel, but he gave them limited responsibilities. In all of this Garfield was aided by the patriotism which Wilson generated around this war "to make the world safe for democracy."

✽   ✽   ✽

The widespread fears of a "Coal Trust" were ironically mis-
placed in 1917. The bituminous coal industry faced the crisis
of the First World War a fragmented, highly wasteful, inefficient, and excessively competitive industry. When the war
broke out, the industry had no national trade association,
monopoly structure, or effective leadership. Since the turn of
the century, the large buyers for the railroads, steam plants and
other utilities had been able to pit coal operators against one
another to secure low prices. In most regions, an unstable industry offered its poorly paid workers only a partial work year.[14]

When the war demand for steel and other industrial commodities began to flood into America from Europe, demand
for soft coal skyrocketed and gave the producers a new advantage over buyers. High-cost mines sprang into use, miners
began to work full-time, and prices began to climb. Coal, which
had been averaging $1 a ton, moved to $2.[15] Large buyers
continued to contract for coal at low prices on a yearly basis,
but small purchasers, bidding on the open or "spot" markets,
began to push prices to $5 and $6 in some places.[16]

To control similarly rising food prices, Wilson appointed
Herbert Hoover as food administrator shortly after the declaration of war on April 6, 1917. Congressman Asbury F. Lever
of South Carolina introduced a bill empowering the administration to control price and production of foodstuffs and other
"necessaries." Public outcries against "speculators" and "hoarders"
of both food and fuel mounted.[17]

Concurrently, through the Council of National Defense (CND)
and its Advisory Commission, the administration attempted to
have various industries cooperate in stimulating output and
coordinating industrial resources for war. The coal industry,
through CND member Interior Secretary Franklin K. Lane,
set up a Committee on Coal Production (CCP) comprised of
operators, miners and consumers. Unlike cooperating committees for other industries, the coal men were not unified enough
to exclude labor and consumers. While Congress debated legislation to regulate wheat and coal, the CCP began to work
out ways to stimulate production, insure mines a requisite
number of railroad cars on an equitable basis, and iron out
other transportation problems.[18] Fearful of government control—
particularly after the Federal Trade Commission (FTC) on

June 19, 1917, issued a report suggesting that government might have to fix prices and regulate distribution of coal—the CCP tried to preempt government price-fixing.[19]

With Lane's enthusiastic support, the CCP brought over 400 coal men to late June meetings in Washington to consider production, distribution and prices. Aware that a Federal Trade Commission coal price study was under way, the coal men voluntarily agreed to set a maximum price of $3 a ton, pending completion of the FTC study. Lane intimated that such patriotic action would not be considered a conspiracy in restraint of trade.[20]

Other Wilsonians, particularly Secretary of War Newton D. Baker, Attorney General Thomas W. Gregory, and Secretary of the Navy Josephus Daniels, damned the maximum price as a greedy, profiteering move. They did not seem to realize that the maximum attacked the main problem of excessive prices in spot markets and that three-fourths of all American coal was under yearly contract at approximately $2. Baker denounced the CCP price as "exorbitant and excessive," threw the CCP into disarray, and destroyed the initial cooperative relationship between the operators and the government.[21] Unfounded fears of a conspiracy to restrain trade and concern over conflict of interest initially destroyed a budding cooperative enterprise in war mobilization. Wilson seemed determined to prevent any operator influence on his administration.

Now pictured as unpatriotic, the coal men watched impotently as Congress added Section 25 to the Lever Bill, giving the president power to fix coal prices. Wilson signed the Lever Act on August 10, 1917, and eleven days later unilaterally lowered coal prices by one-third. Following August 21, 1917, no coal could sell at more than $2 a ton.[22]

The Lever Act not only empowered Wilson to "establish and maintain governmental control" over coal, to fix prices for coal and coke "wherever and whenever sold," to license operators "to regulate the method of production, sale, shipment, distribution, apportionment, or storage" of coal or coke, but also to requisition the businesses of those who conducted their firms "in a manner prejudicial to the public interest."[23] No other industry was "controlled, regulated, and directed as specifically and definitely and in such detail as was coal."[24] Victims of retail speculators and general concern about a "Coal Trust," the coal producers fell under a tough regulatory act.

Despite the prominence and expertise Francis S. Peabody had shown as head of the CCP—a command which had impressed senate investigators—Wilson naturally refused to appoint the author of the $3 maximum to head the FA. He chose instead his old friend Garfield, who was then serving on Herbert Hoover's price stabilization committee for wheat.[25] Wilson also passed over his own son-in-law William Gibbs McAdoo and progressive William T. Colver of the FTC, who sought to have the government pool all coal production and resell it. Although Garfield once headed a syndicate that opened some Ohio coal mines, he was not identified with the industry.[26]

Son of President James A. Garfield, the fuel administrator brought a legal and education career to the Wilson administration. Garfield had earned his BA at Williams College, his father's alma mater, and returned to St. Paul's, his own preparatory school, as a teacher of Latin and Roman history. He went on to receive his law degree from Columbia University and did further legal study at Oxford University and London's Inns of Court. In Cleveland, Ohio, his brother James R. Garfield, friend Frederick C. Howe and he formed a lucrative law practice. He organized the Cleveland Trust Company and opened the Piney Fork Coal mine in southeastern Ohio.

A reformer, Garfield battled "Boss" McKisson and his reign in Cleveland, formed the Cleveland Municipal Association to enlist the interest of the better-educated Clevelanders in running their city, was treasurer of the Cleveland Humane Society, and was director and president of the Cleveland Chamber of Commerce. His interests in politics, his character and his abilities impressed Woodrow Wilson, then president of Princeton, enough to offer Garfield the chair of politics in 1903. Garfield taught at Princeton for five years and then assumed the presidency of Williams College, from which he took a leave of absence during the war.[27]

Garfield put the operators on notice by comparing some of them to the robber barons of the Rhine.[28] He excluded coal men from his early appointments and turned instead to the Geological Survey for experts on coal statistics and to lawyers, mining engineers and professors for his personal advisors.[29] The industry bemoaned the "serious lack of experienced coal men" on his staff. He retaliated by threatening to nationalize the mines. Garfield set out to force the operators to cooperate on his terms.[30]

The government did not negotiate decisions on coal prices as it had in other industries but based them on the FTC's cost statistics. Garfield and his staff prevented profiteering and still increased production. To stimulate production from high-cost mines, he agreed to selective price increases for particular producing districts. The FA approved these increases only after careful statistical investigation by FTC agents and after devising a complicated system of pricing that secured the highest productivity without allowing excess profits to low-cost mines. The FA enforced its maximums in the courts.[31] Despite the increases, the Wilson administration held coal prices down. Before control, weighted average prices for all bituminous coal had risen 105 percent from the 1913–1914 base; under the Fuel Administration the increase was cut to 11 percent.[32] Company returns on investment dropped sharply under FA controls.[33]

As the winter of 1917–1918 came on, Garfield discovered that the overthrow of the CCP approach, shortages in New England and the Midwest, and the $2 price had retarded production. One of the worst winters in memory, railroad snarls and interagency confusions and rivalries brought the nation to a crisis in January 1918. To free the rails for coal shipment to port cities in order to bunker outgoing ships laden with war material, Garfield issued a drastic order shutting down industry east of the Mississippi for five days. The shutdown did little besides raise a merited howl of indignation and spark a barrage of comments about college professors running governmental bureaus.[34]

The winter crisis forced Garfield to rely more on the industrialists. In mid-January 1918, former CCP leader Francis S. Peabody, a group of coal operators and the Railway War Board proposed a zone plan which would restrict purchasers of coal to local producing districts, reduce cross-hauling, end congestion in the Appalachian gateways to the West, and decentralize the entire FA distribution organization. Following discussions with Railroad Administrator McAdoo and the president, Garfield implemented the zone plan.[35]

Zoning coal destroyed coal markets that had developed over

years. Senator Henry Cabot Lodge, who made partisan attacks on government mismanagement during the war, and various operators whose markets were eroded criticized the scheme mercilessly. But the zone system worked. It required, however, hiring administrators in every district to bring buyers and sellers together and to insure that essential war industries were supplied with coal.

Garfield called on a rising organizational genius in the industry, James D. A. Morrow, to head the distribution program. Morrow, a former commissioner of the Pittsburgh Coal Producers' Association, had worked as assistant secretary in the FTC and had been general secretary of the industry's fledgling trade group, the National Coal Association.[36]

To staff distributional offices throughout the industry the FA needed $1.5 million more than Congress had appropriated. Morrow convinced Garfield that the lack of appropriation could be overcome by giving the jobs to the industry's regional trade association personnel. If a trade association did not exist in a particular area, operators could be encouraged to form one. Trade association agents knew the coal business better than some political appointee might, they already had the confidence of the major buyers and sellers, and they had learned over the years not to play favorites in arranging contracts. Moreover, regional trade association offices had the ability to handle the statistical information on production, prices and contracts. Garfield accepted Morrow's suggestion. Trade association volunteers became distribution agents for the Fuel Administration.[37]

State fuel administrators—usually politicians unconnected with the industry appointed by the Wilson administration on recommendation of state party leaders—made the priority decisions. Their industry-donated counterparts, the distribution agents, kept careful track of coal production and movement, then allocated coal to particular war-related industries. Most often they merely saw to it that the producers with coal to sell reached consumers who were contributing to the war effort.[38] Garfield had kept both prices and priorities in governmental hands. He confined industry assistance to rearranging distribution channels.

Tumulty's initial concern thus proved unfounded. The FA had no major conflict-of-interest problems. In fact, the journalist who uncovered the use of the coal personnel and touched off Tumulty's fears became a convert to the Fuel Administration's techniques.

William Hard, progressive journalist who investigated the zone plan for the *New Republic*, a journal critical of Wilson's early mobilization efforts, praised Garfield's use of coal association personnel as free government bureaucrats. The district representative, he wrote, "one of the most important of Dr. Garfield's subordinates, . . . operates the levers of the whole machinery which delivers coal. . . . He is nominated by the local coal industry, and he is supported by it. He is supported by it at considerable expense. . . . This is something more than bureaucracy. . . . It illustrates . . . the principle . . . that the coal industry, as an industry, shall undertake a certain collective responsibility and shall then, with its own force and its own initiative, discharge that responsibility."[39]

Speaking to consumers, Hard continued, "If you are assigned to Zone P, you get your coal from mines in Zone P. And you may know a nice, hard-pressed coal-operator in Zone B or K or M who would be willing to let you have a thousand tons below cost, but it does you no good. It would clutter up the railways. It would interfere with the routing-schemes by which the Railway Administrator and the Fuel Administration save a great many miles of haulage every day." The laws of supply and demand have been "slaughtered," wrote Hard, "not by Bolsheviki but by fellows getting five thousand and twenty thousand and fifty thousand dollars a year who are now working as volunteers for Mr. McAdoo and Dr. Garfield." The FA zone system, concluded Hard, "is the triumph of organized units over unorganized individualism."[40]

In a June 1918 article directed at the operators across the country, *Coal Age* boomed Garfield's leadership. "Many people have believed," wrote the editor, "that the production and national distribution of coal could not be systematized." Yet because of Garfield's zoning and statistical program, "before the snow flies again, Dr. Garfield and his associates will have definite figures showing the production and consumption of coal in every zone, and these data will enable them to ship coal promptly from one region where there is an abundance to other districts where a shortage exists." To those angry about losing traditional markets, the journal suggested: "We must adapt our lives to a new order of things."[41] Garfield had co-opted the coal men into giving time of enormous value to the Fuel Administration, and he had won their respect. The "Coal Trust" had been kept at bay. The administration avoided co-option and conflict of interest and secured cooperation.

Generalizing from the experience of the Fuel Administration becomes precarious, for circumstances for coal were in many ways unique. Among industries important to the war effort, coal was singularly disorganized before the war. The patriotic war fervor generated by the administration gave the government moral force which could not have been maintained for a long time or in peace.[42] The moralism of the administration itself—whether Garfield, Baker or Wilson is taken as the example—has until recent days been unsurpassed. The Wilsonians eyed coal operators suspiciously, destroyed their attempt to cooperate through the Council of National Defense fuel committee, and kept them from positions of power until the government's lack of expertise forced it to bring coal people into the administration. It took a combination of patriotism, moralism and industry disorganization to avoid both co-option and conflict of interest and to achieve industry cooperation in the regulation of coal during the First World War.

NOTES

1. Gabriel Kolko's *The Triumph of Conservatism* (Chicago, 1967), although overargued, is perhaps the best example of recent writing of 1962); Grant McConnell, *Private Power and American Democracy* (New York, 1976); James Weinstein, *The Corporate Ideal in the Liberal State: 1900–1918* (Boston, 1968); Melvin I. Urofsky, *Big Steel and the Wilson Administration: A Study in Business-Government Relations* (Columbus, Ohio, 1969); Robert H. Wiebe, "The House of Morgan and the Executive, 1905–1913," *American Historical Review* LXV (October 1959), 49–60; G. C. Davis, "The Transformation of the Federal Trade Commission, 1914–1919," *Mississippi Valley Historical Review*, XLIX (Dec. 1962); Grant McConnell, *Private Power and American Democracy* (New York, 1966); and Ari and Olive Hoogenboom, *A History of the ICC: From Panacea to Palliative* (New York, 1976).

2. Development since the Second World War of what some call a "military-industrial complex" or system of "Pentagon capitalism" or the "new industrial state" has meant that it has become difficult to separate the interests of particular industries from that of the state. Most analyses

of these developments, however, credit the state—or more precisely the Department of Defense—with holding the trump cards, the contracts. See "President Eisenhower's Farewell to the Nation," *Bulletin* (U. S. Department of State), XLIV (Feb. 6, 1961); J. William Fulbright, *The Pentagon Propaganda Machine* (New York, 1971); John K. Galbraith, *The New Industrial State* (New York, 1967); Robert L. Heilbroner, *The Limits of American Capitalism* (New York, 1966); Seymour Melman, *Pentagon Capitalism: The Political Economy of War* (New York, 1971).

3. *Business Week,* Nov. 13, 1943, p. 116; Oct. 9, 1943, p. 108.

4. Richard Polenberg, *War and Society: The United States, 1941–1945* (Philadelphia, 1972), p. 91.

5. Melvin Urofsky has written that "the demands of the industry had guided WIB [War Industry Board] decisions as much as had the necessities of war. Even in the most controversial phase of the entente, as we shall now see, the 'controlling' agency followed the wishes of the 'controlled'." *Op. cit.,* p. 191; Robert D. Cuff, *The War Industries Board: Business-Government Relations during World War I* (Baltimore, 1973), pp. 204–19.

6. *Ibid.,* pp. 58–70, 128–30, 227–28, 236–40; Robert D. Cuff and Melvin I. Urofsky, "The Steel Industry and Price-Fixing During World War I," *Business History Review,* XXXIX (Autumn 1970), 291–306.

7. Paul A. C. Koistinen, "The 'Industrial-Military Complex' in Historical Perspective: World War I," *Business History Review,* XLI (Winter 1967), 378–403. Kostinen points out that a manager for John Deere became the chief of the Agricultural Implements and Wood Products Section of the WIB, the former president of the Fiske Rubber Company the chief of the Rubber and Rubber Goods Section, and the former treasurer of the Studebaker Corporation the head of the Automotive Products Section.

8. *Literary Digest,* XXIV (1902), 824.

9. B. R. Tillman to W. W. Finley, president, Southern Railway Company, May 22, 1913; B. R. Tillman to Daniel Willard, president, Baltimore & Ohio Railway Company, June 5, 1914; B. R. Tillman to J. C. McReynolds, Attorney General of the United States, May 29, 1914 and July 15, 1914; draft of Senate Resolution 291 on "the power and influence of the so-called Coal Trust," in Department of Justice Central Files, Classified Subject Files, Correspondence, File 60–187–13, Record Group 60 (henceforth RG 60), National Archives (henceforth NA), Box 607.

10. *The New York Times,* Apr. 10, July 7, and June 28, 1917; Frank M. Swacker to G. Carrol Todd, assistant to the U. S. Attorney General, Feb. 24, 1917, including "Memorandum Regarding Alleged Combination in Restraint of Trade in Bituminous Coal. . . ." Department of Justice Central Files, Classified Subject Files, Correspondence, File No. 60–187–16, RG 60, NA. The government lost all cases.

11. Evans Wolley to Tumulty, Sept. 23, 1918, Woodrow Wilson Papers, Manuscript Division, Library of Congress (henceforth Wilson Papers), Reel 293 (Microfilm).

12. Tumulty to Wilson, Sept. 23, 1918, Wilson Papers, Reel 293.

13. U. S. Congress, Senate, Committee on Interstate Commerce, *Increased Price of Coal: Hearing pursuant to S. Res. 126*, 66 Cong., 1 Ses., Aug. 26, 1919–May 3, 1920; Garfield to Senator Thomas J. Walsh, Sept. 25, 1918, Wilson Papers, Reel 293.

14. On the structure of the industry, see William Graebner, "Great Expectations: The Search for Order in Bituminous Coal, 1890–1917," *Business History Review*, XLVIII (Spring 1974), 49–73; *Coal Age*, VIII (Sept. 18 1915), 153; X (Nov. 25, 1916), 801.

15. Paul W. Garrett, *History of Government Control of Prices* (Washington, 1920), pp. 153–70.

16. David I. Wing, "Cost, Prices, and Profits of the Bituminous Coal Industry," *American Economic Review*, XI (Mar. 1921), 77.

17. Seward W. Livermore, *Politics is Adjourned: Woodrow Wilson and the War Congress, 1916–1918* (Middletown, Conn., 1966), Chap. 4. John Bruce Mitchell, "The Coal Hold-Up," *Forum*, LVIII (Nov. 1917), 528–38, writes, "This [coal shortage] is a case of holding everyone guilty until he is proven innocent." Then as now the public sought a scapegoat for a fuel crisis. During the fuel crisis of 1973–1974, people told Gallup pollsters that they believed that three groups were most responsible for the crisis: the oil companies (25 percent of responses), the federal government (23 percent of responses), and the Nixon administration (19 percent of responses). Only 7 percent in December 1973 blamed the Arab oil-producing nations. Multiple answers were permitted. *Gallup Opinion Index*, No. 104 (Feb. 1974), pp. 4–5. See also Robert Sherill, "Breaking up Big Oil," *New York Times Magazine*, Oct. 3, 1976, pp. 15 ff.

18. U. S. Congress, Senate, Committee on Interstate Commerce, *Price Regulation of Coal and Other Commodities, Hearing on S. 2354 and S. J. Res. 77*, 65 Cong., 1 Ses., 1917; *Coal Age*, XI (May 5, 1917), 782; (May 12, 1917), 817–18; Walter S. Gifford to Newton D. Baker, May 25, 1917, Wilson Papers, Reel 238.

19. Federal Trade Commission, *Report on Anthracite and Bituminous Coal, 1917*.

20. *Coal Age*, XI (June 30, 1917), 1124; (July 7, 1917), 15; *The New York Times*, June 28–29, 1917; *Cong. Record*, 65 Cong., 1 Ses., LV, Pt. 5, 5318.

21. Baker quoted in Garrett, *op. cit.*, pp. 158–59; Wilson to FTC member J. Franklin Fort, July 2, 1917, in Ray Stannard Baker, *Woodrow Wilson, Life and Letters* (8 vols.; Garden City, N. Y., 1927–1939), VII, 140–41; Wilson to Baker, personal and confidential, June 29, 1917, Newton D. Baker Papers, Manuscript Division, Library of Congress (henceforth Baker Papers), Box 4.

22. Livermore, *op. cit.*, p. 56; Lever Act, 40 Stat., 276 ff.; *Coal Age*, XII (August 25, 1917), 321.

23. Lever Act, 40 Stat., 284–86.

24. James D. A. Morrow testimony in U. S. Congress, Senate, Commit-

tee on Manufactures, *Publication of Production and Profits in Coal*, Hearings on S. 4828, 66 Cong., 3 Ses., 1921, p. 212.

25. Herbert Hoover, *The Memoirs of Herbert Hoover*, Vol. I: *Years of Adventure, 1874–1920* (New York, 1952), pp. 243, 253, 262–63.

26. Newton D. Baker to Wilson, June 27, 1917, Baker Papers, Box 4.

27. Robert D. Cuff, "The Wilsonian Managers" (unpublished manuscript in author's possession), pp. 3–13; *National Cyclopedia of American Biography* (New York, 1954), XXXIII, 154–55; Garfield testimony in Senate Committee on Manufactures, *Publication of Production and Profits*, p. 1290; Wilson to Garfield Dec. 3, 1918, Wilson Papers, Reel 293; Thomas R. Shipp, "Dr. Garfield, Fuel Administrator," *The World's Work*, XXXV (November 1917), 99–100.

28. Evans Wolley to Tumulty, Sept. 23, 1918.

29. Garfield to Daniels, Mar. 3, 1921, Harry A Garfield Papers, Manuscript Division, Library of Congress (henceforth Garfield Papers), Box 86; U. S. Fuel Administration (henceforth FA), *Final Report of the Fuel Administrator*, p. 26.

30. *Coal Age*, XII (Sept. 8, 1917), 412. On the Senate floor Henry Cabot Lodge asked rhetorically, "Who is the fuel controller, Mr. President? A college president who never saw a coal mine, probably, in his life and knows no more about coal than when he sees it burn in the stove. His appointment was not calculated to inspire confidence among the businessmen of America, particularly the coal operators." *Cong. Record*, 65 Cong., 2 Ses., LV, Pt. 2, 1091.

31. FA, *Final Report of the Fuel Administrator*, pp. 240–43; FA, *Report of the Engineers' Committee*, by Cyrus Garnsay, Jr., et al., 1918; *The New York Times*, Mar. 11, 1918.

32. Garrett, *op. cit.*, pp. 24, 153, 170. Charles Van Hise estimated that without the price controls, coal would have been at least two dollars higher during the war. *Conservation and Regulation in the United States during the World War* (Washington, 1917), p. 168.

33. U. S. Coal Commission, *Report*, 68 Cong., 2 Ses., 1925, pp. 2517–24, 2677–93; FTC, *Preliminary Report on Investment and Profit in Soft-Coal Mining*, 1922, pp. 3–12.

34. James P. Johnson, "The Fuel Crisis, Largely Forgotten, That Chilled Us in 1918," *Smithsonian*, Dec. 1976, pp. 64–71.

35. FA, *Report of the Distribution Division*, 1921, pp. 5–10, 25–27; J.D.A. Morrow to Garfield, Jan. 22, 1918, Records of Harry Garfield, Fuel Administrator, General Correspondence, Record Group 67, Federal Records Center, Box 11.

36. Garfield memorandum, Aug. 29, 1919, Garfield Papers, Special Correspondence, Box 93; *Coal Age*, XII (Aug. 25, 1917), 321; (Feb. 9, 1918), 290.

37. A. G. Gutheim, "The Transportation Problem in the Bituminous Coal Industry," *American Economic Review*, XI (March 1921), 99; FA, *Report of the Distribution Division*, pp. 25–27; Morrow to Hard, Sept. 13, 1918. The irony of Wilson's administrator using the agencies that

Wilson's Justice Department had taken to court was not lost on the operators.

38. William Hard, "Socialistic Coal," *The New Republic*, XVII (Nov. 16, 1918), 64–65; Sidney A. Hale, "The Coal Problem of Today," *World's Work*, XXXVI (July 1918), 318–28; Livermore, *op. cit.*, p. 41.

39. Hard, *op. cit.*, p. 65; On Hard and his contacts within the Republican opposition to Wilson, see Livermore, *op. cit.*, p. 86, and Paul W. Glad, "Progressives and the Business Culture of the 1920s," *Journal of American History*, LIII (June 1966), 75–89. Hard's initial questions over the propriety of the use of trade association personnel led him, apparently, to pass Morrow's letter explaining it to Senator Lodge. After seeing the FA offices and interviewing officials, Hard concluded that there was no conflict of interest and wrote the glowing accounts quoted above. Wolley to Tumulty Sept. 23, 1918; Tumulty to Wilson, Sept. 23, 1918.

40. Hard, *op. cit.*, pp. 64–66; also Hard, "Coal Why Not More?" *The New Republic*, XVI (Oct. 5, 1918), 276–78, and Hard, "Coal," *The New Republic*, XVI (Sept. 21, 1918), 226–27.

41. *Coal Age*, XIII (June 8, 1918), 1043.

42. McConnell has written of the similar patriotism and service offered by businessmen during the Second World War: "Most historians and other writers on this general experience have dwelt on the impressiveness of the achievement and on the dedication of the men who made it possible. With little question, such evaluation is just. Excellent work was done by many of the businessmen who came to Washington and served in discomfort and at real sacrifice. The advisory committees also undoubtedly gave selflessly and in a manner which served the nation well. Some of the suspicions that were directed against men in these positions were very probably unjustified." *Private Power*, pp. 262–63. An attempt by Garfield to recreate the cooperative spirit among the industrialists after the war fell on deaf ears.

Abraham S. Eisenstadt

POLITICAL CORRUPTION IN AMERICAN HISTORY: SOME FURTHER THOUGHTS

The questions that Watergate presents to the historian analyzing American political corruption are clear enough. To what extent does the Watergate phenomenon inhere in American politics? Is Watergate a uniquely American adventure? Or is it yet another act in the universal drama of man transgressing? If so, is American political corruptibility beyond reformation? Is the response to Watergate, no less than the episode itself, part of a recurrent cycle of American corruption and reform?

If the reform phase of the cycle is now in progress, what are its antecedents, and how does it relate to earlier drives for restoring American politics to honesty? Is today's reform a latter-day expression of what the Puritans of the 1630s stood for when, as Thomas Shepard put it, they proclaimed "the necessity of reformation of the Church" and "in zeale of the Truth preached or professed against the corruptions of the times"?[1] Is it a variant form of the colonists' declaration of independence from Britain, which, in John Adams's hopes, would "inspire us with many virtues, which we have not, and correct many errors, follies, and vices," affording Americans, "who were addicted to corruption and venality," "a purification from our vices, and an augmentation of our virtues"?[2] Is it comparable to the reform movements of the antebellum age, when, as Horace Greeley saw it, "the perilous conflict with Wrong and Woe is our most conclusive evidence that Wrong and Woe shall yet vanish forever"?[3] Or is it like the Progressive movement, which, in Theodore Roosevelt's words, sought to "drive the special interests out of politics," and which regarded "executive power as the steward of the public welfare"?[4]

That Americans are now in a surge of reform is richly evident. In the past few years, forty-nine states have passed new campaign finance laws. The American Congress is drafting a strict code of ethics, senators arising in turn, like Roman censors or French Girondins, to call for ever greater probity. But how far can reform carry? Laws do not create morality: if anything, they testify to its absence. Senator Sam J. Ervin of North Carolina, the patriarch who called Richard M. Nixon's sinners to justice, knew better than most the true nature of their sin. "The presidential aides who perpetrated Watergate," he said, "were not seduced by love of money, which is sometimes thought to be the root of all evil. On the contrary, they were instigated by a lust of political power, which is at least as corrupting as political power itself."[5] But if Senator Ervin was right, how can one legislate against another Watergate? How would laws be passed limiting the corruption of lusting for power, to say nothing of the corruption of possessing it? And what should one suggest if he turns from the president's aides to the president himself? Nixon Agonistes was the central figure in the Watergate drama. How could one hope to contain by law the psychic needs that drove a Nixon, knowing that the men who rise high in American politics are, by their nature, far more likely to be natives of Egocentralia than travelers from Altruria?

Granted at once that political corruption is not a uniquely American disease, it would be well to begin by defining it in general terms and then see how far those terms are applicable to American experience. Political corruption means that a public official has perverted the office entrusted to his care, that he has broken a public trust for private gain. To discuss corruption in a polity is, then, to discuss the standards of right and wrong in that polity. To say that the acts of officials holding public office are corrupt is to do two things: obviously, it is to blame them for subverting the moral standards governing the way they conduct their office; but no less importantly, it is to speak of the moral rules by which the community operates and, in effect, to look beyond the public office to the nature and purposes of the polity. It is, thus, to say what one considers to be the ends to which the polity is dedicated and the means by which those ends are to be achieved.

Each polity in every age has its own ideas of what the good society should be, of what role the public official should play in achieving the good society, and therefore of what misplaying of his role can validly be called corruption. When one talks about corruption in American politics, he must therefore refer the concept of corruption to the particularities of the American system: that is, to the premises, values and institutions that form the essence of the American polity. For that reason political corruption in the United States can best be understood if it is seen in a comparative perspective: if American democracy is contrasted with European, and particularly with British, aristocracy. For this perspective, one must consult America's most intelligent foreign visitors, particularly Alexis de Tocqueville and James Bryce. It was the concluded sense of both that America's best men did not go into politics. Did this mean that America had a politics of mediocrity or did it mean, as Andrew Carnegie suggested, that it had settled political institutions over which there was no longer any controversy?[6] Carnegie's suggestion offers another clue to the problem of American political corruption. It is fair to say that American parties and politics have expressed a contest not over ideologies but over alternatives, not between classes but between blocs of interests. The system itself has not been called into question, but only the corrupt way it is said to have been run. Thus the system is safeguarded, put beyond discussion. The system has not been called corrupt; instead the accusation is shifted onto those entrusted with conduct of the system.

In the American polity, there is a difference between the preachments about corruption and its actual practice, between the morals spoken of and the acts performed. A people of pieties, Americans are given to preachment; indeed preachment is often enough the atonement for the practice. In analyzing the problem of corruption in American politics, one therefore has to distinguish between the actuality of corruption and the cry of corruption. The first occurs where the rules of the game have without question been broken, where the transgressor has been caught *flagrante delicto*, with his morality down. Among classic examples are the activities of the Tweed Ring,

the Crédit Mobilier, the Whiskey Ring, the municipal directorates
of Lincoln Steffens's day, the Harding boys, Estes Kefauver's
internal revenue collectors, and that marvel of self-unmade men,
Spiro Theodore Agnew. But in a liberal democracy such as
America's, the cry of corruption is a far more prevalent phenomenon than particular proven acts of corruption. The cry is most
generally raised by those who are out of power and are trying
to get in. Where the premises on which a polity rests are
generally accepted, as they have been in America, the only
question that can legitimately be raised is not about the nature
of government but about its conduct. The cry of corruption
is inherently moral, of course, but its importance is that it
touches upon the ultimate morality in a system like America's.
To say that those in power are not abiding by the rules of
the game means that they are distributing advantages in-
equitably and unfairly; it means, even more pointedly, that by
subverting the rules they may be destroying the game.

In every American age, there has been a group that has
sounded the cry of corruption: the cry that political values
are being debased, the political system subverted, public officials bought out. This group is the American gentility. It is
they who have articulated the republic's ideals, who have
denounced corrupt men and corrupt practices. Who are they,
and what do they believe? They are neo-Puritans, descendants,
in variant forms, of John Winthrop. The gentility has had its
spokesmen in every American generation: its Cottons, its
Mathers, its Hutchinsons, its Galloways, its Ticknors, its Fenimore Coopers, its Parkmans, its Adamses, its Cabots and Lodges,
its Eliots and Morisons. They have always constituted an Eastern
establishment. New England was their initial habitat but, as
they migrated or as groups in other regions took up their outlook, their influence exercised an expanding dominion. They
command America's prestigious divinity schools, prestigious
schools of higher learning, prestigious journals and newspapers.
They believe in private property, an ordered society, civic and
moral education, a respect for institutions, good character as
the essence of good leadership, and, of course, the claims of
status and genealogy. The code they subscribe to is one summed
up in the phrase "bourgeois morality." They stand for an adjustive conservatism and have perennially been America's

genteel reformers. They stand for civic virtue, high-mindedness, a respect for the past, a disinterestedness in public affairs: they stand, in a word, for themselves. What they have decried as corrupt practices were, in some measure, actions that were not done their way. Those they decried as corrupt were not infrequently men they had lost out to. The gentility's cry of corruption has been, again in measure, a heart-rending lament over losing their superintendence of American politics.

In a society endlessly changed by newer ideas and forms of capitalism and democracy, they are constantly at war with the group they regard as the most subversive—the *nouveaux riches*. The gentility fear the influence of new money upon politics. They are also apprehensive about the democratic process. They share with Robert Lowe and the Adullamites the worry that democracy is too fragile to be handled by the people. They worry about a constant erosion of the people's deference to the gentility. Still, their enemies are not the masses but the selfish men, as they see them, who for their own gain would mislead the masses. From the viewpoint of foreigners, they are our best men, the elite that most closely approximates the English or continental European aristocracy. In sum, America's gentility believes that wealth corrupts and democracy is corruptible, that America needs a class of public philosophers or philosopher-kings to give civic lessons to the people and superintend the conduct of the *nouveaux riches,* and that they themselves—men of genteel origins and education—are precisely the class that could best satisfy these needs.[7]

Having said that the American idea of political corruption is particular to the United States, I should like to consider some of the principal factors in American society, factors that have generated political corruption and determined the way Americans perceive it. These factors are American sectarian Christianity, American democracy and law, and the American entrepreneurial ethos. Because the concept and practice of corruption are peculiar to a given polity, it is basic that American political corruption can be properly assayed only if it is compared with that of another polity. Accordingly, where feasible, the American model will be apposed to a European one. This largely accords with Louis Hartz, who, while admitting that the American experience has its own nature, justifiably asks: "How can we

know the uniqueness of anything, except by contrasting it with
what is not unique?" In seeking points of reference for analyzing
American political corruption, the author has been instructed
above all by the intelligence of the man who instructed Hartz,
and indeed a whole generation, and who is still the best guide
to a comparative study of American institutions and ideas—
Alexis de Tocqueville.

✿   ✿   ✿

America is a Christian commonwealth. The founding of its
polity was an incident in the drama of the European reformation. To say that Americans are a Christian people is at once
to define their perception of corruption and the role it has
played in their history. Christianity informs their public life
with a type of moral code; the degree to which their officials
fulfill the code determines the Americans' sense of the officials'
probity or corruption. The early growth of Christian sectarianism
in English North America meant that the Americans were to
follow a different route in church-state relations from the Erastian one taken by most European polities. The dominant role
of the state in Europe since the Reformation meant that morality
in politics was whatever the state's governors said it was. In
this way, the concept of corruption in a European polity has
been, in some measure, an expression of its concept of *raison
d'état*. In America, the triumph of Protestant sectarianism led,
paradoxically, not only to the separation of church and state
but also to the rule of a Christian ethos in the conduct of
public affairs. In an Erastian order of politics, the question of
corruption is to a considerable extent foreclosed. But in an
essentially sectarian order, the question is not only not foreclosed, it is constantly open.

America's religion has shaped its politics: America's politics
is, in a basic way, its religion. Both facts help explain the
American view of political corruption. With Americans politics
serves a triple function: it is the agora of democracy, wealth-
seeking, and religion; in the American polity, the three are in-
separable, indeed almost indistinguishable. In the absence of
an established faith, the many sects joined a community of
belief in the American political system. Participatory democracy
was a translation of participatory communion. The relation

between church and state in America originated in the fact that *raison d'état* had very often been synonymous with *raison de foi*. Far from a sharp demarcation between church and state, or more accurately, between churches and polities, there was an interplay between them where God was politicized and politics deified.[8] G. K. Chesterton described America as "a nation with the soul of a Church."[9] Robert N. Bellah has emphasized the fact that America has a civil religion, whose key components are biblical archetypes: "Exodus, Chosen People, Promised Land, New Jerusalem, Sacrificial Death, and Rebirth."[10] Drawing on Tocqueville, Cushing Strout has traced the impact of American Christianity on American democracy.[11]

Indeed, in trying to understand how and why Christian belief in the United States could serve as a form of politics, one can do no better than refer to Tocqueville's own words:

Christianity has therefore retained a strong hold on the public mind in America, and . . . its sway is not only that of a philosophical doctrine which has been adopted upon inquiry, but of a religion which is believed without discussion. In the United States, Christian sects are infinitely diversified and perpetually modified; but Christianity itself is an established and irresistible fact, which no one undertakes either to attack or to defend. The Americans, having admitted the principal doctrines of the Christian religion without inquiry, are obliged to accept in like manner a great number of moral truths originating in it and connected with it. . . . In the United States, religion is therefore mingled with all the habits of the nation and all of the feelings of patriotism, whence it derives a peculiar force.[12]

It has thus been long understood that politics in America has been a form of civic faith, in which one may find secular variants of special providences, epiphanies and Feasts of Fools, indeed the whole panoply of political sacraments, including extreme unctuousness, double crosses, and the worst sin of all— venality. In the morality play that American politics has been, it was inevitable that the cry of corruption should be so frequently sounded and the prosecution of corruption so zealously pursued. Francis Grund, an Austrian who settled in the United States during the Jacksonian period, spelled out the impact of religion on public office. To violate morality, he said, is to violate religion and, in effect, "to subvert the political institutions of the country." Proof of "the high premium at which morality

is held in the United States consists in its influence on the
elections of officers." In Europe, said Grund, the statesman's
"wanderings are forgotten" in the face of the good he has done
for his nation. But

no such compensation takes place in the United States. Private virtue
overtops the highest qualifications of the mind, and is indispensable to
the progress of the most acknowledged talents. . . . The moment a candidate is presented for office, not only his mental qualifications for the functions he is about to assume, but also his private character are made the
subject of criticism. Whatever he may have done, said, or listened to . . .
is sure to be brought before the public.[13]

Corruption is the other side of virtue. Americans hear the
perennial cry of corruption because theirs is the land of the
perennial reformation. It is basic to their ideology that life is a
constant struggle for sanctification, that grace is theirs not by
right but, at the very best, by achievement. When Americans
say that the Puritan idea of election is made universal, they
are saying that the possibility of access to grace is extended
to all members of the community. But, by that very token, the
struggle for sanctification also becomes universal, and the dangers
of corruption become more widespread. The growth of the
democratic ethos is at once religious and political, so that in
talking of American political corruption, it is almost impossible
to draw a line between the democratic and Christian concepts
of value, however much the concepts are redefined from one
age to the next. Where the ways to grace are thrown open, and
the ways to wealth multiply, indeed where the acquisition of
wealth becomes a sacrament, then the corruptibility of men
becomes a central feature of American life. To the degree that
Americans are the people of the perennial reformation, it is
part of their ethos that they must constantly struggle to purge
politics of evil men and evil ways.

In this quasi-religious drama of politics, the gentility have
served as the keepers of the American conscience. They have
measured their ideas of political conscience against the tenets
of their belief: in a rationalized Christianity, in faith tempered
by law, in divinity housed in institutions, in devotion enclosed
by science, in godly ways approximated to bourgeois habits.
Descendants of John Calvin, they have always been sure that

they were holier than thou and that no small part of their being so consisted in their possessing the true sense of what holiness was. One hears from their midst the voice of rationalized Christianity and Christian conscience sounded from one American generation to the next: in John Cotton, in Increase Mather, in Charles Chauncy, in Benjamin Silliman, in William Ellery Channing, in Ralph Waldo Emerson, and in their genteel and prosyletizing sermons, books, and periodicals, such as the *North American Review* and the *Atlantic Monthly*. It was their moral standard which, more than anything else, defined for Americans their sense of corruption.

They worked both elements of Christianity—the idea of individual salvation and the idea of social justice—into a program for reform. The program was inevitably political and, as Tocqueville would have suggested, associational; it expressed the Americans' particular sense that they were a providential people, singularly blessed and singularly selected for a special mission. In this formulation, the Christian idea has engined all their major reform movements, all their attempts to restore America to its purpose as a polity, a purpose invariably characterized as pristine, hallowed, high and true. The principal leaders of reform, the American gentility, have made each reform movement something of a crusade, with annunciations of what was clearly good and clearly evil, with bills of indictment against the men and institutions that were violating the American moral code, with an impassioned sense of just how paradise had been lost and how it was to be regained. The Puritans' denunciation of sins found its echo in the Declaration of Independence' catalog of royal transgressions, in Theodore Parker's arraignment of the bad merchant, in Henry George's plea for the City of God on earth, in Lincoln Steffens' attacks on the shame of the cities and the enemies of the republic. It was a central theme of each reform movement that American politics had been corrupted, that the money-changers were to be driven from the nation's temple, that the worship of false gods had to be given up, that the conduct of government had to be restored to men of probity and virtue.

Their Christianity has, in sum, been an important factor in Americans' perception of political corruption. These things have been noted: that Christianity has informed the Americans' poli-

tics, that it stands for them as a civil religion, that it has given
them the moral calculus for measuring the good and the bad
in their political lives, that their perennial political creed is
perennial moral reformation, that the superintendents of their
political ethic have been the genteel keepers of their conscience,
and that the latter, more than any other single group, have led
American reform movements, which have undertaken to restore
the morality of a world seemingly lost. Watergate, it is true,
had a dimension that cannot simply or directly be referred to
the religious terms just presented, a dimension involving the
struggle for power between two parties and the genuine fear
of a power that corrupts and a corruption that empowers. But
one misses a significant aspect of Watergate if he does not *also*
see it as a Christian morality play, a struggle between the
antinomians and those who insist upon fulfilling the moral law,
and a contest between the fundamentalism of the Sun Belt and
the rationalized Christianity of the Eastern Establishment.

*   *   *

How far has the American idea of political corruption been
shaped by the fact of American democracy? To put the problem
another way: which was more given to corruption, a democratic
society or an aristocratic? This question, a vital one during the
first century and a half of American history, usually involved
a contrast between America and Britain. For the larger part,
it was the sense of the principal British and American commentators that corruption was more characteristic of democracy
than of aristocracy. True enough, the Founding Fathers decried
British political corruption and hoped to install, at home, a
republic of virtue; but they were all too familiar with the
failures of human nature[14] and, having created a national government based on democracy, they sought nothing so much as
to restrain it. In the Jacksonian era, the Reform Bill of 1832
undertook to shift the locus of power in the British constitution
and to do so, in significant measure, by reducing the element
of corruption in the British electoral process. At the same time,
it impressed Tocqueville that European aristocracy was far less
susceptible of corruption than American democracy.[15] James
Fenimore Cooper, who had begun in the 1820s by refuting
British criticisms and by citing the virtues of life in the United

States, came to the point in the 1830s where he was largely preoccupied with the vices of American democracy.[16] Charles Dickens went to Washington, D.C., with no great expectations, to put it mildly; but his tale of one city showed the hard times the English democrat suffered on witnessing the moral level of American public life. With his usual flair for understatement, he described the American Congress:

Despicable trickery at elections; underhanded tamperings with public officers; cowardly attacks upon opponents, with scurrilous newspapers for shields, and hired pens for daggers; shameful trucklings to mercenary knaves, whose claim to be considered is, that every day and week they sow new crops of ruin with their venal types, . . . aidings and abettings of every bad inclination in the popular mind, and artful suppressions of all its good influences: such things as these, and in a word, Dishonest Faction in its most depraved and unblushing form, stared out from every corner of the crowded hall.[17]

Half a century later, Bryce, who found so much to praise in the United States, saw municipal corruption as a major blemish in American institutions. The American gentility agreed with him very largely, calling for civil-service reform to restore politics to honesty. It seemed to commentators on both sides of the Atlantic that British government, still strongly in the hands of the aristocracy, was far more principled and reputable. Half a century after Bryce, Pendleton Herring, then a professor of political science at Harvard, found that corruption was far more prevalent in America than in Britain. He ascribed this continuing difference to two factors: that America had failed "to reconcile the inequalities of private wealth with democratic doctrines of political equality" and that the British parties paid off their wealthy supporters with honorific titles.[19]

To say, from looking at Britain and America, that the politics of aristocracy is cleaner than the politics of democracy is to make the contrast too convenient. There is very likely nothing inherently pure or corrupt about either form of government, except for the minor consideration that both are run by men and men are something less than angels. If corruption inheres in man rather than in types of government, then the problem becomes one of finding the forms of venality that are particular to a given type. Andrew Carnegie believed that American and British leaders were both open to bribery, the first selling out

for money, the second for titles.[20] For those less inclined than
Carnegie was to acclaim the virtues of American democracy,
it may appear that, during the age from Waterloo to Watergate,
the Americans showed a greater proclivity to political corruption
than the British. The reason may be that purchasing men with
a peerage or knighthood is not only part of a spectacular ritual
but actually fulfills the aristocratic idea, whereas purchasing
men in a democracy by any means violates the democratic idea.
It is important too that, in the nineteenth and twentieth centuries, British aristocrats, *malgré eux*, had both to superintend
the democratization of their polity and to defend their own
interests. The circumstance left them little opportunity for practicing the old-time corruption. Their formula, worked to a fine
art by Sir Robert Peel, Lord Palmerston and William Gladstone,
was to practice some democracy and to preach much morality.
At the time of America's Tweed Ring, its Crédit Mobilier, its
robber barons and its great barbecues, Gladstone was running
the British government on the premise that godliness was next
to financial cleanliness.

To judge how far American democracy has been a factor in
American political corruption, it would be well to return to
the subject of Watergate, which stands as the emblem of
American corruptibility. Seen as a product of its time and place,
Watergate signifies not so much a democracy that is endemically
corruptible as an executive leadership that has been exotically
altered. Those who occupied the White House after the Second
World War were, as they are now called, imperial presidents.
The course of events had thrust the United States into the
center of world conflict and had, inevitably, invested its president with a responsibility and power which he alone could
handle but for which his office was not designed. The imperial
presidency contradicted the office which the Founding Fathers
had contrived and the nation had for almost two centuries lived
with. From having served largely domestic purposes, it became
significantly international; from having been a check on democratic power, it became an instrument of quasi-autocratic power;
from having been an office open to public light, it became one
that often could function best behind closed doors. Of course,
the actual uses of his power would depend on the person of
the president. But whoever the occupant of the White House

has been, America's imperial presidents have expressed some
of the essential qualities of American democracy: the Americans'
sense of mission, their belief that their polity is a model worth
emulating, their almost paranoid fear of foreign threat, their
malaise about coexisting with alternative political ideals. Thus
it is fair to say that, to some degree, Watergate inheres in the
structure and ideas of American democracy. It is not merely
that American presidents have, for the larger part, been plain
men, if not necessarily men from Plains. The question posed
by an age of American world power is whether the responsibility
of empire can be discharged without having an imperial president, or, to put it another way, whether in retreating from the
imperial presidency Americans may not also be retreating from
the responsibilities of empire, responsibilities which are at once
military and moral.

One cannot ask about the importance of democracy as a
factor in American political corruption without also asking about
the importance of American law. American constitutionalism and
jurisprudence form the centerpiece of American democracy. To
understand the history of the American polity, one could find
no better source than the history of American law. It is a
commonplace that law frames social institutions; law and society
are virtually synonymous. Law expresses the polity's mores and
defines its goals. New societies, new laws; as a society changes,
so do its laws; and as the laws change, so does the society. From
the writing of Roscoe Pound, Morris Raphael Cohen, J. Willard
Hurst, and indeed, Oliver Wendell Holmes, Jr., Americans have
long understood the adjustive vitality of their legal system. For
parallel appraisals of English law, recourse for many a decade
has been to the dazzling, breathtaking exegeses of Frederic
William Maitland. From these scholars it has been learned that
laws are not per se corrupt but that they are a society's moral
code and that, accordingly, one society's probity is another's
corruption.

What are the particularities of American society that its laws
would express? American constitutionalism besepeaks the premises of a liberal bourgeois polity. It embraces the ideals of
private property and of written laws as their best guarantee.
To say that America is a polity of laws and not of men is to
record the Americans' quest for protection against what they

regarded as the arbitrariness of the monarch, his ministers, and
the High Court of Parliament. But, at bottom, the insistence
on the primacy of laws over men begs the question, for it is
men who make laws and interpret them. Charles Evans Hughes
uttered the famous words: "The Constitution is what the judges
say it is." Henry Steele Commager's was the brilliant perception
that the Supreme Court has long been sitting as a continuous
constitutional convention. J. Willard Hurst said that "the most
creative, driving, and powerful pressures upon our law emerged
from the social setting." All understood the theme that America
is a polity of the men who superintend its laws and that the
Americans' sense of corruption varies with the precepts of their
legal superintendents and of the mores to which the latter
subscribe.[21]

America has been the paradigmatic liberal polity. Its citizens
have formulated constitutions that delimit the scope of public
power. But an empire of liberty is also an empire of corruptibility. The positive law governing public power can, as has
been noted, be drafted and interpreted to satisfy the interests
of influential individuals and groups. Thus, when Oliver Wendell
Holmes (in *Lochner* v. *New York*) argued that "the fourteenth
amendment does not enact Mr. Herbert Spencer's *Social Statics*,"
he was on the dissenting side of the court, and testifying in
effect that that was precisely what the amendment was doing.
The American empire of corruptibility extends, moreover, not
merely to the social activities the law deals with but also to
those it does not. The liberal polity rests on the concept of
limited jurisdiction. Self-interest rushes in where legislation fears
to tread. The critics of this aspect of liberal society have been
legion. In the 1850s George Fitzhugh denounced the liberal
polity, because it permitted the strong and shrewd, using the
premises of liberalism, to enslave the poor and weak. "Labor
makes values and Wit exploitates and accumulates them," he
said, noting that he was adding his voice to a chorus of critics,
including Charles Dickens, Bulwer-Lytton, Thomas Carlyle, Tory
conservatives and Christian Socialists. The critics of American
liberal bourgeois polity have surely increased since Fitzhugh's
day, and the theme they have regularly reiterated is that its
laws no less than their application are corrupt: that the legal
premises of American society rob the many and enrich the few.

It is hardly necessary to cite a long catalog of those who have questioned the probity of American laws, but the spectrum of opinion is wide, and one can start by citing Henry Steele Commager, Thurman Arnold, Herbert Marcuse, John Kenneth Galbraith, Gunnar Myrdal and John Rawls.

American law is, like all others, essentially the law of property relations. In a polity that is not authoritarian or aristocratic, lawyers have played a role that is, as Tocqueville well understood, quasi-aristocratic. They discharge functions elsewhere performed by dispensers or superintendents of justice based on legal codes, *droit administratif*, or His Majesty's equity and common law—codes, in effect, that derive from the superiority and the exclusivity of a central jurisdiction. The primary function of American lawyers is to serve the interests of property by defending them in court or by making the laws that govern the disposition of property. It is nothing fortuitous that, in this republic of property, the lawyers are also the politicians. They serve in American legislatures, on all levels; they staff the administrative agencies; they staff the judiciaries. They make the laws, they superintend the laws, they interpret the laws. They go from America's best law schools into its most important administrative agencies and they are purchased from the agencies by the highest salaries that the corporations running the American economy can offer. It takes a narrow definition of corruption to say that their activities fall outside the definition. In a liberal bourgeois polity such as America's, they are, as a group and as servants of powerful private interests, probably the most prominent purveyors of corruption.

This is hardly to say that all lawyers are corrupt. It is merely to suggest that the function of law in a polity like America's— to defend the interests of private property—makes laws and lawyers particularly open to corruption. In choosing between the service of public and private interest, it is hard to resist the temptation of money. It is easy to cover one's perception of both interests with a thick cloud of Bernard Mandeville and Adam Smith and to say that in promoting private property one may also advance public causes. And indeed, in some respects, one may. But relatively few lawyers either study their philosophy or probe their conscience. For every Louis D. Brandeis, America has a thousand ambulance-chasers, petty-claims pettifoggers,

land conveyancers, business barristers and, of course, corporation lawyers. For some sense of the topography of this world,
one would have to look into the edifice complex of the Wall
Street law firms, the plushly carpeted offices of their Washington,
D.C., unindicted coconspirators, and the far from fictive society
of Louis Auchincloss. It would be too simple to call this world
a Sodom of corruption. In a polity where the key maxim is that
money talks, it is not easy to say just where the talkers and
what they say have crossed the line of corruption.

Keepers of the American conscience, the gentility has had a
decided sense of the impact of democracy, as a type of government, on political corruption. For more than a century after
the War of 1812, the gentility believed that to be rid of corruption democracy had to be revitalized and the civil service
staffed with competent men. Outlawing the spoils was a program for supplanting vice with virtue. Revitalizing democracy
meant, for the gentility, that elections had to be freed from
purchase or covert control and that government officials had
to be made responsive to the public interest. Jacksonian reformers and Progressives alike invented a variety of devices
whereby the people could speak their voice. To the genteel
reformers, it seemed clear that men with special interests, above
all the *nouveaux riches*, had subverted the political process.
Two steps had to be taken to restore the conduct of government
to probity: fully disclosing the political activities of the special
interests and restoring to public affairs the direct role of the
people. These ideas persist. Reformers have in recent years
sought to control campaign contributions, to publicize the
influence of industry and industrialists on politics, to unlock
the grip of bureaucracy on civic life, to give localities and
communities what is uncharmingly called in computerized jargon
"an input into the decision-making process." What also persists,
with even greater emphasis than before, is the gentility's sense
that democracy is a delicate mechanism, that educating the
citizen, while necessary, may not be enough to keep the mechanism from being misused, that the American political world
has to be made safe not only from plutocracy but also from
democracy, and that the best guarantors of America's political
probity are its philosopher-kings, its gentility.

*　*　*

No less than religion and democracy, the entrepreneurial ethos has been a factor in American political corruption. It was a regular lament of European observers that America's most qualified citizens were largely absent from its government. The sociology of talent is surely germane to a discussion of political corruption. When Bryce said that America's best men did not go into politics, he was merely being polite. Other British visitors—Basil Hall, Frances M. Trollope, Frederick Marryat, even Charles Dickens—had said that its worst men went into politics. Why was American government an art for men of secondary talents? The reason is not hard to find. The best men went into money, either to amass it or to preserve it. Where possible, they used their talents and their money to influence the less talented and less affluent men who went into politics.

In any polity, talent seeks its own level. What that level is depends of course upon social ideals and mores. This phenomenon has been studied by Max Weber and Joseph Schumpeter.[22] It was, in one form or another, well understood by earlier political philosophers, including Tocqueville, Montesquieu, Aristotle and Plato. The failure of the revolutions of 1848 in the German states offers a classic example, commented on by several historians, including A. J. P. Taylor, of the forced diversion of talent from politics to economics. The thesis here is that the defeated German bourgeois liberals, men of education, drive and ability, turned their energies from government to production, rapidly making the expanding Prussian polity the principal European industrial power.[23] French history had earlier offered another version of the same principle: that talents are energized by social ideals and that they conform to the prescriptions of power within a given polity. France, the prime revolutionary nation of continental Europe, extended two guiding ideals to its sister polities of the early nineteenth century: the first, that of a *carrière ouverte aux talents*, coming out of the 1790s, was political and democratic; the second, the exhortation of *enrichissez-vous*, coming out of the regime of Louis Philippe, was economic and bourgeois. Both meant a breaking-down of the barriers that had hitherto confined social energies; both meant that France had moved from an aristocratic to a bourgeois democratic age; and they also meant that these energies would be evident in newer pursuits, consonant with the change of public law and social ideals.

American energies and talents went into enterprise. American politics was part of the domain of American entrepreneurship. This of course reversed the continental concept, in which political authority dictated to enterprise under maxims of *raison d'état* and civic needs. The English revolution of the seventeenth and eighteenth centuries marked something of a departure from this concept, bringing about a rough equation of civism and individualism, of free politics and free enterprise. English America was one of the by-products of this revolution. It was fundamental to its polity, as Tocqueville emphasized, that America had become a democracy without having had a democratic revolution. But, by the same token, it was hardly less fundamental that the Americans had become a nation of entrepreneurs without having had a capitalist revolution. Almost from the beginning, the business of America was entrepreneurship and the business of entrepreneurship was self-promotion.

The bourgeois liberal democratic form of polity that France largely achieved and that Germany largely failed to achieve had long been the central fact of American experience. This surely is what Bernard Bailyn urges as the essential nature of the American Enlightenment and the American Revolution.[24] It is not too difficult to cite the conditions that made America fairly early the land where one could find *carrières ouvertes aux talents* and where one could pursue Poor Richard's maxim: *enrichissez-vous*. Thrust upon a continent of stupefyingly abundant natural resources, the Americans were virtually from the start, in David Potter's phrase, a people of plenty.[25] Coming out of the English group of merchant adventurers, they were oriented for life as a venture in acquisition.[26] Raised in the ways of English law, they knew how to protect the citizen against the jurisdiction of the polity and particularly how to protect the citizen's acquisitions.[27] In religion, they were, as Edmund Burke described them, the dissidence of the dissenters, and no conviction was stronger among them than that they were a providential people in a promised land. They were, in terms that would be understood today, a race of liberated men. But to be free from a complex of social institutions and ideals is not necessarily an ennobling experience, however rhapsodically the historians, Americans' tribal bards, have sung it. The way to liberty is, too, the way to wealth and the way to wealth is very often the way to corruption.

One is fairly safe in arguing that, in politics, wealth corrupts and great wealth corrupts greatly. Where social purpose was largely identified with individual acquisition, who could say just at what point political morality ended and political corruption began? Read the life and doings of Benjamin Franklin, and say with a certainty, if you can, whether the civic community he inhabits is a land of milk and honey or a land of bilk and money. The real point to be made about the role of money in American life is that, in the absence of any other universal sacrament, acquiring money became its own virtue and building one's treasury of merits was translated almost inevitably into building one's treasury. It is not necessary, to make this point, to cite the classic examples of Russell H. Conwell and the Right Reverend William Lawrence, Episcopal bishop of Massachusetts. It would be better to conjoin Tocqueville and Veblen and understand that, in a polity that recognized virtually no other distinction among men than their wealth, everyone tried to make money and everyone tried to consume it conspicuously. If one traces the line from John Cotton's *On Christian Calling* to Henry David Thoreau's *Walden*, he can see how the American idea changed from virtue being its own reward to reward being its own virtue.

The gentility has always pointed out just how corrupt the American way to wealth was becoming. The Puritan jeremiads of the 1670s denounced the lustful display of nakedness among women and the naked lust for money among men. Emerson said no less in 1841 in "Man the Reformer":

The ways of trade are grown selfish to the borders of theft, and supple to the borders ... of fraud. ... It is only necessary to ask a few questions as to the progress of the articles of commerce from the fields where they grew, to our houses, to become aware that we eat and drink and wear perjury and fraud in a hundred commodities. ... The general system of our trade ... is a system of selfishness, ... a system of distrust, of concealment, of superior keenness, not of giving but of taking advantage.[28]

And who could have pronounced a more devastating jeremiad than Walt Whitman in *Democratic Vistas*:

Society, in these States, is canker'd, crude, superstitious, and rotten.... The depravity of the business classes of our country is not less than has been supposed, but infinitely greater. The official services of America, national, state, and municipal, in all their branches and departments, except the judiciary, are saturated in corruption, bribery, falsehood, malad-ministration; and the judiciary is tainted. The great cities reek with respectable as much as non-respectable robbery and scoundrelism.... In business (this all-devouring modern word, business), the one sole object is, by any means, pecuniary gain. The magician's serpent in the fable ate up all the other serpents; and moneymaking is our magician's serpent, remaining today sole mast of the field. The best class we show, is but a mob of fashionably dress'd speculators and vulgarians.[29]

In analyzing the impact of economic factors on political cor-ruption, the prime concern is with the struggle between the entrepreneurial ethos and the social ethos, between individuality and community, between the demands of the ego and the restraints of the superego. What promoted the entrepreneurial ethos also promoted the tendency to political corruption. What restrained the entrepreneurial ethos also restrained the tendency to political corruption. The concern at this point is to say just what is meant by the American entrepreneurial ethos, to consider the factors that have promoted it, and then to consider the factors that have restrained it. The key argument here will be that the growth of American society generated forces that undid the restraints upon entrepreneurship and that, in conse-quence, the tendencies to political corruption were enhanced.

The entrepreneurial ethos is the root ideal of the American polity. By its terms, man strives to achieve and to gain. What Americans call the acquisitive instinct is very much part of their idea of entrepreneurship. Based on the premise that *laborare est orare*, the idea is in this sense religious. Working is indeed the hallmark of American identity: America's emblem is the leather apron rather than silk breeches. Franklin's "Information for Those Who Would Remove to America" put it clearly: "America is the Land of Labour. . . . Every one will enjoy securely the profits of his Industry. . . . People do not inquire concerning a stranger, What is He? but What can he do?... Industry and constant Employment are great preservatives of the Morals and Virtue of a Nation."[30] The last sentence says, clearly enough, that working for oneself is its own morality. Indeed, there is a significant psychological dimension to the idea of entrepreneurship. Carefully detailing the metamorphosis a European went through after settling down on American soil, J. Hector St. John Crèvecoeur concluded that he had become a new genus of creation, *homo americanus*, veritably a new man. Francis Grund, a contemporary of Tocqueville's, saw the psychological dimension of entrepreneurship from a related, but slightly different, angle: "Business is the very soul of an American: he pursues it not as a means of procuring for himself and his family the necessary comforts of life, but as the fountain of all human felicity."[31]

The American entrepreneurial spirit expanded in a favoring environment. The tribes of transplanted Englishmen brought to the shores of North America a store of values which, even under less propitious conditions, would have prepared them for a heady adventure. They were keenly property-minded; they knew the common law and the shield of rights it afforded them; they wished to set limits to superior jurisdictions; they went at the world around them with an associative, collegial, civic consciousness; but they stood before each other and before God with a sense of their individuality and a moral enthusiasm that made overcoming life's travails part of their endless rendezvous with divinity.

It was natural enough, with the almost incontinent expansion of their entrepreneurial ethic, that Americans should come to perceive that life was an individual adventure in self-promotion, that he who would seek could also find, that providential institutions no less than providential resources had set a rich table of possibilities before them. It was no less natural that the adventure would define its own morality, that the Americans' sense of civic restraint would relax as their access to riches expanded. Despite occasional voices to the contrary, they did not see their roads to success as morally questionable or their changing morality as corrupt. The fact was that political corruption inhered in the American concept of entrepreneurship, expanding to the measure of an expanding entrepreneurship.

The idea of entrepreneurship was a counterpart to the idea of community, both belonging to a larger complex of premises to which the Europeans who settled seventeenth and eighteenth century English America subscribed. The conditions in the American environment promoted the rapid, luxuriant growth of the

entrepreneurial ethos. But no less important in promoting that
growth was the dissolution of the complex of premises to which
the entrepreneurial ethos belonged. As these related ideas lost
meaning and vitality, the idea of entrepreneurship lost its confine-
ments. Because the composite of ideas added up to a moral
code, its transformation signified the advent of a new morality.
The sins of the fathers were not only *not* visited upon the sons,
they became, in many respects, the sons' redeeming virtues.
The rules of the game had changed: yesterday's usurer and
purveyor of false goods was today's captain of industry and
financial wizard. To use a simple Freudian analog: the older
superego no longer stood sentinel upon the ego. The decline
of the older values liberated the entrepreneurial ethos for a
freewheeling political playmanship. It was a far cry indeed
from John Winthrop's General Court to Nelson Aldrich's Senate.

What were the restraints upon entrepreneurship that slackened
in the course of successive American eras? Briefly, some of the
more salient ones were the following. The Puritan concept of
a demanding God yielded to the Enlightened idea of a benevo-
lent God. The idea of sanctification, a daily struggle against
sin, gave way to a less constraining adherence to civic responsibilities. The limited community of saints, which one entered
only after a long period of probing, extended its membership
to the point where sainthood had lost both its exclusivity and
its meaning. As one can gather from the writings of Perry
Miller, Puritanism, as an ethical imperative—with economic,
social and political dimensions, no less than theological—was
significantly transformed from 1630 to 1730. For some of this
transformation, one would do well to consult Richard L. Bushman's very fine analysis of how, after 1690, Connecticut's "close-
knit, tightly controlled, homogeneous community . . . became
more open and homogeneous" and how the colony of steady
habits was, by 1765, "moving toward a new social order, toward
the republican pluralism of the nineteenth century."[32] When
colonial America became an independent metropolis, another
bond upon entrepreneurship came loose. Belonging to an imperial order imposed upon the Americans a variety of constraints,
among them surely the direction of their enterprise. In colonial
days, American energy and capital were segmented; they were
oriented to the transatlantic world. After being dislodged from

the British matrix, American entrepreneurship ventured abroad on its own and poured its vast capacities into a greatly expanding internal market. It grew in exponential proportions and grew by what it fed on.

Winthrop's America was a society of deference; Whitman's America was a society of democracy. The transition from deference to democracy meant a loosening of the bonds on entrepreneurship. However much one may question J. Franklin Jameson's argument that the revolutionaries ushered in a new social order, there can be little doubt, as Bailyn has suggested, that they sought to realize the egalitarianism proposed by Enlightened philosophy. One has only to read James Fenimore Cooper's *Homeward Bound* and *The American Democrat* to know how vast a difference he found between the status-respecting America he had left in 1826 and the status-rejecting America he returned to in 1833. The point is simple enough: in a polity of deference, the entrepreneurial ethic had been confined by the politics of deference; in a polity of democracy, entrepreneurship was unfettered, becoming a surging power answerable only to itself. The consequences of this unfettering and this surging were clearly put by *The American Review* in 1845:

To get, and to have the reputation of possessing, is the ruling passion.... There are no bounds among us to the restless desire to be better off.... There are no established limits within which the hopes of any class of society must be confined, as in other countries.... While the commercial spirit in this extravagant form gives a certain sobriety and moral aspect to society, it occasions an excessive barrenness of real moral excellencies.... Our souls are partial, and therefore barren.... Every one minds his own business, to the extreme peril of his soul.[33]

Perhaps the most important single factor altering the entrepreneurial ethic was the growth of a continental industrial economy and the decline, in relative importance, of the local economy. An immediate contact between producers and consumers depended on an immediate morality. Local government responded to the interpersonal relations of the locality. As markets widened, contacts between producers and consumers widened into a long chain of impersonal relations. With the emergence of a national market economy, political control passed inevitably into the hands of the national legislature. James Madison's tenth paper in *The Federalist* could never have conjured up the industrial and financial faction that later regularly tried, and often managed, to corrupt the American Congress. Not even Alexander Hamilton could have anticipated the growth of a massive bureaucracy, on all levels of government, so susceptible of economic influence that one 'could hardly say whether government superintended industry or was merely another of industry's many activities. There is no need to go through the litany of Populist and Progressive indictments to understand that the entrepreneurs of the age were the first beneficiaries of the new nationalism and the new freedom and that, having this legacy to stand on, they brought buying and selling public officials to a fine art.

In considering how far economic factors have produced political corruption, the following observations have been made:

- That what is called political corruption is part of the way a polity looks at itself and thus part of the polity's mores and ideology;

- That American political mores and ideology, however continuous their language and symbols, are continuously being redefined;

- That the prime force in American economic life is what is called here the entrepreneurial ethic;

- That American economic life has always rested on two sets of moral imperatives or ethical codes, the entrepreneurial and the communal;

- That the entrepreneurial and the communal ethic, however piously regarded as coordinate and complementary, have generally been antithetical forces, with the ascendency of the one signifying the decline of the other;

- That the entrepreneurial ethic, as a drive for personal gain, is a perennial source of political corruption;

- That the triumph of the entrepreneurial ethic was favored by America's geography and its vast natural resources;

- That the triumph was guaranteed by the dissolution, in successive American generations, of that complex of older, essentially European, mores in which entrepreneurship had been only one major component;

- That the entrepreneurial ethic emerged as the most important single force in American political life during the years after American independence, and particularly after the end of the War of 1812.

Europe's passage from medievalism to modernity was a drama of alarums and excursions, of profound social conflict and revolution. In America, one could find an equivalent of the major European transitions—from *Gemeinschaft* to *Gesellschaft*, from association to anomie, from aristocracy to democracy, from communalism to individualism, from mercantilism to industrial and finance capitalism, from Erastianism to sectarian liberty. But the transitions were far less profound or problematic for Americans. Conceived in a medieval matrix, American life began with a rejection of its parenthood. For America, Old World institutions and ideals were not so much essences to be transformed as trappings to be shed. In its passage from medievalism to modernity, European morality, defending a polity of Establishments, argued that the good of one should be subservient to the good of all. By contrast, defending a polity where many major institutions of central jurisdiction were never established or were early disestablished, American morality argued that the good of one was largely synonymous with the good of all. It would be fruitless to judge which polity achieved the most morality and the least corruption, all the more so if judgment is based on the premise that to evaluate the morality one must first look at the moralizer. And yet it is fair to say that, even in its own terms, American morality suffered a clear declension from earlier standards. The entrepreneurial ethos never disclaimed its role in the commonwealth, its link with public felicity, its responsibility to the general good. But the republic of virtue which the Founding Fathers envisioned has long since passed, even as an aspiration. From the War of 1812 to today, American morality and American corruption have been the by-products of a surging entrepreneurial ethic, working at present through sophisticated corporate forms and sloganeering as people's capitalism, with powerful lobbyists in the nation's capital never quite honestly answering the questions, whose corporations and which people?

*　*　*

So far the argument here has been that political corruption in America has had its own essential nature, one that has been determined in the main by three principal factors: American sectarian Christianity, American democracy and law, and the American entrepreneurial ethos. It has been contended that each society has a particular concept of political virtue, and the aim has been to define the concept that is uniquely American by comparing the American polity with European models. Merely to discuss episodes of American political corruption per se is to discuss them *in vacuo*, without referents, without plottings and ultimately, then, without definition.

Two questions remain to be considered. How is the recurrence of periods of pronounced political corruption in American history to be explained? And how, in the light of some of the suggestions already offered, is the American response to Watergate to be assayed? With regard to the first question, corruption has been defined as the breaking of the rules of the game of the polity. It is axiomatic that rules are always being broken. The problem is to understand why the breaking of rules proliferates so much that corruption becomes a predominant aspect of a period. It is safe to say that widespread corruption signalizes a deeper strain in the polity. To put it in general terms, the political institutions can no longer accommodate the newer economic and social actualities of the nation. Political mores are in conflict with the altering conditions of society. Indeed, what is called corruption is in no small measure the moral charge that the older political codes are not being observed, that the older political prescriptions are not being fulfilled.

Moreover, when speaking of corruption in American political history, may one not be speaking of the faulty way politicians are handling functions they were not meant to perform? The history of American politics is, in many ways, the story of the expanding functions of government and of the increasing role of the national government. America's ever-changing economy and society throw up new needs. At every point of American history, there is a wide gap between these needs and the effectiveness of politics and politicians in serving them. The lack of service is described as delinquent and morally wrong. And whatever service *is* performed is perforce *ad hoc*, inconsistent with accepted institutions, extralegal if not quite illegal, and in any event censurable. In such times, therefore, official acts of omission and commission evoke charges of corruption. One ought then to consider how far what is called corruption is to be found in the differential between existing political forms and newer social needs. In every epoch, the discrepancy between the two has to be corrected. The attack on the discrepancy marks an era when the government is attacked for its inefficiency and confusion, when moral outrage is voiced, when the cry of corruption becomes loud and widespread. The resolution of the discrepancy marks an era of reform, of reconstructing the bureaucracy, making government more responsive to social needs, and coordinately sounding the high moral purpose of fulfilling the American democratic ideal.[34]

To be more specific, look more closely at the Gilded Age. By all odds, it is the age that is considered to have been one of the most corrupt in American history. What then was there about those decades that might explain the comparatively high incidence of political corruption? The suggestion is that the new society and the modes of conduct it created were being judged in terms of the older political mores. Radical changes were shaping a new America. There is no need to rehearse the catalog of transformation to be found readily enough in the standard texts: in Allan Nevins's *The Emergence of Modern America*, in Samuel P. Hays's *The Response to Industrialism*, in John A. Garraty's *The New Commonwealth*, in Carl N. Degler's *The Age of the Economic Revolution*, in Robert H. Wiebe's *The Search for Order*. In sum, major national problems were emerging which national politics could nowhere accommodate and for which therefore a new system of national politics had to be devised.

The American transformation was hardly unique. In different parts of the Western world similar tendencies were in motion. In *Gemeinschaft und Gesellschaft*, which appeared in 1887, Ferdinand Tönnies described the movement from a "community" of mutual aid, trust and interdependence to a "society" where self-interest was the primary concern.[35] A decade later, in his study *Suicide*, Emile Durkheim contended that, as the rules of social conduct changed, the status of men as moral individuals was significantly undermined.[36] Looking at the American scene from a slightly different angle, Wiebe has found that the older order of insular communities was falling apart during the late nineteenth century and that Americans were searching for a new order. Borrowing from Tocqueville, it might be suggested that the associative institutions of the United States, local and moral agencies that he so much admired for their role in the United States of the 1830s, were ill equipped to handle the national problems of the United States of the 1880s.

The gentility, voicing the moral consciousness of the nation, brought American politics and politicians under heavy indictment. In their charges, the gentility regularly sounded two themes: that the political system was ineffectual and that the politicians were corrupt. Variously phrased, one can hear these themes in Henry Adams's *Democracy*, in Bryce's *The American Commonwealth*, in Charles Francis Adams's *Chapters of Erie*, in Lincoln Steffens's *The Shame of the Cities*, and of course in the pages of Edwin L. Godkin's *The Nation* and Samuel Bowles's *Republican*. In all of these ring the cries of righteous indignation, the unequivocating appeals to codes of ethics, the denunciation of practices that are called ungentlemanly and unworthy, the philippics of a group of high-minded individuals who are as sure of their own morality as they are of the immorality of their opponents. Looking beneath the surface of the indictments, one sees the keepers of the nation's conscience denouncing the violation of the rules of a game that had been played locally rather than nationally and that had hitherto involved local economic agencies and local political jurisdictions. A new economy and a new society were demanding new rules for what was in effect a new game. The indictment of the new capitalists and the new politicians was drawn up largely in terms of an older political morality, in terms, that is, of a local Christian mercantile community. To this degree, then, the Gilded Age—America's great age of political corruption—was a figment of the gentility's moral imagination.

The second question is how, in terms of some of the ideas advanced, is the American reaction to Watergate to be perceived?

This question invites a second question: What was Watergate? It was, in fact, at least two events: an actual violation of the political rules and a television drama. To some degree, the wide public airing of Watergate amplified the enormity of the corruption and insured strong corrective measures. As a television spectacle, Watergate was an engrossing political soap opera about the lives of Richard Nixon, Richard Nixon. It was stupendous public theater, a morality extravaganza played on the hippodrome of a million TV screens. As democracy's *Everyman,* it simplified reality almost to the point of transcending it. It came straight out of the American Christian literary tradition— out of the Puritan jeremiads and Michael Wigglesworth, Nathaniel Hawthorne, Herman Melville, Lewis Wallace and Charles M. Sheldon.[37] Which playwright could have written a drama so full of naked ambition, Christian piety, lust for power and tragic betrayal as the daily episodes of "As the Watergate Turns"? Watching it with fascinated revulsion, Americans could not but feel that all the president's men were satanic minions, that the president himself was villainy incarnate, that the highest office in the land had been lamentably stained, and that strong spiritual cleansing was called for.

As an actual violation of the rules of politics, Watergate had of course major consequences. Nixon's sins could not be ignored—they were cardinal, even for politicians, men hardly distinguished for acts of selfless virtue; they were Nixon's, a president so lacking in charisma or even confidence that his office had become a fortress of unsplendid isolation; they were Republican, and Democrats would have been fools to let their smashing national defeat in 1972 go unchallenged, without at least imputing to the opponents the charge that dirty tricks and tricky Dick had done them in. And the sins, finally, were too public to be passed over. Reforms were called for and they were made. Measures were taken to curb the imperial presidency. Campaign finance laws were almost universally enacted. Legislators were put under stricter ethical codes. It is too early to say just how far this neoprogressive movement will go.

And yet, as some commentators have noted, the movement does not seem to be going very far at all. Congressmen are balking at limitations on their earnings. They are reluctant to offer the electorate a full disclosure of their assets. Little, if anything, will be done to answer Lowell Weicker's charge that men of wealth now dominate the Senate. There is remarkable foot-dragging on probing the allegation that forty Congressmen were in the pay of the South Korean Central Intelligence Agency, which, if true, could send one-tenth of the American House of Representatives to prison. Joseph Crangle has fumed at Senator Daniel P. Moynihan's recommendation that three Republican federal prosecutors be permitted to finish out their terms, because the recommendation meant that party patronage would have to yield, at least for a while, to proven official competence. No action is being taken to curb the powerful influence of politically connected lawyers who, as Frank Lynn puts it, "constitute almost a hidden government." David Broder, of the *Washington Post*, says that "the changes wrought by recent electoral reforms were not as extensive as the furor created by Watergate might have indicated." In the view of Professor Joel L. Fleishman of Duke University, there are distinct limitations to recent reforms. The abuses continue. Indeed, some of the great gurus of America's Eastern gentility are warning that, in responding to Watergate, Americans may be going too far the other way. Says Anthony Lewis, the spirit incarnate of pious liberalism: "There is in fact a real danger of overreaction by Congress to the Executive sins of recent years." And Elliott Richardson, the veritable Mr. Clean of the Nixon administration, warns: "New kinds of excesses have developed in this post-Watergate period as the pendulum has swung in reaction to the original abuses of power." Quoting Algernon Swinburne, he urges the Americans to shun "the sexless orgies of morality," not—it is well understood—because he would have them abjure sex but because he would apparently not have them waste it on mere morality.[38]

Can it be sensibly expected that political abuses will not continue? No human polity is addicted to virtue, and the American polity, the product of the special factors that have shaped it, has its special way both of practicing corruption and of raising the cry that corruption is being practiced. It is not unfair to suggest that, meanwhile, back at the ranches of American political life, on the municipal, county, state and federal levels, the corruption, however tempered, goes on with impressive vitality. The men running the political show can only hope that idiocies like the break-in at Watergate will either not recur or not be handled so ineptly; that another wild bit of vaudeville like the act put on in 1971 and 1972 by the crazies of the Oval Office will not soon hit the boards of the Presidential Palace; and in particular that a man with such obvious paranoid strains as Richard Nixon will either not become president or, since some of America's best paranoiacs are presidents, will never have to go through the drama of public exposure with his moralities all the way down. In a sense, this could mean that the purgation of trial by television served not so much to preclude future Watergates as to make it possible for them to continue in quieter, more fragmented, less flagrant, more covert ways. And should it surprise anyone if they did continue? No less than other polities, democracy in America has its inherent flaws. And the men who superintend the American democracy are, as the Founding Fathers well understood they would be, far, far less than angels.

NOTES

1. "A Defence of the Answer," in Perry Miller and Thomas H. Johnson, eds., *The Puritans* (rev. ed.; 2 vols.; New York, 1963), I, 118.

2. Charles F. Adams, ed., *The Works of John Adams* (10 vols.; Boston, 1850–56), IX, 417–20.

3. *Recollections of a Busy Life* (New York, 1868), p. 527.

4. William E. Leuchtenburg, ed., *The New Nationalism* (New York, 1961), pp. 27, 36.

5. Peter Lisagor, "From Triumph to Tragedy," *The 1975 World Book Year Book* (Chicago, 1975), p. 62.

6. *Triumphant Democracy or Fifty Years' March of the Republic* (New York, 1886), pp. 471–73.

7. The role of the gentility in American life has long been recognized. Foreign and domestic commentators (Tocqueville, Grund, Hall, Chevalier, Fenimore Cooper, to name but a few) were fully aware of this role. The gentility has been the subject of particular study during the past two decades. Richard Hofstadter emphasized their centrality in the Progressive movement in *The Age of Reform* (New York, 1955). Stow Persons, *The Decline of American Gentility* (New York, 1973) is the most important recent book on the subject. Other valuable contributions include John Tomisch, *A Genteel Endeavor: American Culture and Politics in the Gilded Age* (Stanford, 1971); Barbara Miller Solomon, *Ancestors and Immigrants* (Cambridge, Mass., 1956); and John G. Sproat, *"The Best Men": Liberal Reformers in the Gilded Age* (New York, 1968).

8. The transformation and secularization of American Christianity (and particularly American Puritanism) are discussed in Perry Miller, *The New England Mind from Colony to Province* (Cambridge, Mass., 1953), pp. 464–85; Charles A. Barker, *American Convictions, Cycles of Public Thought 1600–1850* (Philadelphia, 1970), pp. 111–15, 180–84; Alan Heimert, *Religion and the American Mind from the Great Awakening to the Revolution* (Cambridge, Mass., 1966), Chap. V; Gordon S. Wood, *The Creation of the American Republic 1776–1787* (Chapel Hill, 1969), pp. 114–18; Rush Welter, *The Mind of America 1820–1860* (New York, 1975), Chap. X; and Robert T. Handy, *A Christian America: Protestant Hopes and Historical Realities* (New York, 1971), Chap. II.

9. Cited by Sidney E. Mead in Russell E. Richey and Donald G. Jones, eds., *American Civil Religion* (New York, 1974), p. 45.

10. Quoted in Richey and Jones, *op. cit.*, p. 40. See also Robert N. Bellah, "Civil Religion in America," *Daedalus*, Vol. XCVI, No. 1 (Winter 1967), 1–21.

11. *The New Heavens and the New Earth: Political Religion in America* (New York, 1974).

12. Alexis de Tocqueville, *Democracy in America*, ed. Phillips Bradley (2 vols.; New York, 1945), II, 6.

13. *The Americans in Their Moral, Social, and Political Relations* (New York, 1837, 1968), pp. 165–67.

14. Roy P. Fairfield, ed., *The Federalist Papers* (Garden City, N. Y., 1961). As notable examples of their view, see in particular Papers 10, 15, 16, 17, 31 and 51.

15. *Op. cit.*, I, 225–26.

16. In 1838, Cooper published two of his strongest indictments of American political mores: *The American Democrat*, a tract of "censure" and "instruction," and *Home as Found*, a novel less censorious or angry.

17. *American Notes* (Gloucester, Mass., 1968), pp. 141–43. The original edition appeared in 1842.

18. *The American Commonwealth* (rev. ed.; 2 vols.; London, 1891), I, Chaps. 51, 52; II, Chaps. 62–64. In this edition, Chap. 52, "An American View of Municipal Government in the United States," was written by Seth Low, who had been the reform-oriented mayor of the city of Brooklyn.

19. *The Politics of Democracy: American Parties in Action* (New York, 1940), pp. 345–47.

20. *Op. cit.*, p. 481.

21. Cited in my prefatory comments to a very illuminating essay by John P. Roche, included in my *American History: Recent Interpretations* (rev. ed.; New York, 1969), II, 51.

22. See Weber's lecture, "Politics as a Vocation," in H. H. Gerth and C. Wright Mills, eds., *From Max Weber: Essays in Sociology* (New York, 1946), pp. 83 f. On Schumpeter, see his *Theory of Economic Development* (Cambridge, Mass., 1934), pp. 74–94, and also "The Creative

Response in Economic History" in Richard C. Clemence, ed., *Essays of J. A. Schumpeter* (Cambridge, Mass., 1951), pp. 216–26.

23. A. J. P. Taylor, *The Course of German History* (New York, 1946), pp. 88–89, 110–11.

24. "Political Experience and Enlightenment Ideas in Eighteenth-Century America," *American Historical Review*, LXVII (January 1962), 339–51.

25. The perception of America as a cornucopia was indeed the spur to the late sixteenth century English colonizing movement, as is evident from the contemporary accounts cited in Louis B. Wright, ed., *The Elizabethans' America* (Cambridge, Mass., 1966).

26. For the sources and patterns of English colonization, see A. L. Rowse, *The Expansion of Elizabethan England* (London, 1955), particularly Chap. VI; David Beers Quinn, *England and the Discovery of America, 1481–1620* (New York, 1974); and Louis B. Wright, *Religion and Empire: the Alliance between Piety and Commerce in English Expansion, 1558–1625* (Chapel Hill, 1943), Chap. I.

27. See Barker, *op. cit.*, pp. 16–20, 226–33; George Lee Haskins, *Law and Authority in Early Massachusetts: A Study in Tradition and Design* (New York, 1960), Chap. X; and Daniel J. Boorstin, *The Americans: The Colonial Experience* (New York, 1964), pp. 195–205.

28. Ralph Waldo Emerson, *Nature, Addresses and Lectures*, ed. Edward Waldo Emerson (Boston, 1904), pp. 230–32.

29. Walt Whitman, *Complete Poetry and Selected Prose*, ed. James E. Miller, Jr. (Boston, 1959), p. 461.

30. Benjamin Franklin, *Representative Selections*, ed., Chester E. Jorgenson and Frank Luther Mott (rev. ed.; New York, 1962), pp. 451–57.

31. *Op. cit.*, p. 202.

32. *From Puritan to Yankee: Character and the Social Order in Connecticut, 1690–1765* (Cambridge, Mass., 1967), preface.

33. Quoted in Edwin C. Rozwenc, ed., *Ideology and Power in the Age of Jackson* (Garden City, N. Y., 1964), pp. 48–54.

34. In formulating this suggestion, I am drawing on some of the ideas offered by Arthur M. Schlesinger, Sr., in "The Tides of National Politics" in his *Paths to the Present* (rev. ed.; Cambridge, Mass., 1964), pp. 89–103. In that essay, the older Schlesinger argued that there have been alternating currents of conservatism and reform in American political history. Arthur M. Schlesinger, Jr., has excellently amplified his father's thesis, using it to explain the sources of the New Deal in *Columbia University Forum*, II (Fall 1959), 4–12.

35. A brief statement of some of his key concepts, which he wrote near the end of his life, may be found in Tönnies, *Community and Society (Gemeinschaft und Gesellschaft)*, trans. and ed. Charles P. Loomis (East Lansing, 1957), pp. 246–59.

36. See in particular the concluding section of *Suicide: A Study in Sociology*, trans. and ed. John A. Spaulding and George Simpson (Glencoe, 1951), pp. 386–92.

37. For a brief survey of the vogue of popular religious literature in the United States, see Frank Luther Mott, *Golden Multitudes* (New York, 1947), Chaps. 3, 26, 28.

38. *The New York Times*, March 10, 1977; March 6, 1977; Oct. 17, 1976; April 7, 1977; Jan. 23, 1977.

THE CONTRIBUTORS

EDWIN G. BURROWS is Assistant Professor of History, Brooklyn College, City University of New York. B.A., Michigan State University; M.A., Ph.D., Columbia University. Author: "The American Revolution: The Ideology and Psychology of National Liberation," *Perspectives in American History*, VI (1972); "Military Experience and the Origins of Federalism and Antifederalism" in Jacob Judd and Irwin Polishook, eds., *Aspects of Early New York Society and Politics* (Tarrytown, N. Y., 1973); *Against Dependency: Psychohistorical Essays in American Political Culture* (New York, forthcoming).

ABRAHAM S. EISENSTADT is Professor of History, Brooklyn College, City University of New York. B.A., Brooklyn College; Ph.D., Columbia University. Author: *Charles McLean Andrews: A Study in American Historical Writing* (New York, 1956); "American History and Social Science," *Centennial Review* (1963); "The World of Andrew Carnegie, 1865–1901," *Labor History* (1969); "The Special Relationship: Commager's *Britain through American Eyes*," *Massachusetts Review* (1977); "Affirmation and Anxiety: The American Idea in the Late Nineteenth Century" in Howard H. Quint *et al.*, eds., *Main Problems in American History* (4th ed.; Homewood, Ill., 1977). Editor: *American History: Recent Interpretations* (2 vols.; 2nd ed.; New York, 1969); *The Craft of American History: Selected Essays* (2 vols.; New York, 1966). Coeditor: "The Cromwell-AHM Series in American History" (12 vols.; New York, 1967–).

ARNOLD J. HEIDENHEIMER is Professor of Political Science, Washington University, St. Louis. B.A., Cornell University; M.A., American University; Ph.D., London School of Economics. Author: *Adenauer and the CDU* (New York, 1960); *The Governments of Germany* (New York, 1961); *Business Associations and the Financing of Political Parties: A Comparative Study of the Evolution of Practices in Germany, Norway and Japan* (The

Hague, 1968). Editor: *Political Corruption: Readings in Comparative Analysis* (New York, 1970).

ARI HOOGENBOOM is Professor of History, Brooklyn College, City University of New York. A.B., Atlantic Union College; M.A., Ph.D., Columbia University. Author: *Outlawing the Spoils: A History of the Civil Service Reform Movement, 1865–1883* (Urbana, Ill., 1961); (with William Sachs), *The Enterprising Colonials: Society on the Eve of the Revolution* (New York, 1965); (with Philip S. Klein), *A History of Pennsylvania* (New York, 1973); (with Olive Hoogenboom), *A History of the ICC: From Panacea to Palliative* (New York, 1976). Editor: (with Olive Hoogenboom), *The Gilded Age* (Englewood Cliffs, N.J., 1967); (with Olive Hoogenboom), *An Interdisciplinary Approach to American History* (Englewood Cliffs, N. J., 1973).

JAMES P. JOHNSON is Associate Professor of History, Brooklyn College, City University of New York. A.B., Duke University; M.A., Ph.D., Columbia University. Author: "Drafting the NRA Code of Fair Competition for the Bituminous Coal Industry," *Journal of American History*, LIII (Dec. 1966), 521–41; "Reorganizing the United Mine Workers of America in Pennsylvania during the New Deal," *Pennsylvania History*, XXXVII (April 1970), 117–32; "The Attempt of the National Recovery Administration to Raise Bituminous Coal Prices" in Frank B. Evans and Harold Pinkett, eds., *Research in the Administration of Public Policy* (Washington, 1975), pp. 51–63; "Theories of Labor Union Development and the United Mine Workers, 1932–33," *The Register of the Kentucky Historical Society*, April 1975, pp. 151–70; "The Fuel Crisis, Largely Forgotten, That Chilled Us in 1918," *Smithsonian*, Dec. 1976, pp. 64–71; *Westfield: From Settlement to Suburb* (Kenilworth, N. J., 1977); "Integrating Educational Theory and History," *The History Teacher*, May 1977, pp. 425–33.

MORTON KELLER is Spector Professor of History, Brandeis University. B.A., University of Rochester; M.A., Ph.D., Harvard University. Author: *In Defense of Yesterday: James M. Beck and the Politics of Conservatism* (New York, 1958); *The Life Insurance Enterprise, 1885–1910: A Study of the Limits of Cor-*

porate Power (Cambridge, Mass., 1963); *The Art and Politics of Thomas Nast* (New York, 1968); *Affairs of State: Public Life in Late Nineteenth Century America* (Cambridge, Mass., 1977).

MARY-JO KLINE is the Editor of the Papers of Aaron Burr, New-York Historical Society. B.A., Barnard College; M.A., Ph.D., Columbia University. Editor: *Alexander Hamilton: A Biography in His Own Words* (New York, 1973); (with Lyman H. Butterfield and Marc Friedlaender), *The Book of Abigail and John: Selected Letters of the Adams Family, 1762–1789* (Cambridge, Mass., 1975); (with Robert J. Taylor and Gregg Lint), *The Papers of John Adams* (2 vols.; New York, 1977).

ROBERT MUCCIGROSSO is Associate Professor of History, Brooklyn College, City University of New York. B.A., Syracuse University; M.A., Ph.D., Columbia University. Author: "The City Reform Club: A Study in Late Nineteenth Century Reform," *New-York Historical Society Quarterly* (1968); "American Gothic: Ralph Adams Cram," *Thought: A Review of Culture and Idea* (1972).

LINDA LEVY PECK is Assistant Professor of History, Purdue University. B.A., Brandeis University; M.A., Washington University; Ph.D., Yale University. Author: "Problems in Jacobean Administration: Was Henry Howard, Earl of Northampton, a Reformer?" *The Historical Journal* (1976); "Biography and History: The Problem for Tudor Historians," *Reviews in European History* (1977); "Court Patronage and Government Policy: The Jacobean Dilemma" in *Patronage in Renaissance Europe* (Washington, forthcoming); "Corruption at the Court of James I: The Undermining of Legitimacy," Festschrift in honor of J. H. Hexter (forthcoming).

EDWARD PESSEN is Distinguished Professor of History, Baruch College and the Graduate School, City University of New York. B.A., M.A., Ph.D., Columbia University. Author: *The Most Uncommon Jacksonians: The Radical Leaders of the Early Labor Movement* (Albany, N. Y., 1967); *Jacksonian America: Society, Personality, and Politics* (Homewood, Ill., 1969); "The Egalitarian Myth and the American Social Reality," *American Histor-*

ical Review (1971); "The United States from 1816 to 1850" in *Encyclopædia Britannica* (15th ed.; Chicago, 1974), *s.v.* "United States, History of the," XVIII, 961–67; *Riches, Class, and Power before the Civil War* (Lexington, Mass., 1973); "The Social Configuration of the Antebellum City," *Journal of Urban History* (1976); *The Many-Faceted Jacksonian Era* (Westport, Conn., 1977). Editor: *New Perspectives on Jacksonian Parties and Politics* (Boston, 1969); *Three Centuries of Social Mobility in America* (Lexington, Mass., 1974); *Jacksonian Panorama* (Indianapolis, 1976).

ARTHUR M. SCHLESINGER, JR., is Albert Schweitzer Professor of Humanities, Graduate School, City University of New York. B.A., M.A., Harvard University; Hon. L.H.D., Muhlenberg College and Tusculum College; Hon. LL.D., Bethany College; Hon. D.C.L., University of New Brunswick. Pulitzer Prize (two), Francis Putnam Prize, Bancroft Prize, Gold Medal of the National Institute of Arts and Sciences, National Book Award. Author: *The Age of Jackson* (Boston, 1945); *The Vital Center* (Boston, 1949); *The Age of Roosevelt* (Boston, 1957–60); *The Politics of Hope* (Boston, 1963); *A Thousand Days: John F. Kennedy in the White House* (Boston, 1965); *The Bitter Heritage: Vietnam and American Democracy* (Boston, 1967); *The Crisis of Confidence: Ideas, Power and Violence in America* (Boston, 1969); *The Coming to Power: Critical Presidential Elections in American History* (New York, 1972); *The Imperial Presidency* (Boston, 1973); *Robert Kennedy and His Times* (Boston, 1978). Editor: (with Morton White) *Paths of American Thought* (Boston, 1970); (with Fred L. Israel) *The History of American Presidential Elections* (New York, 1971); *The Dynamics of World Power: A Documentary History of United States Foreign Policy, 1945–1972* (New York, 1972); (with Roger Bruns) *Congress Investigates: A Documented History, 1792–1794* (New York, 1975).

JEROME L. STERNSTEIN is Associate Professor of History, Brooklyn College, City University of New York. B.A., Brooklyn College; Ph.D., Brown University. Allan Nevins Prize of the Society of American Historians for biography of Nelson W. Aldrich. Author: "Another Look at the Hayes-Tilden Election Night Conspiracy,"

Journal of Southern History (1966); "King Leopold II, Senator Nelson W. Aldrich, and the Strange Beginnings of American Economic Penetration of the Congo," *African Historical Studies* (1969). Associate Editor: *Encyclopedia of American Biography* (New York, 1974).

HANS L. TREFOUSSE is Professor of History, Brooklyn College, City University of New York. B.A., City College of New York, M.A., Ph.D., Columbia University. Author: *Germany and American Neutrality, 1939–1941* (New York, 1951); *Ben Butler: The South Called Him Beast* (New York, 1957); *Benjamin Franklin Wade: Radical Republican from Ohio* (New York, 1963); *The Radical Republicans: Lincoln's Vanguard for Racial Justice* (New York, 1969); *Impeachment of a President: Andrew Johnson, the Blacks, and Reconstruction* (Knoxville, 1975). Editor: *What Happened at Pearl Harbor?* (New York, 1958); *The Cold War* (New York, 1964); *Background for Radical Reconstruction* (Boston, 1970); *Reconstruction: America's First Effort at Racial Democracy* (New York, 1971); *The Causes of the Civil War* (New York, 1971); *Lincoln's Decision for Emancipation* (Philadelphia, 1975); *Toward a New View of America: Essays in Honor of Arthur C. Cole* (New York, 1977).

MELVIN R. WILLIAMS is Assistant Professor of History, Brooklyn College, City University of New York. B.A., M.A., North Carolina Central University; M.A., Ph.D., Johns Hopkins University. Author: "A Blue Print for Change: The Black Community in Washington, D. C., 1860–1880," *Records of the Columbia Historical Society of Washington* (1972); "Humanizing Influences during the American Revolutionary Era," *North Carolina Central Review* (1973).